MW00723428

ZAGATSURVEY®

1998 UPDATE

WASHINGTON, D.C. BALTIMORE RESTAURANTS

Edited and Updated by
Olga Boikess

Contributing Editor for Baltimore
Marty Katz

Published and distributed by
ZAGAT SURVEY, LLC
4 Columbus Circle
New York, New York 10019
Tel: 212 977 6000
E-mail: zagat@zagatsurvey.com

Acknowledgments

Besides thanking the nearly 3,200 Washington/Baltimore restaurant-goers who shared their dining experience with us, we are especially grateful to Alicia Ault, David Belchik, Jay Block, Tom Bryant, Al and Ellen Butts, Karen Cathey, Fred Deutsch, Gary and Maryanne Ehrlich, Lorraine Fitzsimmons, Gail Forman, the Justin Franks, Phyllis Frucht, Carol Gitter, Bill Greene, Henry Hopkins III, Jim Jacobi, Rochelle Jaffe, Barbara Johnson, Jane and Danny Katz, Bill Kopit, Stanley Levy, Mary Martin, Carrie Matthews, Karen H. Seidenberg, Robert Singleton, Jerry Stein, George D. Stewart, and Bob and Bonnie Temple for their support. Our special thanks go to Jami Yuspa for her editorial assistance.

Contents

INDEXES (Cont.)

Introduction

This is not an all-new *Survey*. It is an *Update* reflecting significant developments since our last *Washington, D.C/Baltimore Restaurant Survey* was published. We have included a section of "1998 Additions" (see pages 19–28 for Washington, 165–173 for Baltimore, Annapolis and the Eastern Shore), covering some 95 key places that were not in the previous *Survey*. We have also made changes throughout the book (excluding indexes) to show new addresses, phone numbers, chef changes, closings, etc.

As a whole, this *Update* covers over 1,000 restaurants in the Washington, Baltimore and Annapolis area, with input from nearly 3,200 people. We want to thank each of our participants. This book is really "theirs." By regularly surveying large numbers of local restaurant-goers, we think we have achieved a uniquely current and reliable guide. We hope you agree. On the assumption that most people want a quick fix on the places at which they are considering eating, we have tried to be concise and to provide handy indexes.

We are particularly grateful to Olga Boikess, a Washington lawyer and avid restaurant-goer, who has organized, edited and updated this *Survey* since it was first published in the fall of 1986. Our special thanks also go to contributing editor Marty Katz, photographer and writer, for his insights on the Baltimore food scene.

We invite you to be a reviewer in our next *Survey*. To do so, simply send a stamped, self-addressed, business-size envelope to ZAGAT SURVEY, 4 Columbus Circle, New York, NY 10019, so that we will be able to contact you. Each participant will receive a free copy of the next *Washington, D.C./ Baltimore Restaurant Survey* when it is published.

Your comments, suggestions and even criticisms of this *Survey* are also solicited. There is always room for improvement with your help.

New York, New York   Nina and Tim Zagat
October 2, 1997

Foreword

Inside (as outside) the Beltway, restaurants play an increasingly important role in our lives. Most of us eat out, or carry-in, about as often as we cook. And as more of us work at home, we rely on restaurants, hotel lounges and coffee bars for business and social reasons as much as for sustenance. This dynamic shift in our dining patterns has led to a sustained boom in the restaurant industry, with a profusion of new eateries opening each year.

The nation's capital benefits from an impressive diversity of contemporary bistros, fusion diners, noodle houses and wrap shops — all responding to these needs in different ways. Their common denominator is wholesome, affordable food served in settings suitable for anything from a snack to a serious meal.

Among the most successful versions of this format are eye-catching updates of the classic American grill as exemplified by new-to-the-area branches of The Daily Grill, the District ChopHouse & Brewery and McCormick & Schmick's, which join perennials like the Carlyle Grand Cafe, the Occidental Grill and Old Ebbitt Grill in offering congenial, generously portioned, business-class dining at prices that don't offend clients eyeing the bottom line.

The region has always been a mecca for talented international chefs bringing inexpensive exotic cuisines within reach of our increasingly sophisticated dining public. Lately, however, the distinction between ethnic eateries and mainstream restaurants is blurring as the former outdo the latter in cutting-edge decor and marketing. New Georgetown hot spot Bangkok Bistro joins the already hopping Busara and the suburban-smart Tara Thais as a case in point. At the same time, contemporary American, French, Italian and Japanese chefs are borrowing techniques and ingredients from around the world. Just look at the menus at new ventures like Isabella, Starland Cafe and Tahoga, or at Sushi-Ko where D.C.'s top toques go for 'East meets West' Japanese fare.

At the Gen X end of the eating spectrum, Wrapworks and Zuki Moon are new examples of recent trends to either roll flavorful ingredients into meal-sized edible packages, or ladle them into big bowls. Along with coffee bars and cafe/bakeries like the new Bread Line and the expanding Firehook Bakery, their inventive fare, low-key, attractive premises, long hours and low prices are enticing enough to turn such casual establishments into virtual communal dining/living rooms.

Some of Baltimore's best eating has always taken place in neighborhood-oriented, family-run spots known for homey food and square-deal prices. Happily, many of its most successful recently opened restaurants – notably, Black Olive, Mamie's, San Sushi and Yianni Cafe – basically represent a new generation of hard-working, hands-on enterprises.

At the same time, Baltimore's need for anytime-dining-and-gathering is being met by the likes of Donna Crivello (Donna's at various locations) and One World Cafe, along with youngsters such as City Cafe and countless others. And blockbusters like the Cheesecake Factory and the new Hard Rock Cafe, with their highly visible settings and broad menus, will always find a niche in this popular tourist town.

In sum, each year brings D.C. and Baltimore diners whole new worlds of exciting dining possibilities to meet almost any need or whim. We hope this *Update* will guide you to many wonderful discoveries.

Washington, D.C.   Olga Boikess
October 2, 1997

Key to Ratings/Symbols

This sample entry identifies the various types of information contained in your Zagat Survey.

(1) Restaurant Name, Address & Phone Number

(2) Hours & Credit Cards

(3) ZAGAT Ratings

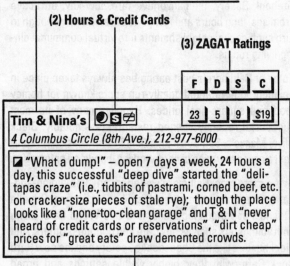

F	D	S	C
23	5	9	$19

Tim & Nina's ◖ Ⓢ ⊅

4 Columbus Circle (8th Ave.), 212-977-6000

◪ "What a dump!" – open 7 days a week, 24 hours a day, this successful "deep dive" started the "deli-tapas craze" (i.e., tidbits of pastrami, corned beef, etc. on cracker-size pieces of stale rye); though the place looks like a "none-too-clean garage" and T & N "never heard of credit cards or reservations", "dirt cheap" prices for "great eats" draw demented crowds.

(4) Surveyors' Commentary

The names of restaurants with the highest overall ratings, greatest popularity and importance are printed in **CAPITAL LETTERS**. Address and phone numbers are printed in *italics*.

(2) Hours & Credit Cards

After each restaurant name you will find the following courtesy information:

◖ .... *serving after 11 PM*

Ⓢ .... *open on Sunday*

⊅ .... *no credit cards accepted*

(3) <u>ZAGAT Ratings</u>

Food, **Decor** and **Service** are each rated on a scale of **0** to **30**:

F	D	S	C

F	....	*Food*
D	....	*Decor*
S	....	*Service*
C	....	*Cost*

23	5	9	$19

0 - 9	....	*poor to fair*
10 - 15	....	*fair to good*
16 - 19	....	*good to very good*
20 - 25	....	*very good to excellent*
26 - 30	....	*extraordinary to perfection*

▽ 23	5	9	$19

| ▽ | .... | *Low number of votes/less reliable* |

The **Cost (C)** column reflects the estimated price of a dinner with one drink and tip. Lunch usually costs 25% less.

A restaurant listed without ratings is either an important **newcomer** or a popular **write-in**. The estimated cost, with one drink and tip, is indicated by the following symbols.

–	–	–	VE

I	....	*$15 and below*
M	....	*$16 to $30*
E	....	*$31 to $50*
VE	....	*$51 or more*

(4) <u>Surveyors' Commentary</u>

Surveyors' comments are summarized, with literal comments shown in quotation marks. The following symbols indicate whether responses were mixed or uniform.

| ◩ | .... | *mixed* |
| ■ | .... | *uniform* |

Washington's Favorites

Upper map (Washington D.C. metropolitan area):

Miles 0—3

Detail to left

MARYLAND

Bethesda ⊛

Old Angler's Inn
Potomac ★

495

McLean ⊛

WASHINGTON NATIONAL AIRPORT

Carlyle Grand Cafe
Shirlington ★

Arlington

Washington D.C. ★

Potomac River

95

VIRGINIA

⊛

L'Auberge Chez Francois
Great Falls ★

7

Reston ⊛

Tysons Corner

The Inn at Little Washington
60 miles ★

⊛ Indicates home to one or more of the top 40 most popular restaurants

Lower map (Washington D.C. detail):

Washington D.C.

Rhode Island Ave.

Vermont Ave.

H St.

M St.

13th St.

S St.

16th St.

18th St.

Hampshire Ave.

City Lights of China

I Matti

Lebanese Taverna ★

New Heights ★

Cheesecake Factory ★

Austin Grill ★

Wisconsin Ave.

Morton's ★

1789 ★

Massachusetts Ave.

Nora ★

Jockey Club ★

Citronelle ★

Georgetown

Obelisk

Asia Nora

Galileo

Provence

Vidalia

Le Lion D'Or

Prime Rib

I Ricchi
The Palm
Sam & Harry's

Georgia Brown's

Morrison-Clark Inn

Ruppers

Gerard's Place

Bombay Club

Kinkead's

Taberna del Alabardero

Legal Sea Food

Kramerbooks

White House

Old Ebbitt Grill

Les Halles

Red Sage

Capitol Grille

Jaleo

701

Pennsylvania Ave.

The Mall

Constitution Ave.

E St.

K St.

Virginia Ave.

Theodore Roosevelt Island

Potomac River

Washington's Favorite Restaurants

Each of our reviewers has been asked to name his or her five favorite restaurants. The 40 spots most frequently named, in order of their popularity, are:

1. L'Auberge Chez Francois	21. Morrison-Clark Inn
2. Kinkead's	22. Old Angler's Inn
3. Inn at Little Washington	23. Lebanese Taverna
4. Galileo	24. Taberna del Alabardero
5. Vidalia	25. Capital Grille
6. Citronelle	26. Palm
7. Nora	27. Ruppers
8. Carlyle Grand Cafe	28. Morton's of Chicago
9. Prime Rib	29. Old Ebbitt Grill
10. I Ricchi	30. 701
11. Red Sage	31. Sam & Harry's
12. Gerard's Place	32. Georgia Brown's
13. Provence	33. New Heights
14. Bombay Club	34. Austin Grill
15. Jaleo	35. I Matti
16. Obelisk	36. City Lights of China
17. Le Lion D'Or	37. Les Halles
18. Cheesecake Factory	38. Jockey Club
19. 1789	39. Legal Sea Food
20. Rio Grande Cafe	40. Asia Nora

It's obvious that most of the restaurants on the above list are among the most expensive, but Washingtonians love a bargain. Were popularity calibrated to price, we suspect that a number of other restaurants would join the above ranks. Thus, we have listed over 150 "Best Buys" on pages 17 and 18.

Top Ratings*

Top 40 Food Ranking

29 Inn at Little Washington
28 Makoto
   L'Auberge Chez Francois
27 Kinkead's
   Obelisk
   Seasons
   Le Lion D'Or
26 Gerard's Place
   Prime Rib
   Galileo
   Citronelle
   L'Auberge Provencale
   Rupperts
   Nora
   Taste of Saigon
   Patisserie Cafe Didier
   Morton's of Chicago
25 Morrison-Clark Inn
   1789
   Rabieng

   Tachibana
   I Ricchi
   Peking Gourmet Inn
   Taberna del Alabardero
   Haandi
   Vidalia
   Provence
   Duangrat's
   Pizzeria Paradiso
   Four & Twenty Blackbirds
   Pesce
   New Heights
   City Lights of China
   Pilin Thai
24 Melrose
   Sushi-Ko
   Bombay Club
   Jockey Club
   La Bergerie
   Le Refuge

Top Spots by Cuisine

Top Additions
   Addie's
   Cesco
   Isabella
   McCormick & Schmick's
   Tahoga

Top American (New)
27 Kinkead's
   Seasons
26 Rupperts
   Nora
25 Morrison-Clark Inn

Top Bar-B-Q
22 Rockland's
20 Red Hot & Blue
19 Starke's Head Hog BBQ
   Houston's
18 Old Glory BBQ

Top Breakfast†
26 Patisserie Cafe Didier
23 La Colline
   La Brasserie
19 Parkway Deli
   Old Ebbitt Grill

Top Brunch
27 Kinkead's
   Seasons
26 Citronelle
25 Morrison-Clark Inn
   New Heights

Top Business Lunch
27 Kinkead's
   Seasons
   Le Lion D'Or
26 Gerard's Place
   Prime Rib

---

* Excluding restaurants with low voting.

† Other than hotels.

Top Chinese

25 Peking Gourmet Inn
City Lights of China
23 Mr. K's
22 Fortune
Good Fortune

Top Continental

24 Jockey Club
Ritz-Carlton Grill
23 Ritz-Carlton Restaurant
22 Tivoli
— Baron's

Top Creole/Cajun/
New Orleans

24 R.T.'s
22 Warehouse Bar & Grill
21 Cajun Bangkok
Louisiana Express Co.
20 219

Top Family Dining

24 Lebanese Taverna
21 Rio Grande Cafe
20 Red Hot & Blue
Outback Steakhouse
19 Hard Times Cafe

Top French Cafe/Bistro

24 Le Refuge
Village Bistro
23 Le Gaulois
Bistrot Lepic
Lavandou

Top French Classic

28 L'Auberge Chez Francois
27 Le Lion D'Or
24 La Bergerie
23 La Miche
La Colline

Top French (New)

26 Gerard's Place
Citronelle
25 Provence
24 Maison Blanche
Cafe Bethesda

Top Hamburgers

23 Carlyle Grand Cafe
22 Occidental Grill
21 Mike's American Grill
Artie's
19 Old Ebbitt Grill

Top of the Hill

23 La Colline
La Brasserie
21 Two Quail
20 La Lomita
B. Smith's

Top Hotel Dining

27 Seasons/Four Seasons
26 Citronelle/Latham
25 Morrison-Clark Inn
24 Melrose/Park Hyatt
Jockey Club/Ritz-Carlton

Top Indian

25 Haandi
24 Bombay Club
Bombay Bistro
22 Bombay Palace
Aditi

Top Italian

27 Obelisk
26 Galileo
25 I Ricchi
23 Goldoni
Il Pizzico

Top Japanese

28 Makoto
25 Tachibana
24 Sushi-Ko
23 Tako Grill
22 Hisago

Top Mex/Tex-Mex

21 Rio Grande Cafe
Mi Rancho
20 Lauriol Plaza
La Lomita
Enriqueta's

Top Middle Eastern

24 Lebanese Taverna
23 Moby Dick
Kazan
22 Pasha Cafe
Bacchus

Top Pizza

25 Pizzeria Paradiso
22 Coppi's
21 Faccia Luna Pizzeria
Eye St. Cafe
Red Tomato Cafe

Top Saturday Lunch
27 Kinkead's
26 Citronelle
   Taste of Saigon
   Patisserie Cafe Didier
25 Rabieng

Top Seafood
25 Pesce
23 Blue Point Grill
21 Sea Catch
   Legal Sea Food
   Crisfield

Top Southeast Asian
23 Asia Nora
   Germaine's
21 Oodles Noodles
   Straits of Malaya
— Raku

Top Southern
25 Morrison-Clark Inn
   Vidalia
22 Georgia Brown's
20 B. Smith's
18 Union St. Public Hse.

Top Southwestern
22 Red Sage
   Gabriel
20 Santa Fe East
   Cottonwood Cafe
18 Stella's

Top Steakhouses
26 Prime Rib
   Morton's of Chicago
24 Sam & Harry's
   Ruth's Chris
23 Capital Grille

Top Thai
25 Rabieng
   Duangrat's
   Pilin Thai
24 Tara Thai
23 Crystal Thai

Top Vegetarian Friendly
21 Greenwood's
19 Zed's
   Vegetable Garden
— Planet X
— Thyme Square

Top Vietnamese
26 Taste of Saigon
22 Cafe Dalat
   Queen Bee
   Cafe Saigon
   Saigon Gourmet

Top Worth a Trip
29 Inn at Little Washington/
   Washington, VA
26 L'Auberge Provencale/
   White Post, VA
25 4 & 20 Blackbirds/
   Flint Hill, VA
   Stone Manor/
   Middletown, MD
23 Bleu Rock Inn/
   Washington, VA

Top Yearlings/Rated
24 Cashion's Eat Place
23 Goldoni
   Jin-ga
   Bistrot Lepic
22 T.H.A.I.

Top Yearlings/Unrated
   Bangkok St. Grill
   Cafe Atlantico
   Lespinasse
   Raku
   Thyme Square

Top 40 Decor Ranking

29 Inn at Little Washington
27 Willard Room
  L'Auberge Chez Francois
26 Taberna del Alabardero
  L'Auberge Provencale
  1789
  Morrison-Clark Inn
  Seasons
  Bombay Club
  Red Sage
25 Ritz-Carlton Grill
  Makoto
  Coeur de Lion
  Jockey Club
  Capital Grille
  Prime Rib
  Ritz-Carlton Restaurant
  Asia Nora
  Jin-ga
24 Old Angler's Inn

Provence
Bleu Rock Inn
Jefferson
B. Smith's
Two Quail
Le Lion D'Or
Melrose
Sequoia
701
T.H.A.I.
Gadsby's Tavern
Nora
23 Hibiscus Cafe
Goldoni
Galileo
Shelly's Woodroast
New Heights
I Ricchi
Busara
Occidental Grill

Top Outdoor

Bleu Rock Inn
Coco Loco
Gerard's Place
Inn at Glen Echo
La Brasserie
L'Auberge Chez Francois

Old Angler's Inn
Perry's
Radio Free Italy
Sequoia
701
Straights of Malaya

Top Rooms

Asia Nora
Bombay Club
B. Smith's
Coeur de Lion
Inn at Little Washington
Jockey Club
Lespinasse
Makoto
Morrison-Clark Inn

Old Ebbitt Grill
Provence
Red Sage
Ritz-Carlton Grill
Ritz-Carlton Restaurant
Seasons
1789
Taberna del Alabardero
Willard Room

Top Views

Bleu Rock Inn
Cedar Knoll Inn
Chart House
Gangplank
L'Auberge Chez Francois

Le Rivage
Perry's
Potowmack Landing
Roof Terrace Ken. Ctr.
Sequoia

Top 40 Service Ranking

29 Inn at Little Washington
27 Makoto
    L'Auberge Chez Francois
26 Seasons
    L'Auberge Provencale
    Le Lion D'Or
25 Prime Rib
    Obelisk
    Taberna del Alabardero
    Bombay Club
    Rupperts
    Ritz-Carlton Grill
24 Jockey Club
    1789
    Four & Twenty Blackbirds
    Willard Room
    Morrison-Clark Inn
    Maison Blanche
    Nora
    Ritz-Carlton Restaurant

Melrose
Kinkead's
Gerard's Place
Coeur de Lion
Sam & Harry's
23 Galileo
    701
    Citronelle
    Bleu Rock Inn
    Jefferson
    Kazan
    Capital Grille
    Mr. K's
    Morton's of Chicago
    Vidalia
    New Heights
    I Ricchi
    Oval Room
    Rabieng
    La Bergerie

Best Buys*

Top 100 Bangs For The Buck

This list reflects the best dining values in our *Survey*. It is produced by dividing the cost of a meal into the combined ratings for food, decor and service.

1. Burro
2. El Pollo Rico
3. Bob & Edith's Diner
4. Pho 75
5. Crisp & Juicy
6. Hard Times Cafe
7. C.F. Folks
8. Pho 95
9. Le Bon Cafe
10. Moby Dick
11. Patisserie Cafe Didier
12. Cafe Saigon
13. Cafe Parisien Express
14. Pilin Thai
15. Florida Ave. Grill
16. Generous George's
17. Delhi Dhaba
18. Full Key
19. Ambrosia
20. Cowboy Cafe
21. La Madeleine
22. Cafe Dalat
23. Ledo Pizza
24. Faccia Luna Pizzeria
25. Haad Thai
26. Rockland's
27. Crystal Thai
28. Silver Diner
29. Oodles Noodles
30. Hunan Number One
31. Taste of Saigon
32. Nam Viet
33. Pizzeria Paradiso
34. Dean & DeLuca Cafe
35. Benjarong
36. Parkway Deli
37. Garrett Park Cafe
38. Coppi's
39. Bombay Bistro
40. T.H.A.I.
41. King Street Blues
42. Luna Grill
43. Little Viet Garden
44. Dusit
45. Rabieng
46. Taipei/Tokyo Cafe
47. Food Factory
48. Mi Rancho
49. Easby's
50. Burma
51. Bertucci's
52. Starke's Head Hog BBQ
53. La Lomita
54. Pizza de Resistance
55. Vox Populi
56. City Lights of China
57. Cafe Taj
58. Bua
59. Polly's Cafe
60. Haandi
61. State of the Union
62. Pasha Cafe
63. Mike's American Grill
64. Good Fortune
65. Skewers/Cafe Luna
66. Pho Cali
67. California Pizza Kitchen
68. Tara Thai
69. Red Tomato Cafe
70. Hard Rock Cafe
71. El Tamarindo
72. Artie's
73. Queen Bee
74. Thai Kingdom
75. Louisiana Express Co.
76. Eye St. Cafe
77. House of Chinese Gourmet
78. Hsiang Foong
79. China Chef
80. Calvert Grille
81. Saigon Gourmet
82. Austin Grill
83. Shelly's Woodroast
84. Bugaboo Creek Steak Hse.
85. Duangrat's
86. Foong Lin
87. Old Glory BBQ
88. Full Kee
89. Kabul Caravan
90. Rio Grande Cafe
91. Panjshir
92. Mick's
93. Nam's
94. Meskerem
95. Cactus Cantina
96. Aditi
97. Fortune
98. Sala Thai
99. Hunan Lion
100. Houston's

---

* Excluding coffeehouses.

Additional Good Values
(A bit more expensive, but worth every penny)

A&J Restaurant	Lauriol Plaza
Aangan	Lebanese Taverna
Aegean Taverna	Lite 'n' Fair
Amphora's Diner Deluxe	Malik
Arucola	Mama Wok & Teriyaki
Bangkok St. Grill	Mare E Monti
Bistro	Martin's Tavern
Bistro Bistro	Metro 29
Bistro Francais	Miss Saigon
Blue Plate	Music City Roadhse.
Bombay Club	Old Hickory Grill
Bread Line	Paolo's
Burrito Brothers	Pasta Plus
Busara	Perry's
Cafe Deluxe	Pesce
Cafe Mileto	Pho
Cajun Bangkok	Planet X
California Tortilla	Rhodeside Grill
Canton Cafe	Saigon Inn
Capitol Wrapps	Saigonnais
Caravan Grill	Southside 815
Carlyle Grand Cafe	Spices
Cheesecake Factory	Sunny Garden
Chicken Place	Sushi Chalet
Clyde's	Sushi Sushi
Del Ray Garden and Grill	That's Amore
Eat First	Tom Tom
Ecco Cafe	Umberto's
Enriqueta's	Union Street Public Hse.
Eurogrill	Vegetable Garden
Hibiscus Cafe	Vienna's Grille
Il Pizzico	Wrapworks
Il Raddichio	Wurzburg-Haus
Jaleo	Zed's
La Fourchette	Zuki Moon

Washington, D.C.
1998 Additions

R | C

A&J Restaurant 🆂⊄

† | |

1319-C Rockville Pike, Rockville, MD, 301-251-7878
This pleasant Rockville Pike Taiwanese tea house defines
cheap eats, serving some of the area's most authentic
dim sum and meal-sized noodle dishes for a pittance
($1.25-$4.95); its day-long dim sum menu ranges from the
familiar to exotic vegetables and meats, making it a smart
move to ask about what's on other peoples' plates.

Addie's

††† | M

11120 Rockville Pike (Edson Ln.), Rockville, MD, 301-881-0081
Rookie chef-owners Jeff and Barbara Black's cheerful
cottage adds a serious New American dining dimension
to the ethnics and generics dominating Rockville Pike;
powered by their professionalism and energy, this human-
scale spot serves Downtown food at suburban prices,
doesn't take reservations and is often jammed.

Amphora's Diner Deluxe 🆂◗

† | |

1151 Elden St. (Alabama Ave.), Herndon, VA, 703-925-0900
This enormous neon-and-silver beacon glows round-the-
clock, attracting hungry Herndon to its Greek-accented
fare; the ambitious, mega-size, 300-item menu is firmly in
the hands of a diner-dynasty family that's already been
successful with a Vienna progenitor.

Bangkok Bistro 🆂

† | |

*3251 Prospect St., NW (bet. Wisconsin Ave. & 33rd St.),
202-337-2424*
Strategically placed to share Cafe Milano's overflow (and
the parking lot across the street), Georgetown's new
Thai is hot; among its assets are a modish setting with
wraparound windows overlooking the passing scene
and a lovely courtyard patio; the visuals are even more
sizzling than the cool, contemporary victuals.

Barcelona 🆂

†† | M

*815 King St. (bet. Columbus & Alfred Sts.), Alexandria, VA,
703-548-1670*
Sample an array of 'little dishes', paella or a regional Iberian
entree at this tapas bar and taberna in Old Town Alexandria;
travelers who have toured the tascas (tapas bars) in its
namesake city swear that it tastes like the real thing.

Bistro Med (CLOSED) † | M |
7403 Coleshire Dr. (Anderson Rd.), VA, 703-827-2627
A spin-off of Arlington's successful Village Bistro bids for
McLean and Tysons Corner customers with moderately
priced Continental fare served in a traditional, European-
feeling room; although its garlicky specialties fit into the
current vogue for all things Mediterranean, its location in
a nondescript Pimmit Hills strip mall (near those tony
'hoods) does not.

Blue Plate ⑤ ‖ | I |
2002 P St., NW (bet. New Hampshire Ave. & 20th St.),
202-293-2248
The talents responsible for Obelisk and Pizzeria Paradiso
(this *Survey's* No. 1 Italian, and pizzeria, respectively)
reinvent homespun American eats – grilled cheese with
roasted veggies on homemade bread, chocolate cake and
freshly churned ice cream – at this svelte modern diner
off Dupont Circle; while its low prices are nostalgic, the
focus on quality ingredients, knowledgeable service and
anytime dining is very up-to-date.

Bread Line ‖‖ | I |
1751 Pennsylvania Ave., NW (bet. 17th & 18th Sts.), 202-822-8900
Inspired by the world's bread-based street foods (and the
World Bank across the way), Mark Furstenberg's (ex
Marvelous Market) new bakery/cafe serves made-from-
scratch bagels, sourdough breads, Danish and English
muffins for breakfast and piadina (Italian grilled wraps),
empanadas, sandwiches and soul-warming soups at
lunch; as you'd expect from this artisanal baker, the food
is unbelievably fresh.

Cafe Nunziata ⑤ (CLOSED) † | M |
555 Quince Orchard Rd. (Clopper Rd.), Gaithersburg, MD,
301-208-9292
At a major Gaithersburg intersection, this spacious,
contemporary Italian has something for everyone: a sociable
bar, attractive indoor and outdoor settings for business,
gala or casual meals and dancing and live entertainment; its
menu moves from creative pizzas, pastas, subs and salads to
well-conceived meat and seafood entrees.

Canton Cafe ⑤◑ ‖ | I |
Twinbrook Shopping Ctr., 2007 Viers Mill Rd. (Twinbrook Pkwy.),
Rockville, MD, 301-309-3888
Hanging BBQ ducks, bowls of congee and Chinese music
make you feel like you're in Canton rather than a bright,
spacious Rockville spot; its vast menu offers an imaginative
inventory of Cantonese dishes, from the not-to-be-missed
deep-fried, salt-spiced shrimp to mysterious concoctions
featuring pig intestines or jellyfish.

Canyon Cafe ⑤　t　M
Chevy Chase Pavilion, 5345 Wisconsin Ave., NW, 202-364-0700
Adobe brick, timbers, sunset hues and a chile-spiked
menu lend a Southwestern patina to a Friendship Heights
refueling stop; drawn by the area's upscale shoppers and
moviegoers, this Dallas import slugs it out with several
other nearby eateries for their trade.

Capital Wrapps　t　I
*4733 Bethesda Ave. (bet. Woodmont & Wisconsin Aves.),
301-654-0262*
No one's laying a bad rap on this cheerful Bethesda spot,
which picks up on the latest out-of-hand eating craze with
mouth-stretching roll-ups filled with spicy, health-conscious
ingredients; diners are encouraged to treat the menu's
SW, Thai and Caribbean combos as mere suggestions –
given its low-priced, eat-in/take-out format, why not?

Caravan Grill　t　I
1825 18th St., NW (bet. S & T Sts.) 202-518-0444
It didn't take long for Adams Morgan East to join the trek to
this appealing Persian restaurant with its lavish buffet and
exotic bill of fare; moderate prices, an artful, whitewashed
setting, a delightful patio and a proud host describing each
aromatic dish make for an easy intro to an ancient cuisine.

Cesco　ttt　E
4871 Cordell Ave. (Norfolk Ave.), Bethesda, MD, 301-654-8333
A primo place to sample top Italian toques Roberto Donna's
and Francesco Ricchi's signature dishes (noodles with rabbit
sauce, veal with black truffles) is their upscale Bethesda
joint; it's commodious, comfortable and, best of all (for
suburbanites), doesn't require driving Downtown; however,
given its padrones' popularity, call ahead.

Coco Pazzo ⑤❷ (CLOSED)　tt　E
Union Station, 50 Mass. Ave., NE, 202-898-2430
Manhattan locomotive Pino Luongo roars into Union Station,
streamlining the soaring space occupied by Sfuzzi into a
multilevel see-and-be-seen scene with Tuscan-inspired
cuisine; whereas its Italian name means 'crazy (as in madly
stirring) cooks', its polish and pizazz belie the sobriquet.

Daily Grill ⑤　tt　M
1200 18th St., NW (M St.), 202-822-5282
Everyday eats in slick, saloon surroundings is the concept
of this California-based chain whose massive bar, vintage
photos and wooden booths provide a suitable backdrop for
Connecticut Ave. white-collar biz; modeled after the Brown
Derby and other legendary grills, its all-American menu
features the kind of Cobb salads, steaks, chops and onion
rings that never seem to go out of style.

Dave and Busters 🅂🌀   † M
White Flint Mall, 11301 Rockville Pike (Nicholson Ln.), Rockville, MD, 301-230-5151
Virtual reality rules at this gleaming brass-and-wood Rockville American with lots of high-tech simulation: electronic games, a mock casino, a mystery theater and a massive sports-and-people-watching bar provide diversion; the dining room fuels the frenzy with pizzas and pastas.

Del Ray Garden and Grill 🅂   † I
4918 Del Ray Ave. (bet. Old Georgetown Rd. & Cordell Ave.), Bethesda, MD, 301-986-0606
Across the street from Downtown Bethesda public parking, a pocket-sized patch of green and trim blue-white-and-brick dining rooms give this beguiling Vietnamese a summery air; while its menu holds few surprises, quality ingredients, careful cooking and modest prices make this garden bloom.

District ChopHouse & Brewery 🌀   † M
509 Seventh St., NW (bet. E & F Sts. NW), 202-347-3434
This Pennsylvania Quarter saloon and brewhouse achieves instant Old Washington patina from the historic bank building that houses it and the vintage photos on the walls; its clubby gloss and grill room dining are just the ticket for the sports attending the new MCI arena, not to mention the suits and Shakespeare Theater goers regentrifying this zone.

Faryab Afghan Cuisine 🅂   † I
4917 Cordell Ave. (bet. Old Georgetown Rd. & Norfolk Ave.), 301-951-3484
Bethesda has dozens of ethnic restaurants, but until recently lacked Afghani fare; in this arched, white-walled dining room, admirers of that pungent cuisine enjoy kebabs, along with less-familiar Northern specialties.

Isabella   †† E
809 15th St., NW (bet. H & I Sts.), 202-408-9500
Although the dramatic Byzantine decor, suave servers and elaborate presentations at this modern Mediterranean provide visuals and victuals galore, its prime Downtown address puts the focus on the faces in the room; chef Will Greenwood's departure puts a question mark after its future plans.

John Harvard's Brew House 🅂   † M
1299 Pennsylvania Ave., NW (13th & E Sts.), 202-783-2739
Named for Harvard University's founder, reputedly a patron of suds scholarship, this handsome Downtown brewpub offers a postgrad beer education; its menu of internationally flavored tidbits and entrees is served in a dark wood setting destined for successful informal business meetings.

La Dolce Vita ⑤   † | M

10824 Lee Hwy. (bet Rte. 123 & Main St.), Fairfax, VA, 703-385-1530

A whimsically decorated wood-fired pizza oven is the centerpiece of this sunny, modern Fairfax Italian whose crusty pies, authentically sauced pastas and entrees give suburbanites a taste of the sweet life in Naples, Florence or Rome; yet, here, as in much of newly developed Northern Virginia, such mellow moments take place in a strip mall.

La Provence   † | M

Vienna Shopping Ctr., 144 W. Maple Ave. (bet. Center St. & Courthouse Rd.), Vienna, Va. 703-242-3777

In a Northern Virginia suburb dominated by ethnic eateries and chains, Keo Kountakoun (ex Le Paradise) and his chic wife Marie turn a mundane shopping plaza locale into a brick-walled, candlelit corner of provincial France; suffused with charm, its ambiance is almost as much of a draw as the prettily plated French bistro food.

Maggiano's Little Italy ⑤   † | M

Tysons Galleria, 1790M International Dr. (Rte. 123), Tysons Corner, VA, 703-356-9000

More is more at this Italian extravaganza in Tysons Corner; that goes for the gut busting, family-style platters, the sea of red-checked tablecloths, the noise and the waits; it also applies to the freshly baked breads, mile-high desserts, pastas, pizzas and salads that are featured in its Corner Bakery and Cafe; this is Chicago's Lettuce Entertain You's first area foray – expect more.

Mango Mike's ⑤   † | M

4111 Duke St. (bet. Quaker Ln. & N. Jordan St.), Alexandria, VA, 703-823-1166

Hot colors, comfy couches, sleek design and reggae evoke a casual Caribbean mood at this West Alexandria local; its amalgam of fresh fish, sweet and spicy salsas, rasta pastas and Creole creations, billed as 'contemporary Caribbean cuisine', buttressed by friendly surroundings and rational prices, are well-calibrated to this up-and-coming 'hood.

McCormick & Schmick's ⑤   †† | M

1652 K St., NW (bet. 16th & 17th Sts.), 202-861-2233

With its Edwardian opulence, professionalism, and fresh fish, the K St. link of this West Coast seafood chain became a power institution within days of its November '96 debut; here, pols and partners dine in paneled privacy, commodious booths, or mob its 65-foot mahogany bar for $1.95 meal-sized munchies (3:30-6:30 PM) and "light" (under $10) fare; N.B. Reston gets hooked-up in fall '97.

Mendocino Grille and Wine Bar S ⊥ | E

2917 M St., NW (bet. 29th & 30th Sts.), 202-333-2912
Geppetto's hearty pizzas gave way to designer pastas,
trendy entrees, a cruvinet and some 85 California wines at
its revamped Georgetown location; but while some local
bec fins haven't yet given the nod to this bistro's New
American food, its smashing, open-to-the-street setting
turns everyone's head.

Monroe's S ⊥ | M

1603 Commonwealth Ave. (Monroe Ave.), Arlington, VA,
703-548-5792
Treating customers like family is the stock-in-trade of the
brood responsible for this gleaming Del Ray American
Italian, as well as the nearby, ever-popular Calvert Grille;
with its high chairs, kiddie menu, serve-yourself bottles of
wine and spaghetti standbys, eating here is a lot like eating
at home – i.e. comfy and well-meaning, if not always tip-top.

Old Europe S ⊥ | M

2434 Wisconsin Ave., NW (below Calvert St.),
202-333-7600
Oktoberfest, wild game, new beer and May wine are only
a few of the year-round festivities at this Glover Park
rathskeller, whose wursts, schnitzel, dumplings and open-
handed hospitality remind many Germans of home; in 1998,
this venerable institution, said to be DC's oldest restaurant,
will celebrate its 50th birthday.

Old Hickory Grille S ⊥⊥ | I

15420 Old Columbia Pike (Rt. 198), Burtonsville, MD,
301-421-0204
Down-home BBQ and blackened, Cajun-style eats are fired-
up to order at this Burtonsville storefront cafe whose
homemade jalapeño biscuits, cornbread, fresh salsas and
well-made sides signal that this kitchen cares; it recently
doubled in size without sacrificing either its small-town
feel or old-time prices.

Olde Towne Tavern & Brewing Co. S◐ ⊥ | M

227 E. Diamond Ave. (N. Summit Ave.), Gaithersburg, MD,
301-948-4200
A century-old building in Olde Towne Gaithersburg provides
a smashing pub setting for unwinding, casual dining, live
music (upstairs) and New American eats; its extensive
selection of housemade beers and microbrews is backed
up by the requisite bar food and grills, but crowds, noise
and waits are the downside of its near-universal appeal.

Paul Kee ⬤   ⌗ | I
11305-B Georgia Ave. (University Blvd.), Wheaton, MD,
301-933-6886
Known for its meal-in-a-bowl Hong Kong–style soups and
roast pig, this ordinary-looking Wheaton Chinese cooks
authentically for its native clientele; adventurous diners
can sample its unusual casseroles or ask about daily
specials that feature seasonal produce.

Peking Eastern House S   ⌐ | I
Midway Shopping Ctr., 16041 Frederick Rd. (bet. Redland
& Shady Grove Rds.), Rockville, MD, 301-527-8558
This simple Rockville restaurant caters to the area's sizable
Chinese Muslim community by preparing its Northern
specialties with bean curd and halal (religiously approved)
meat; the place has zilch in the way of atmosphere (and
no pork or booze), but its daily dim sum and lamb dishes
are good enough to give it ecumenical appeal.

Rainforest Cafe S   ⌐ | M
Tysons Corner Ctr., 7928L Tysons Corner Ctr. (Rte. 7),
McLean, VA, 703-821-1900
Spectacular special effects – tropical storms, wild beasties,
live birds, exotic fish and talking trees – dominate this
Tysons Corner mall–based American-Eclectic, where gift
shop browsing vies with trencherman-sized, tropically
themed sandwiches, pastas, salads, seafood and drinks
as the focus of an 'environmentally conscious family
adventure'; the experience is cutesy, crowded, commercial
and by no means cheap – it's also fun.

Rhodeside Grill S⬤   ⌗ | I
1836 Wilson Blvd. (Rhodes St.), Arlington, VA, 703-243-0145
A smashing urban life mural, tasteful pottery and a serious
(yet affordable) American menu signal that this lively
Arlington roadsider is not just a watering hole – its talented
kitchen turns out revved-up staples and imaginative regional
cuisine; the food and service are good enough to be the
evening's entertainment, yet casual enough to accompany
the post–9:30 PM music.

Riverside Grille S   ⌐ | M
Washington Harbour, 3050 K St., NW (30th St.), 202-342-3535
This vast outdoor singles/people-watching scene stretches
along Washington Harbour, with a small, more formal
American dining room inside; here, as at its neighbor and
kin, Tony & Joe's Seafood Place, most customers come
for the show, treating its bar fare, seafood, pastas and
grills as supporting players.

Rock Bottom Brewery ⑤◐　t | M
7900 Norfolk Ave. (St. Elmo St.), Bethesda, MD, 301-652-1311
It's perpetually party-time at this larger-than-life Bethesda
brewpub, sports bar, pool hall, music scene, cigar lounge
and multilevel meetery whose dark-wood-and-stainless-
steel decor and mostly Southwestern menu don't miss a
trendy trick; judging by the massive crowds, this branch
of a Boulder, Colorado, rock-solid chain has hit paydirt.

Saigon Royal ⑤ (CLOSED)　t | ┘
1326 E. Gude Dr. (S. Law Rd.), Rockville, MD, 301-309-0444
Look past the dreary Rockville locale to discover the charms
of this pretty Indochine, whose crisp appointments suit its
zesty, fresh tasting cuisine; soups and seafood spark its
roster of all things Vietnamese.

Serbian Crown ⑤　t | VE
1141 Walker Rd. (Colvin Run Rd.), Great Falls, VA, 703-759-4150
This Great Falls staple for candlelit Continental dining à la
Russe pulls out all the stops – caviar, vodkas, violins and
flaming desserts; perennially popular, notwithstanding its
dressy demeanor and regal rates, it's a clubroom for the
local limo set and a backdrop for their special events.

Starland Cafe ⑤　tt | M
5125 MacArthur Blvd. (Arizona Ave.), 202-244-9396
Potomac is singing about this recent American release
that pays homage to '70s music and Bill Starland's band; the
area has long needed just this blend of casual elegance,
spirited staff and affordable regional cooking; and to crib
from Starland's hit, the patio is an *Afternoon Delight.*

Sushi Sushi ⑤　tt | ┘
*4915 Fairmont Ave. (bet. Norfolk Ave. & Old Georgetown Rd.),
Bethesda, MD, 301-654-9616*
Simply sushi is the story line of this bento box–sized
operation in bustling Bethesda where one can sample
sparkling fresh seafood in subdued Japanese surroundings.

Sweetwater Tavern ⑤　tt | M
*14250 Sweetwater Ln. (Multiplex Dr.), Centreville, VA,
703-449-1100*
3066 Gatehouse Plaza (Gallows Rd.), 703-645-8100
Rapidly developing Centreville and Tysons Corner get in
on the burgeoning brewpub scene at these latest ventures
of trend-smart Great American Restaurants Inc. (responsible
for the successful Carlyle Grand Cafe and Silverado);
accoutrements range from a grain silo to Western-theme
props and vittles.

Tahoga S   ††† | E

2815 M St., NW (bet. 28th & 29th Sts.), 202-338-5380
Named for the Indian village that pre-dated Georgetown, this
sleek townhouse's sculpted interior and New American
food (scallops with corn-pancetta relish) is all very 20th
century; its air of casual refinement facilitates on- and
off-duty meetings and its secret garden is truly a find.

Umberto's S   †† | M

*7745 Tuckerman Ln. (Seven Locks Rd.), Potomac, MD,
301-983-5566*
It's close to home, family friendly, realistically priced and
serves well-prepared, generously portioned versions of the
Italian owner's mother's recipes; no wonder this Potomac
favorite recently had to let out its belt and expand.

Vox Artis   †† | M

839 17th St., NW (bet. 17th & I Sts.), 202-974-4260
Mirrors, murals, French windows and polished wood give
this Farragut Square brasserie its Parisian sensibility, while
its fish soup conjures up the south of France; here, Jacques
Bourgeois offers the serious suits who frequent his casual
cafe, Vox Populi, the next level of gourmet Gallic.

White Tiger S   † | I

301 Massachusetts Ave., NE (3rd St.), 202-546-5900
Congressional staffers hunting for an affordable lunch in
pleasant surroundings should check out this classy Indian; it
offers lots of savory vegetarian and nonvegetarian choices
and one of Capitol Hill's nicest sidewalk cafes.

Wrapworks S   † | I

1079 Wisconsin Ave., NW (bet. M & Potomac Sts.), 202-333-0220
1601 Connecticut Ave., NW (Q St.), 202-265-4200
*Reston Town Ctr., 1820 Discovery St. (Reston Pkwy.), Reston, VA,
703-318-5200*
Wrapping trendy fusion combos (i.e. Southwestern, Asian
and Mediterranean) in tasty casings for portable, anytime
eats, these syndicated cafes are riding the latest culinary
wave; an instant twentysomethings hit, their utilitarian
premises are as packed as their colorful tortillas.

Zuki Moon S   ††† | I

*George Washington University Inn, 824 New
Hampshire Ave., NW (bet. I & K Sts.), 202-333-3312*
At her serene Foggy Bottom Asian noodle house, Mary
Richter's (ex Cities) riffs on popular Far Eastern cuisines
feature udon (thick noodles) in broth topped with fish, meats
and crisp veggies, as well as tempura, grills and serious
sweets; for those in tune with her 'less-is-more' sensibility,
such simple, sophisticated dining is the perfect prelude
(or coda) to a nearby Kennedy Center event.

Alphabetical Directory of Washington, D.C. Restaurants.

Washington, D.C.

	F	D	S	C

Aangan S
17 | 16 | 18 | $21
4920 St. Elmo Ave. (bet. Old Georgetown Rd. & Norfolk Ave.), Bethesda, MD, 301-657-1262

■ "Undeservedly overlooked", this Bethesda Indian's "fresh and subtle" dishes suit an "American palate", while its colonial courtyard setting feels "sunny" on the darkest winter day; "very pleasant" (if "slow") service makes it a "warm and welcoming" "discovery."

Aaranthi S
▽ 18 | 14 | 17 | $19
Danor Plaza, 409 Maple Ave. E. (Beula St.), Vienna, VA, 703-938-0100

☑ This suburban sibling of the well-thought-of Georgetown Indian, Aditi, receives mixed notices; while some delight in finding the same "delicious food" and a staff "that enjoys giving" good service, others insist it "must be adopted."

Aditi S
22 | 16 | 19 | $20
3299 M St., NW (33rd St.), 202-625-6825

■ "A step above the usual Indian", this second-story dining room produces "nicely representative" fare at lower-caste prices; despite the "lack" of decor, most rate it "worth the parking nightmare" in Georgetown (high praise).

Aegean Taverna S
17 | 15 | 17 | $17
2950 Clarendon Blvd. (Garfield St.), Arlington, VA, 703-841-9494

☑ "Pleasant patio dining" and being treated "like family" enhance the appeal of the "consistent" food dished out at this Clarendon Hellene; though a few find the fare "boring", it's welcome in an area with "few Greek choices"; the mood is "understated" – that is, "until the belly dancer arrives."

Alamo S
▽ 13 | 17 | 13 | $16
1063 31st St. (M St.), 202-342-2000

☑ A newish Georgetown "neighborhood drop-in" joint where the Tex-Mex vittles don't live up to the "painstakingly detailed Western decor"; it tastes like a case of "too much tequila for the chef" or simply a kitchen that "needs to work out the kinks."

Alamo ● S
13 | 18 | 14 | $17
100 King St. (Union St.), Alexandria, VA, 703-739-0555

☑ A party-prime corner location in Old Town, "amazing margaritas" and country-rock bands are the "primary draws" of this Tex-Mex; happily, few of its youngish partisans get past the "great chips and salsa" sober enough to taste the "predictable" entrees.

Ambrosia ◑⋻
| 19 | 6 | 17 | $11 |

Congressional South, 1765 Rockville Pike (bet. Twinbrook Rd. & Alpine Dr.), Rockville, MD, 301-881-3636

■ "Long lines" tell the story about this great Greek "dive" in Rockville – the food is "good, cheap" and "plentiful", and the "factory setting" has so little atmosphere that it's considered "colorful" (or "depressing"); go for the "best gyro platter in the area" or lamb "done any way."

America ◑S
| 13 | 18 | 15 | $19 |

Union Station, 50 Massachusetts Ave., NE (North Capitol), 202-682-9555
Tysons Corner Ctr., 8008-L Tysons Corner Ctr. (Rte. 7), McLean, VA, 703-847-6607

◪ The terrific "*Mr. Smith Goes to Washington* views" from this Union Station megadiner, and Capitol gazing from its sidewalk cafe, are tempered by a "way-too-ambitious" American menu and "waiters with a bad attitude"; less demanding patrons point out it's "fun for out-of-towners" and "there's something for everyone"; P.S. the "barnlike cave" in Tysons Corner has a similar "luck-of-the-draw" menu sans the people-watching and pols.

American Grill ◑S
| 19 | 17 | 17 | $29 |

(fka Cafe Pierre)
Loews L'Enfant Plaza Hotel, 480 L'Enfant Plaza, SW, 202-484-1000

◪ An "oasis" in the L'Enfant Plaza "concrete jungle", this hotel dining room's "imaginative" Contemporary American menu and restful surroundings are a welcome respite; while not perfect, it's worth considering for a quiet lunch or dinner – especially since they "make one great dark chocolate cake."

Andalucia S
| 20 | 18 | 20 | $30 |

Shoppes of Bethesda, 4931 Elm St. (Arlington Rd.), Bethesda, MD, 301-907-0052
12300 Wilkins Ave. (Parklawn Dr.), Rockville, MD, 301-770-1880

■ These "congenial" Spaniards rank among suburban Maryland's "classier restaurants" despite their "commercial zone" (Rockville) and "glorified storefront" (Bethesda) settings; host-owner Joaquim Serrano establishes a "refined" environment in which to enjoy "straightforward" classics and "expertly prepared fish" – when he's around, things seem especially well-oiled.

Appetizer Plus S
| – | – | – | M |

1117 N. 19th St. (Lynn St.), Rosslyn, VA, 703-525-3171
Known for its "inexpensive" but uninspired all-you-can-eat sushi, this Rosslyn Japanese is a "good value" if you're not expecting thrills or frills; go hungry and be prepared to wait.

Aquarelle 🆂   <u>-</u> <u>-</u> <u>-</u> <u>E</u>

Watergate Hotel, 2650 Virginia Ave., NW (New Hampshire Ave.), 202-298-4455

Following the much-publicized departure of superchef Jean-Louis Palladin from its kitchen, this dining room refocuses on its paintable Potomac River vistas complemented by classically based New American food and appointments; its new toque, Robert Wiedmaier, earned high marks at Cafe on M for his flavor palette and presentations.

Argentine Grill 🆂   <u>16</u> <u>14</u> <u>16</u> <u>$20</u>

2433 18th St., NW (Columbia Rd.), 202-234-1818

◪ At one of the "best sidewalk spots in Adams Morgan", local gauchos sample the cuisine of Argentina; although some find the service "surly" and the hearty fare focusing on chewy (read "tough") steaks and grilled specialty meats "much ado about nothing", the "lively" weekend scene is more like the "real thing" – "to South America we go."

Arizona (CLOSED)   <u>-</u> <u>-</u> <u>-</u> <u>I</u>

1211 Connecticut Ave. (M St.), 202-785-1211

Write-ins alerted us to "one of the city's best-kept new secrets" – a Southwesterner with lots of style, "unusual tastes" and a below-Dupont-Circle address; its "chicken mole comes with dreamy mashed potatoes" and "you can't beat the ribs."

Aroma 🆂   <u>-</u> <u>-</u> <u>-</u> <u>M</u>

1919 I St. (20th St.), 202-833-4700

Not quite "undiscovered" (but hardly well-known), this intimate K Street–area Indian is one of several "top-notch" subcontinentals to open in the past few years; its classical menu of tandooris, curries and breads offers "delicate, mouthwatering food" at "reasonable prices."

Artie's 🆂   <u>21</u> <u>18</u> <u>20</u> <u>$19</u>

3260 Old Lee Hwy. (south of Fairfax Circle), Fairfax, VA, 703-273-7600

◼ "Consistent", "attractive", "friendly and open late" on weekends are among the "good reasons" this all-purpose American is "often mobbed"; it's probably the best business lunch option in the Fairfax "restaurant wasteland" (though you'll "struggle to hear the deal"), with "addictive rolls", a "great prime rib" and draft microbrews.

Arucola 🆂   <u>16</u> <u>15</u> <u>15</u> <u>$24</u>

5534 Connecticut Ave., NW (Morrison St.), 202-244-1555

◪ "Tasty", "affordable" "meals on wheels" sums up this "trendy" Chevy Chase Italian where rolling carts are laden with pastas and antipasti accompanied by grilled meats and fish; the "smorgasbord approach" encourages family-style dining, but with "kids everywhere", "no reservations and no room to wait", some "only visit for lunch."

ASIA NORA
23 | 25 | 22 | $37

2213 M St., NW (bet. 22nd & 23rd Sts.), 202-797-4860

■ Nora Pouillon makes "exquisite use of small space" to achieve a "Zen"-like serenity at this West End Asian "adventure"; her "cool, fresh" fare synthesizes Japanese, Thai, Indonesian and Indian influences – it's "health-conscious", on the edge, "expensive" and strikes a few as "contrived"; still, you "always run into White House staff" and knowledgeable foodies.

Atami S
18 | 10 | 16 | $20

3155 Wilson Blvd. (Clarendon Metro Stop), Arlington, VA, 703-522-4787

■ The $24.95 "unlimited" sushi special at this "dreary", "no-frills" Clarendon Japanese uses "good-quality" fish and "doesn't try to fill you up on rice"; however, unless you're famished or it's time for "that monthly sushi gorging", tempura, one-dish meals or sushi à la carte are more cost-effective options.

Athenian Plaka S
17 | 18 | 18 | $21

7833 Woodmont Ave. (Fairmont Ave.), Bethesda, MD, 301-986-1337

☑ Although "you can do better" than this "agreeably kitschy" Greek for fine dining in Bethesda, it's not a bad choice "for an outdoor lunch on a sunny day"; you'll get lots of "homey", "garlicky" food in a "cheerful atmosphere."

Au Pied du Cochon ◑S
12 | 13 | 13 | $17

1335 Wisconsin Ave., NW (Dumbarton St.), 202-333-5440

☑ The charms of this "funky", 24-hour French "hole-in-the-wall" in Georgetown are elusive unless you've been there "at 3:30 AM" – supposedly, the "cheap" omelets, eggs Benedict and fries "are better then" and "people-watching" peaks; perhaps it's because late at night it's less obvious that it "needs a good scrubbing."

Austin Grill S
19 | 15 | 17 | $17

2404 Wisconsin Ave., NW (Calvert St.), 202-337-8080
8430 Old Keene Mill Rd. (Rolling Rd.), W. Springfield, VA, 703-644-3111
7278 Woodmont Ave. (Elm Ave.), Bethesda, MD, 301-656-1366

South Austin Grill
801 King St. (Washington St.), Alexandria, VA, 703-684-8969

■ These "high-energy" cantinas "give Tex-Mex food a fresh look" (think "duck tacos", crabmeat quesadillas), swirl "addictive" margaritas and have a "country-western feel" that makes Texans feel "right at home"; they're "crowded" and "too loud to converse", but the Gen X crowd doesn't go here to talk.

Bacchus
22 | 18 | 20 | $25

1827 Jefferson Pl., NW (bet. M & N Sts.), 202-785-0734
7945 Norfolk Ave. (Del Ray Ave.), Bethesda, MD,
301-657-1722 S

■ Patron "loyalty is well deserved" by these "personable"
Lebanese siblings for their "consistently good" food and
"low-key" (if "dated") surroundings; they're "ideal for meze"
(appetizers) and "good for an inexpensive business lunch"
(with "great eavesdropping") in Dupont Circle; "spend a
lot or not much – and get a good meal either way."

Balalayka S
▽ 16 | 18 | 19 | $21

3300 M St., NW (33rd St.), 202-338-4544

☑ Step down into a Russian happening at this M Street
basement cafe, where you'll find "lots of Russians", "very
heavy food", garish decor, "live music" and offbeat fun;
be sure to bring a designated driver.

B & C S (CLOSED)
– | – | – | M

(aka Bread & Circus Cafe)
2323 Wisconsin Ave. (Calvert St.), 202-333-5393

Grocery shopping in Upper Georgetown takes on a new
dimension at this "promising" in-store cafe, which uses
"fresh, wholesome" ingredients from the market in its
pastas, salads and grills; an 'in' spot for "breakfast" or a
"light lunch", it also serves casual dinners.

Bangkok St. Grill & Noodles
– | – | – | I

5872 Leesburg Pike (bet. Columbia Pike & Glen Carlyn
Rd.), Falls Church, VA, 703-379-6707

Head to Falls Church for a quick, inexpensive tour of
Thailand's street-food stalls; here, Duangrat's young sprig
reproduces the vendors' noodle, rice bowl and grill
specialties in a spare, blond wood and white setting; this
place is getting good press.

Bangkok Vientiane S
▽ 18 | 9 | 13 | $15

926 W. Broad St. (bet. West St. & Ospring St.), Falls
Church, VA, 703-534-0095

☑ Laos' location between Vietnam and Thailand explains
the multinational menu and clientele at this Falls Church
Asian; "hot", spicy food is the focus – "all else is left to
chance" (translation: "depressing" decor, "slow service");
while a handful hint it's "gone downhill", most maintain
it's "cheap" and "good."

Bardo Rodeo
9 | 12 | 11 | $13

2000 Wilson Blvd. (1 block east of Courthouse Metro
Stop), Arlington, VA, 703-527-9399

■ One goes to this "postapocalyptic" "playground" in an
"old car dealership painted like an LSD trip" for all-night
pool, "bold" house brews and "raucous fun"; "forget the
food" (mostly "veggie victuals") – this place is a one-of-
a-kind, "love-it-or-hate-it", "great slumming beer joint."

Baron's   – | – | – | M
Sheraton Premiere at Tysons Corner, 8661 Leesburg Pike (Westwood Ctr. Dr.), Vienna, VA, 703-448-1234
At night, soft lights and music provide a "pleasant" backdrop for the Contemporary American fare in this "beautiful", "baronial" Tysons Corner dining room; the venue is best known to locals for the "wonderful selection at Sunday brunch" ($29.95 including champagne) served in the less formal space called Ash Grove.

BeDuCi   21 | 18 | 20 | $30
2100 P St., NW (bet. 20th & 21st Sts.), 202-223-3824
☑ "If only you could eat charm", this Dupont Circle Mediterranean might beat them all – not that a meal here isn't often "delicious" and "delightful"; "given the high price", however, many customers expect better food and comfort; N.B. its spring 1996 move to a bigger space, featuring a notable sidewalk cafe, addressed the latter complaint.

Bei Tempi ⑤   15 | 15 | 17 | $24
4930 Cordell Ave. (Old Georgetown Rd.), Bethesda, MD, 301-718-0344
☑ Regulars sing the praises of the warmth, willingness "to please", "traditional" fare and special deals at this popular, family-run Bethesda Neapolitan, but less-impressed patrons consider the name (which means 'beautiful times') a misnomer.

Belmont Kitchen ⑤   18 | 17 | 17 | $23
2400 18th St., NW (Belmont Rd.), 202-667-1200
☑ Long known for "providing Waspy food" in "DC's most ethnic neighborhood", and for its "people-watching" outdoor brunch, this Adams Morgan "nook" also has a rep for "bad service", but the staff is so "nice" that many overlook it.

Benjarong ⑤   22 | 18 | 20 | $18
Wintergreen Plaza, 855-C Rockville Pike (Edmonston Rd.), Rockville, MD, 301-424-5533
■ There are "some very nice dishes" on the comprehensive menu at this "classy", "reasonably priced" Rockville Thai, along with nice touches, such as artwork on display, that you wouldn't expect to find in a "cheap, ethnic" storefront; admirers judge it the "best Thai in suburban Maryland."

Benkay   15 | 10 | 15 | $18
727 15th St., NW (bet. H St. & New York Ave.), 202-737-1515
☑ Fighting "lines and tourists" for "mass-produced", "mediocre" sushi at this Downtown Japanese's all-you-can-eat buffet isn't ideal, but you "can't beat the price" and the "set meals" are even more of "a bargain"; the utilitarian setting at least has "great TV."

Bertolini's S　　15 17 15 $21

801 Pennsylvania Ave., NW (9th St.), 202-638-2140
White Flint Mall, 11301 Rockville Pike (Nicholson Ln.),
Bethesda, MD, 301-984-0004

◪ These strategically located chain places with upscale decor and "by the numbers" Italian food "aren't restaurants you'd travel miles to go to", but for a "reasonably priced" pizza and salad they're "surprisingly good" – and the "very slow" servers are kind to kids.

Bertucci's S　　17 16 16 $15

1218-20 Connecticut Ave., NW (Jefferson Pl.), 202-463-7733
2000 Pennsylvania Ave., NW (bet. 20th & 21st Sts.),
202-296-2600
8027 Leesburg Pike (off Rte. 495), Vienna, VA, 703-893-5200
7421 Sudley Rd. (Nicholson St.), Manassas, VA, 703-257-5550
13195 Parcher Ave. (bet. Elden St. & Worldgate Dr.),
Herndon, VA, 703-787-6500
6525 Frontier Dr. (Franconia Rd.), Springfield, VA, 703-313-6700
6208 Multiplex Dr. (bet. Rte. 28 & Old Braddock Rd.),
Centreville, VA, 703-803-9300
725-27 King St. (Columbus St.), Alexandria, VA, 703-548-8500

◪ "Popular with families" for what they are – "cheap", "convenient" places for "pretty decent" pizza plus pasta and salads; as with any chain, you'll find "clueless" help, poor housekeeping and "mediocre food" on any given day at any location.

Bice S (CLOSED)　　23 23 21 $39

601 Pennsylvania Ave., NW (Indiana Ave.), 202-638-2423

◪ This "boisterous" Downtown Northern Italian "power" place for "trendy lunches at Fendi prices" has been "much maligned" (i.e. often pronounced "bitchy") despite its "fabulous" risotto, "reliable people-watching" and handsome setting; a Seventh Street corridor pioneer, it is still going strong.

Bilbo Baggins S　　18 18 18 $22

208 Queen St. (Lee St.), Alexandria, VA, 703-683-0300

◪ Fans of this "funky" Alexandria townhouse delight in its "interesting" American and veggie dishes (even when they "don't quite pan out") and don't mind the contrast between the "warm setting" and sometimes "colder-than-your-ex-in-laws" service; while its homemade raisin bread and sticky buns are a "habbit", a "serious" wine list is the sleeper.

Bistro S　　– – – M

ANA Hotel, 2401 M St., NW (24th St.), 202-457-5020
Exciting young chefs are keeping this moderately priced Contemporary American bistro on DC's culinary map; pleasant dining is made more so by the handsome wood and tile interior, secluded courtyard and "very helpful staff; surveyors say the "spectacular" Sunday brunch in the Colonnade room is not to be missed.

Bistro Bistro S   20 | 18 | 18 | $22

*Village at Shirlington, 4021 S. 28th St., Arlington, VA,
703-379-0300*
*Reston Town Ctr., 1811 Library St. (bet. Dulles Toll Rd. &
Reston Pkwy.), Reston, VA, 703-834-6300*
4301 N. Fairfax Dr. (Glebe Rd.), Ballston, VA, 703-522-1800
☑ Designer American bistros with a "solid menu" that try to
create a "neighborhood" feel in "faux-urban" locales;
fans think they're best for hanging out with friends and
"post-movie fare", but detractors decry "bland" food,
"yuppie" pricing and a staff trained for "throughput."

Bistro Francais ●S   20 | 18 | 18 | $26

3128 M St., NW (bet. 31st St. & Wisconsin Ave.), 202-338-3830
☑ "Where else in DC" can you get a real dinner "at 1 AM"?;
the later it gets, the more "wonderfully French" this
Georgetown "standby" becomes as it fills up with chefs,
nightowls and travelers on "late-night flights"; its steak
tartare and pommes frites are as legendary as its prix fixe
deals; "if service were better, it wouldn't seem so authentic."

Bistro Le Monde (CLOSED)   17 | 14 | 17 | $21

223 Pennsylvania Ave., SE (bet. 2nd & 3rd Sts.), 202-544-4153
■ Prompted by congressional gift-ban rules, which are
drying up the Capitol Hill lunch trade, and an increasingly
health-conscious clientele, this House-side Gallic bar and
upstairs bistro (fka Le Mistral) have a new format and menu
of lower-priced salads, pastas and light entrees; downstairs
plays to "staffers and Hill locals", upstairs it's "Hill-itis."

Bistrot Lepic S   23 | 19 | 21 | $34

1736 Wisconsin Ave., NW (S St.), 202-333-0111
■ "Très French" in a "Georgetowny" way, this "charming"
storefront with "true bistro" fare is "just the right size"
("a tad cramped") to be a "wonderful find"; it's "always
crowded, but one is never rushed."

Bistro Twenty Fifteen S   21 | 19 | 21 | $32

*Embassy Row Hilton, 2015 Massachusetts Ave. (off
Dupont Circle), 202-939-4250*
☑ "Hidden" off Dupont Circle, this "quiet, restful"
hotel venue with a new (post-*Survey*) chef seems to
be "struggling to find its image", which is currently
Contemporary American.

Bleu Rock Inn S   23 | 24 | 23 | $44

*Rte. 211 (5 mi. west of Hwy. 522 N.), Washington, VA,
540-987-3190*
☑ With its "romantic" Blue Ridge Mountain prospect, this
French-accented inn is a "delightful" overnight destination;
but its food and hospitality suffer by comparison with the
Inn at Little Washington nearby; surrounded by vineyards
and orchards, it's still a "nice Sunday jaunt" and especially
"lovely" at brunch (which the legendary Inn doesn't serve).

Blue & Gold S — | — | — | M |
3100 Clarendon Blvd. (Highland St.), Arlington, VA, 703-908-4995
Northern Virginia brewpubs are going "upscale" as
evidenced by this "overly ambitious" Clarendon entry; early
samplers report that the "delicious, Cajun-influenced" food
is "pretty pricey"; nevertheless, one "could get comfortable
here" – with earplugs.

Blue Point Grill S 23 | 17 | 20 | $31 |
600 Franklin St. (Washington St.), Alexandria, VA, 703-739-0404
☑ "Browse the antiques on King Street", then drop by
Sutton Place Gourmet for some of the "best seafood in
Alexandria" at its "spartan" cafe; the "exceptionally fresh"
fish doesn't come cheap, and the kitchen and servers
stumble, but more often than not the "innovative menu"
and good wine prevail.

Bob & Edith's Diner ◗S⇄ 15 | 12 | 16 | $9 |
2310 Columbia Pike (Wayne St.), Arlington, VA, 703-920-6103
☑ It's "fast, friendly, filling and 'fordable" – and at 4 AM it
"beats waiting until 'real' places open for breakfast"; this
"classic", "very un-Washington" "grease pit" in Arlington
may also be the only place where "middle-aged women,
bikers and trendy gays fit in with yuppies."

Bombay Bistro S 24 | 13 | 19 | $17 |
3570 Chain Bridge Rd. (Lee Hwy.), Fairfax, VA, 703-359-5810
Bell's Corner, 98 W. Montgomery Ave. (Washington St.),
Rockville, MD, 301-762-8798
■ Respected by the local Indian community for their
"delicious" classics and regional specialties, plus an
"amazingly fresh" buffet lunch, these "always packed"
suburbanites are high on virtually everyone's "cheap
eats" list; if you "love good food more than fine dining",
they're a "real treat."

BOMBAY CLUB S 24 | 26 | 25 | $34 |
815 Connecticut Ave. (bet. H & I Sts.), 202-659-3727
■ One of Downtown DC's top "power-dining" rooms, this
"supercivilized" Anglo-Indian, with its "days of the raj"
opulence, "sophisticated" kitchen and "elegant" manners,
is surprisingly "low-key . . . for the price"; credit its savvy
owner, Ashok Bajaj, who "knows what DC wants."

Bombay Dining S ▽ 23 | 18 | 19 | $23 |
4931 Cordell Ave. (Old Georgetown Rd.), Bethesda, MD,
301-656-3373
■ "Cordial" and a "great value for interesting food" sums
up the attraction of this "excellent" Indian in Bethesda; try
the "best-buy" lunch buffet, then go next door to Travel
Books to plan your trip.

Bombay Palace S   22 | 19 | 20 | $28
2020 K St., NW (bet. 20th & 21st Sts.), 202-331-4200
☑ This K Street Indian with "pretty, pink" decor is "not as upscale as the nearby Bombay Club", but it's "worthy in its own right"; many, in fact, think it's a "better value" and serves the "best traditional Indian food outside an Indian home" (i.e. spicy and rich).

B. Smith's S   20 | 24 | 18 | $28
Union Station, 50 Massachusetts Ave., 202-289-6188
■ Barbara Smith's soulful restaurant in a "majestic" Union Station setting successfully "combines down-home feel with elegance" and "welcomes all"; the "high-end Southern fare" can be "delicious" or "mediocre", but "it's worth the risk to see the room" and the "ultracool evening clientele" – a great choice "for foreign guests."

Bua S   21 | 16 | 19 | $18
1635 P St. (bet. 16th & 17th Sts.), 202-265-0828
■ Although the "atmosphere could use some work", this "relaxed", "reasonably priced" Thai with a "breezy deck" and "fresh, spicy" food is deemed a Dupont Circle East "trade secret" ("like a fishing hole only I know"); one of the few naysayers quips, "tiny portions explain the servers' trim waistlines."

Bugaboo Creek Steak House S   15 | 20 | 17 | $18
6820 Commerce Dr. (Backlick Rd.), Springfield, VA, 703-451-3300
15710 Shady Grove Rd. (Rte. 270, exit 8), Gaithersburg, MD, 301-548-9200
☑ "Kids love" these "goofy" steakhouses for their "Disneyish" decor and "novelty" atmosphere complete with "talking animals", while their parents love the price; the steak and ribs are "ordinary" if plentiful, though occasionally they talk back.

Buon Giorno   20 | 19 | 20 | $32
8003 Norfolk Ave. (Del Ray Ave.), Bethesda, MD, 301-652-1400
☑ In Bethesda, where Italian eateries abound, this family-run "favorite" has "maintained its standard" by staying "consistent", "traditional", "predictable" and "welcoming"; at the same time, it "hasn't improved over the years."

Burma S   21 | 10 | 18 | $15
740 Sixth St., NW (bet. G & H Sts.), 202-638-1280
☑ "Sweet service" and "exotic" fare make this "cheap-eats" Asian seem "far more elegant" than its "simple" decor and "run-down" Downtown "neighborhood would lead you to expect"; note that Burmese food, sometimes described as "Chinese with a kick", is not for "weak palates"; P.S. expect to stay awhile – "quick lunches take two hours."

Burrito Brothers 🅂 ⊄   — | — | — | I |
205 Pennsylvania Ave., SE (2nd St.), 202-543-6835
2418 18th St. (Columbia Rd.), 202-265-4048 ◐
3273 M St., NW (Potomac St.), 202-965-3963 ◐
1524 Connecticut Ave., NW (Q St.), 202-332-2308
1825 I St., NW (bet. 18th & 19th Sts.), 202-887-8266
1815 M St., NW (bet. 18th & 19th Sts.), 202-785-3309
11690 Plaza America Dr., Reston, VA, 703-478-6394
We don't know why we left these sources of "nutritious fast food" served in "basic" spaces off the *Survey*; they provide a "grease-free" "meal of fresh ingredients" at a "terrific price" (under $5) and are "open late."

Burro ⊄   19 | 12 | 15 | $8 |
1621 Connecticut Ave. (bet. Q & R Sts.), 202-483-6861 🅂
1134 19th St. (bet. L & M Sts.), 202-833-5041
2000 Pennsylvania Ave., NW (20th St.), 202-293-9449
■ "Fast food meets great ingredients" at these colorful Tex-Mex takeouts dishing out "cheapo", grando burritos (and low-fat chili, beans and soups) from countertop digs; although some say the "fresh", "healthy" fillings are "not so flavorful", many maintain they're "muy bueno."

Busara 🅂   23 | 23 | 20 | $23 |
2340 Wisconsin Ave., NW (Calvert St.), 202-337-2340
8142 Watson St., McLean, VA, 703-356-2288
■ "Dramatic" neon and black decor, a "hip bar" and a "gorgeous garden" lend a "sophisticated" touch to the "straightforward" yet "yummy" food served at this popular Upper Georgetown Thai; a few find the scenery (walking and otherwise) "flashy but distracting" – "sunglasses optional inside" and at the new Virginia locale.

Cactus Cantina 🅂   18 | 16 | 17 | $18 |
3300 Wisconsin Ave., NW (Macomb St.), 202-686-7222
🔳 This "casual", "everyday" Tex-Mex in Cleveland Park offers "decent, cheap food" and a "great tortilla-making machine" that keeps kids "occupied"; it "keeps expanding", yet it still gets gripes about waits – also "noise", "careless" cooking and being "rushed."

Cafe Asia 🅂   — | — | — | M |
1134 19th St. (bet. L & M Sts.) 202-659-2696
Recommended for a lunchtime "trip around the Far East" or sushi happy hour ($1 a piece) below Dupont Circle; this smart-looking Pan-Asian earns kudos for "nice waiters", "reasonable prices" and "doing everything" pretty well.

Cafe Atlantico   — | — | — | M |
405 8th St., NW (bet. D & E Sts.), 202-393-0812
In summer 1996, this former Adams Morgan hot spot revamped historic Penn Quarter digs into a lively, multilevel happening; DC trendies couldn't wait to check out its worldly Nuevo Latino cuisine and clientele.

Cafe Berlin S

18 | 16 | 19 | $23

322 Massachusetts Ave., NE (bet. 3rd & 4th Sts.), 202-543-7656

■ One of the "best outdoor dining areas" on the Hill makes this German popular with "Senate staffers"; another attraction is the "bargain soup-and-sandwich lunch" plus lightened-up versions of regional specialties like potato pancakes, bratwurst and spaetzle washed down, of course, with an "excellent German beer."

Cafe Bethesda S

24 | 20 | 21 | $35

5027 Wilson Ln. (bet. Old Georgetown & Arlington Rds.), Bethesda, MD, 301-657-3383
121 Congressional Ln. (next to Congressional Plaza), Rockville, MD, 301-770-3185 **(CLOSED)**

■ "Vest pocket" intimacy and "light" cooking are the drawing cards of this Bethesda Contemporary American; however, make sure that "leisurely dining" is in your game plan, as well as paying real money "for a weekday dinner."

Cafe Dalat S

22 | 10 | 19 | $14

3143 Wilson Blvd. (Highland St.), Arlington, VA, 703-276-0935

■ Setting a high "standard" for "good-value" grub, this venerable Vietnamese with a "fall-of-Saigon atmosphere" may be the "friendliest", "cheapest" and tastiest in the Clarendon cheap-eats corridor; fans go so far as to say it's "head and shoulders above its much-talked-about neighbor Queen Bee" (ratings reveal they're neck and neck).

Cafe Deluxe S⊅

18 | 19 | 19 | $21

3228 Wisconsin Ave., NW (Macomb St.), 202-686-2233

■ How could this "buzzing" Cleveland Park youngster miss with its "LA atmosphere", martini and mashed potatoes "comfort food" and sidewalk cafe?; it's a "much-needed", unfussy, "neighborhood bar for the '90s" (albeit "still experimental") – hence the "long waits."

Cafe Milano S

19 | 19 | 16 | $31

3251 Prospect St., NW (bet. Wisconsin Ave. & 33rd St.), 202-333-6183

☑ It's fashionable to trash this "flashy" Georgetowner for its much-publicized, late-night Euro scene ("poseur's palace", "snobissimo"), but whereas celebs and micro-minis are well-seated downstairs, upstairs is "quiet and private" – "pretty agreeable" for a "light" Northern Italian meal; there's also an off-street patio that's "lovely for lunch."

Cafe Mileto S

∇ 17 | 18 | 19 | $19

Cloppers Mill Village Ctr., 18056 Mateny Rd. (Great Seneca Hwy.), Germantown, MD, 301-515-9370

■ This youngster's brick pizza oven, decorative setting and inviting terrace indicate a serious try at bringing Southern Italy to Germantown; neighbors are hoping that the fairly successful efforts to date are "not beginner's luck."

Cafe Mozart ⑤ | 16 | 13 | 16 | $18 |

1331 H St., NW (bet. 13th & 14th Sts.), 202-347-5732

◪ "Indistinguishable from countless in Vienna", this "dusty" old Downtown German deli is one of the few local places where the "best of the 'wurst' [and other hard-to-find groceries] can be found"; it also serves "hearty" Bavarian meals and desserts in a bright, noisy rear dining room to mixed reviews: "disappointing" vs. " a nice alternative."

Cafe New Delhi ⑤ | ▽ 24 | 16 | 21 | $16 |

1041 N. Highland St. (Clarendon Metro Stop), Arlington, VA, 703-528-2511

■ Northern Virginians tell us that this "excellent little" Indian "deserves to be mobbed" for its "especially tasty" vegetable dishes, breads and curries, "modest prices", "friendly" ways and "beautiful calm" that enhances the "wonderful food"; perhaps its "storefront look" keeps the crowds away.

Café Oggi ⑤ | 19 | 18 | 19 | $25 |

6671 Old Dominion Dr. (Lowell & Whittier Aves.), McLean, VA, 703-442-7360

◪ The food is definitely not Milano "modern" ("how do you say très ordinaire in Italian?"), but suburbanites are pleased to have this Italian in McLean; "predictable" and a bit "pretentious", it's also "pretty" and a "change of pace."

Cafe on M ⑤ | 26 | 22 | 23 | $39 |

Westin Hotel, 2350 24th St., NW (M St.), 202-429-0100

◪ Shortly after this suave West Ender was 'discovered', its chef departed, putting the above ratings in doubt; new management is continuing the Contemporary American focus, but we hear that the changes may have blunted its edge; one thing remains the same, however – the "dark", windowless decor.

Cafe Parisien Express ⑤⇗ | 18 | 13 | 14 | $12 |

118 King St., Alexandria, VA, 703-683-3331 **(CLOSED)**
4520 Lee Hwy. (bet. Woodstock & Woodrow Sts.), Arlington, VA, 703-525-3332

■ "In Paris", as in the Northern Virginia suburbs, there are times when you want a "quick", "cheap" meal; these "pleasant", self-serve cafes speak "fast food" with a French accent and "live up to the promise of their name"; now "get rid of the Styrofoam plates."

Cafe Promenade ⑤ | 19 | 21 | 20 | $28 |

Mayflower Hotel, 1127 Connecticut Ave., NW (bet. L & M Sts.), 202-347-2233

■ Long a major power breakfast, lunch and afternoon tea site, this "classy" hotel dining space with "great people-watching" has gotten even better since chef Tino Buggio directed his energies here; his first-class Mediterranean food has "vastly improved" Downtown dining options – and made the above ratings obsolete.

Cafe Riviera ⑤   – | – | – | M
Georgetown Inn, 1310 Wisconsin Ave., NW (bet. Dumbarton & N Sts.), 202-944-9600
A roomy oasis of civility in rowdy Georgetown, the svelte, minimalist setting here provides a welcome respite for shoppers and sightseers, while its recently revamped menu, mostly New American with shades of sunny Provence, lets them opt for a bite or a meal; on-site parking (a Georgetown rarity) is a big deal.

Cafe Rose ⑤   – | – | – | M
Stratford Motor Lodge, 300 W. Broad St. (Little Falls St.), Falls Church, VA, 703-532-1700
This Falls Church motel/restaurant, an Iranian community hub, is a "very good" place to explore Persia's 4,000-year-old cuisine; here, it's prepared for you as for a guest in the owner's "home" (translation: "slow" dining).

Cafe Saigon ⑤   22 | 13 | 19 | $14
1135 N. Highland St. (bet. Wilson & Clarendon Blvds.), Arlington, VA, 703-276-7110
■ One visits this no-frills Vietnamese lunch counter for its "excellent" pho, Hanoi pork and "special items available nowhere else" in Clarendon; "small and efficient", it's a "fun place to eat."

Cafe Taj ⑤   23 | 20 | 21 | $20
1379 Beverly Rd. (Old Dominion Dr.), McLean, VA, 703-827-0444
■ Reviewers in McLean "love" this relatively "unknown", "really good Indian" for its tempting food and "modest" prices; a lovely courtyard and "soothing" postmodern interior and manners bring you as close as you can get to the "Bombay Club . . . in the suburbs."

Cajun Bangkok ⑤   21 | 13 | 18 | $19
907 King St. (Alford St.), Alexandria, VA, 703-836-0038
■ The seemingly "strange" coupling of Cajun and Thai cuisines at this Old Town storefront pleases "spicy food" freaks; highlights of its bipartite menu include crying tiger, pecan-crusted catfish and shrimp étouffe – all authentically prepared and "helpfully" served amid "nonexistent decor."

Calasia (CLOSED)   21 | 17 | 19 | $35
7929 Norfolk Ave. (Cordell Ave.), Bethesda, MD, 301-654-6444
☑ Since its original chef left and key staff followed suit, this "in" place in Bethesda "doesn't meet the expectations" of many surveyors; now its "California food with an Asian flavor or vice versa" is too often "disappointing" and with "only 11 tables" some think service could improve.

California Pizza Kitchen S   18 14 17 $16

1260 Connecticut Ave. (N St.), 202-331-4020
Chevy Chase Pavilion, 5345 Wisconsin Ave., NW (Military Rd.),
202-363-6650
700 King St. (S. Washington St.), Alexandria, VA, 703-706-0404
Village at Shirlington, 4053 S. 28th St. (Randolph St.),
Arlington, VA, 703-845-7770 **(CLOSED)**
12300 Price Club Plaza, Ste. C (W. Ox Rd.), Fairfax, VA,
703-802-2250 **(CLOSED)**
1201 S. Hayes St., Ste. F (12th St.), Arlington, VA, 703-412-4900
Tysons Corner Ctr., 7939-L Tysons Corner (Rte. 7), McLean,
VA, 703-761-1473
Montgomery Mall, 7101 Democracy Blvd. (Westlake Dr.),
Bethesda, MD, 301-469-5090
■ Though "grown-ups" are "embarrassed to admit it, they love the food" at these "Disney-does-nouveau-pizza" kitchens, as evidenced by the highest traffic in the *Survey*; serving pizzas topped with "weird" stuff and staffed by overly friendly "90210 types", their "formula" may be "yup food", but it's a "good deal" if you can deal with the bright lights and "spotless white-tile decor."

California Tortilla S   _ _ _ I

4862 Cordell Ave. (bet. Norfolk & Woodmont Aves.),
Bethesda, MD, 301-654-8226
Bethesda's "healthy" Mexican replaces fat with "fresh" ingredients and "flavorful" seasonings; what's more, it delivers the "whole package" at "cheap prices" in a breezy eat-in/carry-out format.

Calvert Grille S   18 10 19 $15

Calvert Apts., 3106 Mt. Vernon Ave. (bet. E & W Glebe Rd.
& Commonwealth Ave.), Alexandria, VA, 703-836-8425
■ When Del Ray parents "can't find a sitter", they head for the toy-filled "kids' room" at this "neighborhood joint"; Don and Lynn Abram run it like a "big family", serving "quality breakfasts", "stick-to-your-ribs American fare" and well-selected brews at "reasonable prices."

Cambodian   ▽ 15 11 16 $16

1727 Wilson Blvd. (Quinn St.), Arlington, VA, 703-522-3832
◨ This colorful Cambodian "dive" in Arlington is possibly the "best source for a cuisine worth exploring"; most appreciate its low prices and "sweet service", but some find the Chinese-like dishes "unimpressive."

CAPITAL GRILLE S   23 25 23 $41

601 Pennsylvania Ave., NW (6th St.), 202-737-6200
■ Decked out with "all the trappings" of a "clubby", "establishment" stronghold, DC's most Republican restaurant is packed with "fat cats talking on cell phones" and "first-time cigar smokers" ("all under age 25"); it has "great steaks, better drinks", smooth service ("regulars" preferred) and "expense-account" prices.

Capitol City Brewing Co. ⑤   14 | 19 | 15 | $17
1100 New York Ave., NW (bet. H & 11th Sts.), 202-628-2222
2 Massachusetts Ave. (1st St.), 202-842-2337
7735 Old Georgetown Rd. (Fairmont Ave.), Bethesda, MD,
301-652-2282
2700 S. Quincy St. (28th St.), Shirlington, VA, 703-578-3888
◪ "Evenings are a yuppie group grope" at these raucous
brewpubs where soft pretzels and burgers are the menu
highlights and the help can't really cope with the crowds;
still, the "microclimate" keeps "young Republicans",
lawyers and conventioneers "off the street."

CARLYLE GRAND CAFE ⑤   23 | 21 | 21 | $24
4000 S. 28th St. (Quincy St.), Shirlington, VA, 703-931-0777
▥ This "wildly popular" American bistro brings a "gourmet-
for-the-common-man" approach to dining in Shirlington;
chef Bill Jackson gives "fresh ingredients" an "innovative"
twist but "doesn't forget that you have to eat the dish";
however, it's hard to forget that you're in a "suburban sprawl
of a restaurant" with a "food court" feel; sit upstairs.

Cashion's Eat Place ⑤   24 | 21 | 21 | $30
1819 Columbia Rd., NW (bet. Biltmore & Mintwood Sts.),
202-797-1819
▥ Ann Cashion has created a "sophisticated" home away
from home at her "urban" bistro where the bar and open-to-
the-street dining space function as a neighborhood living
room; her modern American "comfort food" is so appealing
that customers, ranging from "Beltway bandits" to "tourists"
to Euro expats, "want to try everything on the menu."

Cedar Knoll Inn ⑤   18 | 20 | 18 | $22
9030 Lucia Ln. (Vernon View Dr.), Alexandria, VA, 703-799-1501
▤ Word has it that this Potomac viewplace, with its
"Elks Lodge" decor, may "not be just for mothers-in-law
anymore"; a 'real' chef and his Mediterranean-American
fare have "vastly improved" dining prospects – though
not to the level of the "lovely" river prospects.

C.F. Folks ⌱   21 | 10 | 18 | $12
1225 19th St., NW (bet. M & N Sts.), 202-293-0162
▤ Just-folks 'do lunch' at this Dupont Circle food stall
(though you're likely to spot boldface names "saving a few
bucks"); its "quirky" proprietor serves up "sandwiches
and sass" along with "terrific" blackboard specials on a
"limited" basis – closed after 3 PM and on weekends.

Chadwick's ◑⑤   14 | 14 | 16 | $17
5247 Wisconsin Ave., NW (Jennifer St.), 202-362-8040
3205 K St., NW (Wisconsin Ave.), 202-333-2565
203 Strand St. (Duke St.), Alexandria, VA, 703-836-4442
◪ Though some say these "comfortable" collegiate pubs
"need a jump start", they're "always dependable", a "good
value" and "handy" for a pre-movie burger and beer.

Chardonnay S   ▽ | 20 | 22 | 20 | $30 |

Doubletree Park Terrace Hotel, 1515 Rhode Island Ave.,
NW (Scott Circle), 202-232-7000

■ Garden ambiance, posh appointments, "good service"
and a "great wine list" recommend this "underrated", easy-
to-reach Contemporary American just off Scott Circle for
a "power lunch" or "romantic" dinner; supporters say it's
"one of the better reasonably priced hotel eateries."

Charlie Chiang's S | 16 | 14 | 16 | $18 |

4250 Connecticut Ave. NW (Van Ness St.), 202-966-1942
1912 I St. NW (bet. 19th & 20th Sts.), 202-293-6000
Village at Shirlington, 4060 S. 28th St. (Quincy St.),
Shirlington, VA, 703-671-4900
660 S. Pickett (Van Dorn St.), Alexandria, VA, 703-751-8888

◪ Despite their "health-conscious emphasis", these
"cheap", "convenient" Chinese get very mixed reviews:
"always fresh", "reliable and consistent" vs. "remarkably
ordinary"; as with many seemingly "Americanized" Asians, it
pays to "ask for specials not on the menu."

Chart House S | 19 | 21 | 19 | $28 |

1 Cameron St. (waterfront), Alexandria, VA, 703-684-5080

◪ "Beautiful locale", "boring food" sums up the majority
opinion on this waterfront viewplace whose steak, seafood
and salad-bar fare, "robotically cheerful" help and long
waits epitomize "chain" dining; still, for some, it embodies
"romance by the water" with "gorgeous" sights, "tasty"
eats and decadent mud pie.

CHEESECAKE FACTORY ●S | 19 | 18 | 17 | $20 |

Chevy Chase Pavilion, 5345 Wisconsin Ave., NW (bet.
Jennifer St. & Western Ave.), 202-364-0500
White Flint Mall, 11301 Rockville Pike (Nicholson Ln.),
Bethesda, MD, 301-770-0999

◪ "Hopeless waits", "gargantuan portions", "monstrous
desserts", an "unabridged" menu – there's "too much of
everything" at these "crowd-pleasers", which is why so
many "love" them; if ever a restaurant chain epitomized
the "homogenization of New America", this is it.

Chesapeake Seafood | 15 | 9 | 14 | $17 |
Crab House S (CLOSED)

3607 Wilson Blvd. (bet. Nelson & Monroe Sts.), Arlington,
VA, 703-528-8888

◪ "Wacky" yet "worth surmounting the language barrier"
for the "cheap", "delicious" Vietnamese seafood dishes
served at this Clarendon hole; the "huge menu" of pho and
American-style fin fare can be daunting, ditto the "drab"
premises and service that's "ok on a good day", but the
Astroturf "patio is a trip."

Chicken Place S   ▽ 19 | 10 | 16 | $13
11201 Grandview Ave. (Reedie Dr.), Wheaton, MD,
301-946-1212
■ Crisp-skinned roasted chicken, "great fries" and unusual
Peruvian sides – "for a very few pesos" you can turn
"weeknight" refueling into a low-budget "adventure" at
these Andean rotisseries; but unless you count the tempting
smells and late-night music and dancing, the ambiance is nil.

China Canteen S   ▽ 23 | 10 | 21 | $15
808 Hungerford Dr. (off Ivy League Ln.), Rockville, MD,
301-424-1606
■ It's not as well-known as it should be, yet Rockville
Sinophiles swear by this "crummy"-looking, "homestyle
Chinese" with its "chalkboard menu and lumpy seats",
"great food, bargain prices and a staff that tries to explain
exotic dishes" – "what more would you want?"

China Chef S   18 | 12 | 17 | $16
11323 Georgia Ave. (University Blvd.), Wheaton, MD,
301-949-8170
☑ Although this Wheaton Cantonese wins local "loyalty" for
its weekend dim sum, lobster special and "doting" on kids,
we also hear the food is "now very ordinary" (like the
decor); nevertheless, it's cheap enough to be worth a try.

China Inn ●S (CLOSED)   19 | 13 | 16 | $19
631 H St., NW (bet. 6th & 7th Sts.), 202-842-0909
☑ It looks "worn", yet this "reliable old Chinatown standby"
is still capable of producing exciting dishes like "spicy
eggplant", "drunken crabs" and daily dim sum; but some
surveyors increasingly find less reason to visit this "shabby
neighborhood" – especially at night.

"Ciao baby" Cucina   18 | 20 | 18 | $26
Washington Sq., 1736 L St., NW (bet. 18th St. &
Connecticut Ave.), 202-331-1500
☑ Young K Street strivers favor this too-"trendy" Italian for
its "high-end" atmosphere and free "happy-hour chow", but
not for the high-end prices (unless "someone else pays")
or "magazine food" ("looks better than it tastes"); there's
a popular lunch buffet and a back room for "celebrations."

Cintra S (CLOSED)   ▽ 23 | 13 | 20 | $22
5216 Wilson Blvd. (bet. Florida St. & George Mason Dr.),
Arlington, VA, 703-525-1170
■ An Iberian addition to the area's international palate,
this Portuguese offers "unusual" food in a Ballston
storefront brightened with ethnic touches; *paelha* and
pork with clams are some of the interesting choices –
along with an interesting bar.

Cities S   20 | 23 | 18 | $28

2424 18th St., NW (Columbia Rd.), 202-328-7194

☑ Newly transformed into a polished enclave for a chic dinner or a laid-back brunch, this open-to-the-street Eclectic-International "brings the world to Adams Morgan;" last spring's redo eliminated the grunge (and the nightclub upstairs), but still left its cooking, which showcases "a different city" every four months, sometimes "uneven and uninspired."

CITRONELLE S   26 | 23 | 23 | $47

Latham Hotel, 3000 M St., NW (30th St.), 202-625-2150

■ Michel Richard's "very Californian" take on French dining (à la LA's Citrus) is the "best expense-account splurge" in Georgetown; filled with "romantic nooks" and "famous faces", it's where the "upscale" crowd goes "when the meal is the main event"; Saturday lunch is a civilized treat.

City Lights of China S   25 | 14 | 19 | $19

1731 Connecticut Ave., NW (bet. R & S Sts.), 202-265-6688

■ "The best Chinese food in DC served efficiently by surly waitresses" is the short of it; the rest of the story on this "cramped", "no-decor" ("but who cares?") Dupont Circle step-down is that in a "town devoid of good Chinese", its "light sauces" and "fresh ingredients" stand out; yes, that was "Mick Jagger"; "quick delivery", too.

Clyde's ◗S   17 | 21 | 18 | $21

Georgetown Park Mall, 3236 M St., NW (Wisconsin Ave.), 202-333-9180
Reston Town Ctr., 11905 Market St. (Reston Pkwy.), Reston, VA, 703-787-6601
8332 Leesburg Pike (Rtes. 7 & 123), Vienna, VA, 703-734-1901
70 Wisconsin Circle (bet. Wisconsin & Western Aves.), Chevy Chase, MD, 301-951-9600

☑ With their commitment to providing "wholesome food" at a "good price", these "handsome", hometown saloons are reinventing themselves while preserving their "great burgers" appeal; the "stunning" new Chevy Chase locale is a "smash" hit, though working out "kinks" – and Georgetown has been impressively overhauled; a few naysayers respond "too bad you can't eat the decor."

Coco Loco   20 | 22 | 18 | $28

810 7th St., NW (bet. H & I Sts.), 202-289-2626

■ A "high-energy", "off-the-wall" South American hot spot where pinstripes, pols and cosmopols find common ground; it has added words like caipirinhas (80-proof, lime-flavored knockout drops), Mexican tapas and churrascaria (an all-you-can-eat "carnivore extravaganza") to the Downtown dining vocabulary; late Saturday night, when Brazilian dancers rev up the room, critics call it "overexposed."

COEUR DE LION ⑤   24 25 24 $43
Henley Park Hotel, 926 Massachusetts Ave., NW (10th St.),
202-638-5200
■ When you "take someone you love" to this "jewel"
set in a Downtown hotel, its "beautiful setting", "romantic"
ambiance, "creative" Contemporary American fare and
after-dinner dancing will burnish your glow; it's also a
"pleasure" for business or brunch and "perfect for
special occasions."

Connaught Place ⑤   ▽ 25 19 24 $21
10425 North St. (Rte. 236 W. & University Dr.), Fairfax, VA,
703-352-5959
■ This "refined" suburban subcontinental rewards those
who "find it" (in Fairfax City) with "first-class food and
service" reminiscent "of London's" famed Anglo-Indian
restaurants; the seafood, chicken tikka and "lamb anything"
are "excellent" – "light", "not oily" and "fresh."

Coppi's ⑤   22 19 18 $18
1414 U St., NW (bet. 14th & 15th Sts.), 202-319-7773
3421 Connecticut Ave. (bet. Porter & Macomb Sts.),
202-244-6437
◪ In the not-quite-gentrified New U area, this brick-oven
pizzeria is "packed" on weekends with a lively mix of
resid'Uers and tourists from the 'burbs; they find plenty of
attitude, along with "creative" salads and toppings and a
deadly Nutella (chocolate-hazelnut paste) calzone; the
Connecticut Avenue spoke also keeps spinning.

Cottonwood Cafe ⑤   20 20 19 $27
4844 Cordell Ave. (bet. Wisconsin Ave. & Old
Georgetown Rd.), Bethesda, MD, 301-656-4844
◪ "Too spicy", "too pricey", "too unvarying" say some
surveyors – so why is this "Red Sage knockoff" usually
packed to the max?; because "Bethesda is desperate
for good Southwestern food" but willing to settle for a
reasonable proxy if it's "close", "friendly" and happens to
have a "great patio."

Cowboy Cafe ⑤   14 12 15 $12
Adams Square Shopping Ctr., 2421 Columbia Pike (bet. S.
Barton & Cleveland Sts.), Arlington, VA, 703-486-3467
4792 Lee Hwy. (N. Glebe Rd.), Arlington, VA, 703-243-8010
6151 Richmond Hwy. (Rte. 1), Alexandria, VA, 703-660-2320
■ "Music rules" at this "terrific neighborhood" hitching
post in S. Arlington, which means that "Thursday night is
pork chops and The Grandsons" (a country-rockabilly band)
or a "good cheap burger" and microbrew; but what locals
like best is that "over the years the staff's enthusiasm has
not waned" – ditto at newer locations; P.S. "nonsmokers
need an iron lung."

Crisfield S
21 | 10 | 16 | $25

Lee Plaza, 8606 Colesville Rd. (Georgia Ave.), Silver Spring, MD, 301-588-1572
8012 Georgia Ave. (East-West Hwy. & Railroad St.), Silver Spring, MD, 301-589-1306

☑ A fried-fish field trip to these Old Maryland culinary "landmarks" may be a "go once" experience given their "high" price tag, "dowdy" appearance and "surly" help; yet they are edible history, with "some of the best seafood on the East Coast" and lots of "character" in the original Silver Spring location; N.B. Lee Plaza has new owners.

Crisp & Juicy S
20 | 5 | 13 | $9

Sunshine Sq. Shopping Ctr., 1331-G Rockville Pike (Congressional Plaza), Rockville, MD, 301-251-8833
Leisure World Plaza, 3800 International Dr. (Georgia Ave.), Silver Spring, MD, 301-598-3333
Lee Heights Shopping Ctr., 4520 Lee Hwy. (Lorcom Ln.), Arlington, VA, 703-243-4222 ⊅

■ This trio of "roadside chicken stands" serving "great", cheap, "greasy" chicken, a "scrumptious" hot sauce and must-try Latin sides are "cheaper and better than eating at home"; although the "lack of any attempt at decor has a certain charm", most prefer takeout.

Crystal Thai S
23 | 17 | 21 | $18

Arlington Forest Shopping Ctr., 4819 Arlington Blvd. (Park Dr.), Arlington, VA, 703-522-1311

■ At this Arlington Thai, crystal chandeliers and white walls contrast pleasantly with "well-prepared" food that's "spicier than at most Thai restaurants"; its "light touch" with traditional recipes and "pauper's prices" please most, but its performance can be "erratic."

Da Domenico
20 | 17 | 20 | $28

1992 Chain Bridge Rd. (Rte. 123), McLean, VA, 703-790-9000

☑ "The veal chop sings" and so does the opera-loving proprietor of this "old-fashioned" Tysons Corner Italian, as he and his "attentive" staff transform an ordinary meal in "dated" surroundings into a "pleasant evening"; however, it is said that "Chef Boyardee could make it at this location."

Dar es Salaam S (CLOSED)
19 | 21 | 20 | $25

3056 M St., NW (bet. 30th & 31st Sts.), 202-337-6680

■ Visit Morocco on M Street at this dramatically lit, authentically crafted replica; recline on pillowed seating and sample multicourse feasts or (mostly) "delicious" à la carte specialties while the belly dancers whirl; it's an "inviting" "getaway" from Georgetown traffic.

Dean & DeLuca Cafe   19 | 14 | 13 | $13

3276 M St., NW (33rd St.), 202-342-2500 S
1299 Pennsylvania Ave., NW (bet. 13th & E Sts.),
202-628-8155
1919 Pennsylvania Ave., NW (bet. 19th & I Sts.),
202-296-4327

▨ "Snack central" for Georgetown shoppers and people-watchers, this "stylish" sidewalk cafe serves tempting sandwiches, salads and light fare based on "what's best that day" in the adjacent gourmet shop; many find it "far too easy to spend too much" despite the "NY" attitude – ditto at D&D's Downtown bean bars.

Delhi Dhaba S   19 | 7 | 13 | $11

7236 Woodmont Ave. (bet. Bethesda Ave. & Elm St.),
Bethesda, MD, 301-718-0008
2424 Wilson Blvd. (bet Barton St. & Clarendon Blvd.),
Arlington, VA, 703-524-0008

■ Blaring Indian MTV sets the tone at these suburban down 'n' Delhis, where "hefty portions" of spicy curries and breads at "rock-bottom prices" substitute for amenities like atmosphere and service; no wonder surveyors say they're strictly for takeout or "on-the-run" meals.

Dixie Grill S (CLOSED)   12 | 15 | 14 | $15

518 10th St., NW (bet. E & F Sts.), 202-628-4800

▨ A "great happy hour" and "shooting pool upstairs" draw Capitol Hill types to this Downtown Confederate pretender; reputedly, presidential "policies are hashed out here over a beer", but only a Republican would call the "greasy" fare real Southern food.

Donatello ◗ S   21 | 18 | 21 | $28

2514 L St., NW (Pennsylvania Ave.), 202-333-1485

▨ "On a summer night", the front porch of this "reliable", "relaxed" West End Italian is awfully "romantic"; it does "great everyday business lunches" and Kennedy Center ticketholders "would be lost" without its pre- and post-theater prix fixe menu, yet it has "never achieved liftoff" – possibly because it's "unexciting."

DUANGRAT'S S   25 | 21 | 21 | $23

5878 Leesburg Pike (Glen Forest Rd.), Falls Church, VA,
703-820-5775

■ One of the *Survey*'s top-rated Thais "never fails to please" with its "fragrant, deliciously flavored" dishes, pastel "elegance", waitresses in "custom dress" and "charming" weekend dance show; it's a "soothing" oasis in Bailey's Crossroads that can be "very impressive" for entertaining "at a fair price."

Duca Di Milano (CLOSED)   18 | 20 | 18 | $34
2 Wisconsin Circle (Wisconsin & Western Aves.), Chevy Chase, MD, 301-656-3822
☑ Shameless glitz, "arrogant" too, yet this Northern Italian haunt of Chevy Chase/Bethesda's "beautiful people" has something "authentically European" about it; what's more, it's capable of producing "very good" – though "variable" of late – food; it's quiet at lunch, "flashy" at the bar.

Dusit 🄢   21 | 16 | 19 | $17
2404 University Blvd. W. (Georgia Ave.), Wheaton, MD, 301-949-4140
☑ In Wheaton, with its wealth of inexpensive ethnic eateries, this "typical lavender" Thai gets good grades for comfort and for some "well-priced" dishes that "really shine", like BBQ beef salad and "satisfying curry"; perhaps naysayers haven't "learned what not to order."

Dynasty ◑🄢   ▽ 18 | 14 | 15 | $15
11123 Viers Mill Rd. (Wheaton Metro Station), Wheaton, MD, 301-942-3070
☑ Dinner at this unprepossessing Hong Kong outpost in Wheaton gives Westerners a chance to try exotic dishes and "authentically" prepared, "great fresh fish" as enjoyed by its Chinese clientele; however, gelatinous sea cucumbers and "goopy brown sauce" may not be your destiny.

Easby's Buffet 🄢   11 | 9 | 11 | $10
8053 Leesburg Pike (Gallows Rd.), Tysons Corner, VA, 703-893-2072 **CLOSED**
1488 Rockville Pike (Montrose Rd.), Rockville, MD, 301-770-7710 **(CLOSED)**
Herndon Ctr., 428 Elden St. (Herndon Pkwy.), Herndon, VA, 703-435-5348 **CLOSED**
☑ Cheaper and easier than eating at home, this suburban family "feeding station" lets you "bulk up" on plain American food at its unlimited "smorgasbord"; but like your "school cafeteria", it elicits such barbs as "what service?"

Eat First 🄢   18 | 5 | 14 | $12
728 7th St., NW (bet. G & H Sts.), 202-347-0936
☑ "Surprisingly novel and tasty dishes" reward frequent visits to this Hong Kong "hole" in Chinatown; the "respectful staff guides you to make interesting choices" and is "kind enough to warn against goose feet . . . and other exotica", yet some would eat here last.

Ecco Cafe 🄢   20 | 17 | 19 | $20
220 N. Lee St. (Cameron St.), Alexandria, VA, 703-684-0321
☑ Credit Diana Damewood's warm "welcome" along with double-sized pastas, pizzas and prize-winning salads for "making this place tick"; although it looks like it was decorated at a "yard sale", it's where they "power lunch Virginia-style" and "Old Town natives" dine "once a week."

El Caribe ⑤   19 | 17 | 19 | $23
3288 M St., NW (bet. Potomac & 32nd Sts.),
202-338-3121
8130 Wisconsin Ave. (bet. Cordell Ave. & Battery Ln.),
Bethesda, MD, 301-656-0888
☑ They may be "tired-looking", but these late-night Latinos are "enjoyable" and "attentive" and produce "interesting", "hearty" plates; "like the Redskins", however, there are "a few great ones" (fried calamari, paella and black beans), plus some "duds."

El Gavilan ⑤   ▽ 18 | 10 | 18 | $16
8805 Flower Ave. (Pine Branch Rd.), Silver Spring, MD,
301-587-4197
■ Among the many Central Americans in this Silver Spring enclave, this one is favored for being relatively "nice-looking" and for "authentic" Salvadoran food that goes beyond "good" fajitas and salsa; on weekends, "loud" music adds another "authentic" note.

El Pollo Rico ⑤ ⑰   23 | 7 | 16 | $10
2915-2917 N. Washington Blvd. (10th St.), Arlington, VA,
703-522-3220
7031 Brookfield Plaza Rd. (Amherst Ave.), Springfield, VA,
703-866-1286
2541 Ennalls Ave., Wheaton, MD, 301-942-4419
■ "Yummy", mouthwatering roasted chickens virtually fly out the door of these high-volume charcoal grills largely because "you don't find better value and your food comes almost before you've finished ordering"; eat "shoulder to shoulder" off "Styrofoam plates" in one of the area's "true democratic restaurants" – or opt for "to go."

El Tamarindo ⑤   17 | 10 | 16 | $14
7331 Georgia Ave., NW (Fessenden Rd.), 202-291-0525
4910 Wisconsin Ave., NW (42nd St.), 202-244-8888 ●
1785 Florida Ave., NW (bet. 18th & U Sts.), 202-328-3660 ●
☑ Rated on a "calorie to dollar ratio", these low-rent Salvadorans zoom off the charts; their "hearty, simple but good" platters are the mainstay of students, moviegoers and hungry families; after midnight, the food, "great music" and goodwill get even better; squeamish diners "bring the Rolaids."

Elysium ⑤   – | – | – | E
Morrison House Hotel, 116 S. Alfred St. (bet. King &
Prince Sts.), Alexandria, VA, 703-838-8000
Although this secluded and "formal" dining room in a posh Old Town hotel has suffered from a series of chef changes, it still can make "special occasions" more so; lately, its Contemporary American food is served in three-, four- or five-course menus, with matching wines, by a staff almost "too attentive" to your needs.

Enriqueta's S
| 20 | 15 | 18 | $20 |

2811 M St., NW (bet. 28th & 29th Sts.), 202-338-7772

◪ One of the area's few "real" Mexicans, it's the place to taste mole and Mayan dishes; but Georgetown parking, too-"quick" service, "close" seating and chairs that could double as "torture devices" do not encourage "lingering."

Eurogrill (CLOSED)
| – | – | – | M |

8401 Connecticut Ave. (Chevy Chase Lake Dr.), Bethesda, MD, 301-907-0368

From offering a "good choice of well-presented food" to garage parking "on a rainy night", this "pleasant suburban Continental" does basic things right; its "fixed-price menus are an outstanding value"– and one reason why its Bethesda neighbors treat the place like their living room.

Evans Farm Inn S
| 13 | 19 | 16 | $25 |

1696 Chain Bridge Rd. (Rte. 123), McLean, VA, 703-356-8000

◪ Despite gripes about its American kitchen mired in the past and the "tired" decor, Ralph and Maria Evanses lovely "bucolic setting" – complete with petting zoo, farms, shops and British pub – has been a heavily trafficked family destination since 1957.

Eye St. Cafe
| 21 | 16 | 18 | $18 |

1915 I St., NW (bet. 19th & 20th Sts.), 202-457-0773

■ Although Mary Richter (ex Cities) has left this "casual" Mediterranean, her legacy makes it a "find" for an uncrowded dinner; the menu features Lebanese vegetarian choices and pizza at lunch, when "too-close" seating and "rushed" service draw fire; still, "in an area [K Street] short on reasonably priced" dining, its customers are forgiving.

Faccia Luna Pizzeria S
| 21 | 15 | 17 | $15 |

2400 Wisconsin Ave., NW (Calvert St.), 202-337-3132
2909 Wilson Blvd. (Filmore St.), Arlington, VA, 703-276-3099

■ "It's the crust"– "oven burnt" – and "fresh", thoughtful toppings that make these "lively neighborhood pizzerias"; but "even if you don't eat pizza", salads, hoagies, pastas, microbrews, "good" sounds, "sports on the tube" and "love-in-bloom photos on the wall" make them great "hangouts"; "slow service" seems to be the only "negative."

Falls Landing S (CLOSED)
| 20 | 21 | 20 | $31 |

Village Ctr., 774 Walker Rd. (Georgetown Pike), Great Falls, VA, 703-759-4650

◪ "Central casting couldn't do Sunday dinner in the '50s more accurately" than this "colonial" Virginian with its blue-haired clientele, "living room"–like decor and cream-sauced seafare; nevertheless, it offers the "freshest fish" and stately treatment in a "serene setting."

Fatt Daddy's 🆂 (CLOSED) 12 | 12 | 12 | $16
316 Massachusetts Ave., NE (bet. 3rd & 4th Sts.), 202-547-7014
⬛ On Capitol Hill, "le bon temps roule" with "very mixed results" at this New Orleans facsimile; while it wins points as an "outdoor option" with "upbeat" help, virtually everything but the location "needs help."

Fedora Cafe 🆂 18 | 19 | 18 | $22
8521 Leesburg Pike (bet. Rte. 123 & Dulles Access Rd.), Tysons Corner, VA, 703-556-0100
⬛ A "comfortable", polished wood and brass backdrop for briefcase dining, after-work unwinding and "pre–Wolf Trap" snacks in Tysons Corner explains this Cal-Ital's "puzzling" (to those inside the Beltway) popularity; while there's nothing wrong with the eats, they're "not the main attraction."

Felix 🆂 21 | 20 | 19 | $30
2406 18th St., NW (Belmont Rd.), 202-48-FELIX
⬛ This "NY chic" New American's "innovative", internationally accented food, "decadent" desserts and "fantasy" cityscape design "have found a good home" in Adams Morgan – but its "NY prices" and "pretensions" have not; check out the "hip" (for DC) weekend music scene.

Fern Street Bistro (CLOSED) ▽ 23 | 17 | 20 | $23
6025-A Burke Ctr. Pkwy., Burke, VA, 703-425-9463
⬛ "Thirtysomethings" in Burke bless this strip-mall site for creating an "exciting atmosphere" with an Eclectic menu and a neat "gimmick" – choosing beer or wine from the adjacent retail store; it's "still a great secret" but small enough that "reservations are a must on weekends."

Filomena Ristorante 🆂 20 | 19 | 19 | $29
1063 Wisconsin Ave., NW (bet. M & K Sts.), 202-338-8800
⬛ The "finomenal" portions of "heavy" pasta dished out at this "gargantuan" Georgetown "tour bus" stop bring groans from some gastronomes; overlook the "hustle and bustle" and "snob attitude", however, and you may be "surprised by who" you see ("Pat Buchanan"); N.B. ask for the presidential table.

Firehook Bakery & Coffeehouse 🆂 24 | 16 | 17 | $9
1909 Q St., NW (19th St.), 202-588-9296
917 17th St. (bet. I & K Sts.), 202-429-2253
106 N. Lee St. (bet. King & Cameron Sts.), Alexandria, VA, 703-519-8020
⬛ From "crusts to crumbs", the "stellar" artisan bread and fresh focaccia from these bakery/cafes, like their "scrumptious" pastries, are "arguably the best" in town; eaten in "warm" surroundings, they give good bang for the buck; 17th Street serves sandwiches and salads.

Fleetwood's S (CLOSED)   14 | 20 | 14 | $23
44 Canal Ctr. Plaza (N. Fairfax Circle), Alexandria, VA,
703-548-6425
◪ "Great" live music and Potomac River views at Mick
Fleetwood's namesake blues club/eatery are "cheapened
by the inexperienced staff" and "uninspiring" American
food; perhaps a recent reorganization will tune up this
"theme restaurant without much of a theme."

Flint Hill Public House S   ▽ 16 | 20 | 18 | $30
Rte. 522 (Rte. 647), Flint Hill, VA, 540-675-1700
■ "Lovely new owners" are turning this turn-of-the century
property into a "wonderful place to visit" (despite some
"iffy" days); everyone from "bikers" to bankers are welcome
to sample the seasonal Contemporary American fare in a
pub or parlor setting that suits a wide range of appetites
and occasions; Blue Ridge Mountain vistas from the
outdoor deck are "worth the trip."

Florida Ave. Grill   19 | 12 | 16 | $13
1100 Florida Ave., NW (11th St.), 202-265-1586
◪ DC's "best greasy breakfast", served at this soul kitchen
in a "borderline" 'hood, includes "waitresses calling you
'baby'", "grits and biscuits buttered to order", photos of
"famous patrons" and "plastic plants"; the food "could be
made with less fat", but then it wouldn't be "great down-
home cooking"; P.S. "it's cheap", too.

Food Factory S⊅   20 | 5 | 11 | $11
4221 N. Fairfax Dr. (Glebe Rd.), Arlington, VA, 703-527-2279
1116 Herndon Pkwy. (Elden St.), Herndon, VA, 703-435-3333
8145-G Baltimore Ave. (University Blvd.), College Park,
MD, 301-345-8888
■ "It's another world" at "Kebabs R Us", a Pakistani
cafeteria in Ballston with less than "zero decor" but "huge
servings" of "great kebabs", breads and spicy curries at
rock-bottom prices; this (or its unrated brethren) is the
place to go when you want to "fill your stomach" and
"can't afford to eat at home."

Foong Lin S   20 | 15 | 20 | $19
7710 Norfolk Ave. (Fairmont Ave.), Bethesda, MD,
301-656-3427
■ Bethesda's "Sunday night" Chinese has "redecorated
into the '90s" ("a welcome change") while preserving
its "retro" menu of standards; prized for its fresh fish,
willingness to "prepare foods as requested" ("Peking
chicken") and "gracious, unflappable" help, it's summed
up by surveyors as "high quality but uninspired."

Fortune S   22 | 12 | 17 | $18 |

Greenforest Shopping Ctr., 5900 Leesburg Pike (Bailey's Crossroads), Falls Church, VA, 703-998-8888
North Point Village Ctr., 1428 Reston Pkwy. (bet. Rte. 7 & Baron Cameron Rd.), Reston, VA, 703-318-8898
■ "Go on Sunday for the full effect" of the "festive", fast-paced scene at these Virginia dim sum palaces where rolling carts serve "fantastic" Chinese tidbits in a "gymnasium" filled with "Chinese families", "Vietnamese weddings" and non-English-speaking waiters; weekday dim sum, backed by a compendium of Chinese seafood dishes, is also "like Taipei."

49 Twelve Thai S   ▽ 19 | 15 | 19 | $19 |

4912 Wisconsin Ave., NW (bet. Ellicott & Fessenden Sts.), 202-966-4696
■ Some say this "very good" Northwest neighborhood Thai where they "really try hard" deserves wider attention for its "beautiful presentation" of assertively seasoned food; although comfortable, "summer dining outside" sums up the decor.

FOUR & TWENTY BLACKBIRDS S 25 | 22 | 24 | $33 |

Route 522 (Rte. 647), Flint Hill, VA, 540-675-1111
■ A reminder of the small-town snugs in rural England, with its wooden tables and rustic charm, this eclectic Contemporary American in the Virginia foothills not only gets rave reviews from media critics, but it also passes the real people test – it's a one-and-a-half-hour drive from DC, yet there's a "line for Sunday brunch."

Four Rivers S   18 | 9 | 16 | $16 |

184 Rollins Ave. (E. Jefferson St.), Rockville, MD, 301-230-2900
■ To find out why this "dumpy" Rockville storefront is "where Chinese eat Chinese", ask for a "suggestion from the Chinese menu" or try one of the Szechuan specialties or "great veggie" choices; food and service is "better and more exciting when in groups" – and you get to sample lots of dishes.

Fran O'Brien's Steak House ◖ S   ▽ 19 | 18 | 19 | $30 |

Capitol Hilton Hotel, 1001 16th St., NW (L St.), 202-783-2599
◩ Making a play for "Duke Zeibert's crowd", ex-Redskin Fran O'Brien has turned a wood-paneled, near-the-White House space (ex Trader Vic's) into a clubby, "old-fashioned" steakhouse/sports bar; its "great ambiance", "mammoth" portions and "good lunch prices" earn yardage but not a touchdown – the final score is "middle-of-the-road political hangout."

Full Kee ◐⑤⇴　　　　　19 | 5 | 14 | $13
509 H St., NW (bet. 5th & 6th Sts.), 202-371-2233
■ One of DC's "best" for Chinese is even better "at 2 AM",
when top chefs drop by this Chinatown Cantonese for clams
in black bean sauce and shrimp dumpling soup; at that
hour, no one cares about "language problems", "abrupt
service" or no booze or decor – the fact is the "food can't
be beat" and "it's cheap."

Full Key ◐⑤　　　　　22 | 8 | 16 | $12
*Wheaton Manor Shopping Ctr., 2227 University Blvd. W.
(Georgia Ave.), Wheaton, MD, 301-933-8388*
☑ "Unusual" meal-sized soups, noodle dishes and "Hong
Kong specialties" that "you have to be adventurous to eat"
establish this Wheaton Cantonese's authenticity; but the flip
side is that it's "tough to communicate" and the 'atmosphere'
is supplied by Chinese families focusing on the "good,
inexpensive" food.

Gabriel ⑤　　　　　22 | 18 | 20 | $26
*Radisson-Barcelo Washington Hotel, 2121 P St., NW (bet.
21st & 22nd Sts.), 202-956-6690*
■ Check out the "intriguing" spread of "inventive" tapas
at this Contemporary Latin's "good-value" buffet lunch
($9.50), "good-time" happy hour (Wednesday-Friday $7.50)
or "lavish" brunch; equally "exciting" entrees can be ordered
full sized or as little plates; though busy, this attractive, "not-
your-average" hotel dining room is still something of a
Dupont Circle secret.

Gadsby's Tavern ⑤　　　　　18 | 24 | 20 | $25
*138 N. Royal St. (Cameron St.), Alexandria, VA,
703-548-1288*
☑ Follow in George Washington's footsteps to this Old Town
restoration and museum for a "history lesson come alive"
with costumed staff, period appointments and colonial food
and drink; while it's a "tourist must", with a great courtyard
for parties, some say the "olde" gimmick must be "backed
up by better food."

Galaxy ⑤　　　　　– | – | – | M
*Tower Square Ctr., 155 Hillwood Ave. (Annandale Rd.),
Falls Church, VA, 703-534-5450*
"Some of the best Vietnamese food" in the area can be
found at this relatively unknown Falls Church Indochinese
whose menu offers a galaxy of regional choices; its
performance is both "high high and low low" ("very spotty"),
but it won't cost much to try your luck; N.B. dine early on
weekends or you'll find yourself a part of the adjacent
nightclub scene.

GALILEO S | 26 | 23 | 23 | $49 |
1110 21st St., NW (bet. L & M Sts.), 202-293-7191
■ The "best Italian moments in town" take place in
Roberto Donna's "handsome", "celebrity"-lined dining
room; his "sophisticated" menus reinterpret Northern
Italian classics "showcasing" the "best of everything" in
that day's market and are backed by an "amazing" wine
list and "attentive" help; "when it's on" (and it almost always
is), it's "excellent."

Gangplank S (CLOSED) | 14 | 17 | 14 | $24 |
600 Water St., SW (7th St. & Maine Ave.), 202-554-5000
◪ In a "lucky" marina setting for catching "tourists and
Arena Stage" ticketholders, this floating fish house baits
its hook with seafood, steak, good parking and "pleasant
river views"; enthusiasts insist it's "far better than its
reputation" (and ratings), while critics quip "throw it back
if it comes out of the kitchen."

Garrett Park Cafe S | 19 | 18 | 18 | $17 |
4600 Waverly Ave., Garrett Park, MD, 301-929-0486
■ A "folksy, small-town" eatery with a "big heart", where
Garrett Park locals linger on the front porch or inside over
thick, "homemade" sandwiches and "tasty" American
entrees – and "hope its being listed here doesn't ruin it";
"charming" and "relaxing", it's a "slow-paced" "time warp."

Generous George's S | 17 | 15 | 16 | $13 |
*7031 Little River Tpke. (John Marr Dr.), Annandale, VA,
703-941-9600*
*Concord Shopping Ctr., 6131 Backlick Rd. (Commerce St.),
Springfield, VA, 703-451-7111*
3006 Duke St. (Roth St.), Alexandria, VA, 703-370-4303
◪ The "bizarre" (to put it kindly) "circus atmosphere" at
these pizza parlors is strictly for "high school dates" and
families with "screaming kids" intent on "scarfing" up
"tons of food" for little dough; only 'George' has the crust
to pile "pasta on pizza" and serve it in surroundings so
"tacky" that it's like "eating in a fraternity basement the
morning after the party."

Genji S | ▽ 22 | 15 | 21 | $20 |
*Lee-Graham Shopping Ctr., 2816 Graham Rd. (Lee Hwy.),
Falls Church, VA, 703-573-0112*
■ Northern Virginians have "been going to this traditional
Japanese forever", which should tell you something
about its "excellent food" and manners; it's located in an
area of Falls Church with a scarcity of nice restaurants and
is quite "good for large parties."

Georgetown Seafood Grill ◐ S   18 | 13 | 17 | $25
3063 M St., NW (bet. 30th & 31st Sts.), 202-333-7038 **(CLOSED)**
1200 19th St., NW (bet. M & N Sts.), 202-530-4430
☑ The original branch of this Georgetown raw bar and
seafooder popular for Sunday brunch and on Saturday
afternoons has closed; however, the new (unrated) below
Dupont Circle location has the space and decor its
predecessor lacked – and nearby office workers to reel in.

Georgia Brown's S   22 | 23 | 21 | $31
950 15th St., NW (K St.), 202-393-4499
■ A "lively mix of patrons" and "hearty helpings" of "good
food" distinguish this high-profile restaurant near the White
House; it "takes chances", playing "imaginative" riffs on
Carolina Low Country cuisine and design elements while
making its diverse clientele feel "comfortable."

Geppetto S   17 | 14 | 16 | $18
*Wildwood Shopping Ctr., 10257 Old Georgetown Rd.
(Democracy Blvd.), Bethesda, MD, 301-493-9230*
☑ It's a toss-up between the thin-crust white pizza
with "tons of garlic" and the deep-dish pie with "mounds
of pepperoni" at this "crowded" and "slow" Bethesda family
place; its efforts at cooking pasta and Neapolitan entrees
are likened to "an Italian opera sung in English – poorly."

Geranio S   22 | 19 | 21 | $26
*722 King St. (bet. Washington & Columbus Sts.),
Alexandria, VA, 703-548-0088*
■ To old-time Alexandrians, this trattoria is one of those
"special places" where a meal is more than the sum of its
parts; at a quiet "winter dinner by the fire", with the pasta
and seafood enhanced by "special attention" from the
staff, it's easy to overlook the rather "shabby decor" and
enjoy food that's "comfortingly pleasing year after year."

GERARD'S PLACE   26 | 21 | 24 | $50
915 15th St., NW (McPherson Sq.), 202-737-4445
■ It's one of the top-rated restaurants in the *Survey*, yet
Gerard Pangaud's fans insist his "intimate", "most Parisian"
Downtown bistro is "underappreciated", raving "best
French food outside Paris", "food graduated from finishing
school, it's so refined", "from pigs feet to mango tart –
wow!"; diners also "love" being treated "like friends."

Germaine's S   23 | 18 | 21 | $32
2400 Wisconsin Ave., NW (Calvert St.), 202-965-1185
☑ You "never know what or who you'll find" in this legendary
lady's Upper Georgetown dining room; her distinctive,
"light but filling" Pan-Asian cuisine has "stood the test of
time" and her "charm" puts everyone, from presidents to
poets, "at ease"; last spring's redecoration could
improve the already "great people-watching."

Ginza's
▽ 20 | 16 | 20 | $24

1009 21st St., NW (bet. K & L Sts.), 202-833-1244

◪ "At least you can get into" this "moderately priced" Midtown Japanese, and "if you know what to order" (ask what the Tokyo business suits are having) you'll do fine; it's said to have "good" cooked entrees and the "best sushi under $30"; neither the setting nor service is noteworthy.

Goldoni ⑤
23 | 23 | 22 | $43

1113 23rd St., NW (bet. L & M Sts.), 202-293-1511

◪ Fabrizio Aielli, a Roberto Donna (Galileo) protégé, has "sculpted" a skylit West End space into a "serious" Italian producing some "outstanding" seafood and pasta dishes; his deft touch with his native Venetian and Nuevo Italian specialties is drawing the area's bec fins; Kennedy Center accessibility is another plus.

Good Fortune ◐ ⑤
22 | 14 | 16 | $17

2646 University Blvd. (bet. Viers Mill Rd. & Georgia Ave.), Wheaton, MD, 301-929-8818

◼ The "best dim sum" in the Wheaton area and some of the best "seafood noodle dishes" are among the highlights of this multiregional Chinese whose "simple interior" is "more tasteful" than most similar places; its "family-style" set-price dinners are a "steal" and a great way to sample the rest of its "extensive menu."

Granja de Oro ⑤
– | – | – | I

2920 Annandale Rd. (Rte. 50), Falls Church, VA, 703-534-5511

The victuals at this Peruvian "chickout" in Falls Church extend beyond "delicious", "cheap", rotisserie chicken to country-style BBQ meats, saltados (sautés), seafood and fried yucca with a green hot sauce that gives customers "new reason to live"; the visuals are watching soccer on the tube and live weekend entertainment.

Greenwood's
– | – | – | M

(nka Greenwood at Cleveland Place)
3529 Connecticut Ave., NW (Porter St.), 202-833-6572

◪ Recently relocated to Cleveland Park (early '98), this sophisticated youngster's fresh approach to seasonal American dining is worth checking out; at its prior locale it had some growing pains, but the Eclectic fare was so interesting that reviewers want it to work.

Grillfish ⑤
– | – | – | M

1200 New Hampshire Ave., NW (M St., NW), 202-331-7310

◪ This West Ender's slogan – 'fresh fish, friendly prices, no tuxedo' – couldn't be more '90s in its casual appeal; the high ceiling, open-bar setting and simple fish and pasta menu seem made to order for neighborhood suits, cliff dwellers and diners on the way to Kennedy Center.

Grill from Ipanema S 20 | 19 | 17 | $25
1858 Columbia Rd., NW (Belmont Rd.), 202-986-0757
■ Something like "Rio de Janeiro", especially after a caipirinha or two, this offbeat Adams Morganite appeals to a "chic" crowd that "dresses for the [black on black] decor"; go early for "Brazilian home cooking", late for "international people-watching"; the unimpressed say the "food isn't as clever as the name."

Guapo's S 17 | 13 | 17 | $17
4515 Wisconsin Ave., NW (Albermarle St.), 202-686-3588
Rio Mall, 9811 Washingtonian Blvd., Gaithersburg, MD, 301-977-5655
■ "Solid margaritas", fajitas and "cheap", "cheese-laden, deep-fried Mexican food" keep these kid-friendly Tex-Mexicans "mobbed on weekends"; the Tenleytown shack looks so "realistic you don't drink the water" – a far cry from its "plastic" Gaithersburg kin.

Gulf Coast Kitchen S 16 | 17 | 16 | $18
7750 Woodmont Ave. (bet. Cheltenham Dr. & Old Georgetown Rd.), Bethesda, MD, 301-652-6278
■ This deliberately "tacky" "Biloxi" boathouse replica is where Bethesda singles "chill with a brew and a po' boy" or oysters from the raw bar and a meal of sides; it's "loud", "young" and "friendly", with sandwiches, salads and Creole plates (introduced post-*Survey*); happy hour on the roof deck is bedlam.

Haad Thai S 23 | 19 | 19 | $18
1100 New York Ave., NW (11th St.), 202-682-1111
■ What a "great addition to Downtown/Convention Center dining" – a "pretty" Thai with "fresh-tasting food", "quick" service, "terrific prices" and tranquility; the "chic", sunset-at-the-beach decor shows what tasteful touches and good lighting can do for a storefront space; reserve for lunch.

HAANDI S 25 | 18 | 22 | $21
Falls Plaza Shopping Ctr., 1222 W. Broad St. (Rte. 7), Falls Church, VA, 703-533-3501
4904 Fairmont Ave. (Old Georgetown Rd.), Bethesda, MD, 301-718-0121
■ "Buried" in the suburbs, these "very small", "very professional" "great values" earn top Indian honors in the *Survey*; their "well-prepared", judiciously spiced food gets a "thumbs up" from natives and novices alike, while their "civilized" manners eclipse "threadbare decor" (Falls Church); as a result, "go early" or wait.

Hard Rock Cafe ◗ S
14 | 21 | 16 | $17

999 E St., NW (10th St.), 202-737-ROCK

☑ You'd be surprised how many "self-respecting residents" consider this Downtown rock 'n' roll "tourist trap" a "fun place" for a burger and fries with "good music" and people-watching; one goes to the "bar upstairs" to avoid the kids; but even there, "sensory overload" is inevitable.

Hard Times Cafe S
19 | 16 | 18 | $13

Woodley Gardens Shopping Ctr., 1117 Nelson St. (Rte. 28), Rockville, MD, 301-294-9720
K-Mart Shopping Ctr., 394 Elden St. (bet. Herndon Pkwy. & Van Buren St.), Herndon, VA, 703-318-8941
1404 King St. (West St.), Alexandria, VA, 703-683-5340
3028 Wilson Blvd. (Highland St.), Arlington, VA, 703-528-2233

■ "On a snowy winter night", nothing beats a bowl of "the best chili in the cosmos", "terrific onion rings" and a beer at these beloved "greasy [literally] spoons"; with "rustic decor" and "1950s country-western music on the jukebox", they're "fun, relaxed" and "still the king of value."

Hautam Kebobs S
– | – | – | M

Ritchie Ctr., 785-D Rockville Pike (Wootton Pkwy.), Rockville, MD, 301-838-9222

Subtly seasoned and precisely grilled kebabs, classically served with freshly baked flat bread and rice, are the specialty of this surprisingly attractive Iranian storefront in Rockville's Ritchie Center; fish, chicken or meat kebabs are featured along with "authentic" appetizers and desserts.

Havana Cafe S
18 | 13 | 16 | $18

3100 Clarendon Blvd. (Washington Blvd.), Arlington, VA, 703-524-3611

☑ "Tasty, homestyle Cuban food" like ropa vieja and black beans and rice, served with "graciousness" in a "pleasant patio setting", generates "lots of activity on an otherwise quiet Clarendon block"; but expats wish it tasted more like old Havana – or even Miami Beach.

Herb's S (CLOSED)
14 | 13 | 15 | $18

Governor's House Holiday Inn, 1615 Rhode Island Ave., NW (17th St.), 202-333-4372

☑ "Theatrical" memorabilia, a "literary atmosphere" and crowd, and half-price burgers on Sunday nights – relics of former owner Herb White's reign – save this "middle-America" Downtown hotel dining room; it's best for a "sunny outdoor lunch" or "late snack", when the "room service" quality of the American fare is less evident and helped by the "friendly" staff.

Hibiscus Cafe
22 ⟧ 23 ⟧ 18 ⟧ $25 ⟧

3401 K St. (34th St.), 202-965-7170

■ Adding a "splash of color" to DC nighttime dining with its crayon bright, "neon and metal" design, "torrid" Caribbean cuisine and "lots of hip folks", this Islander's "hideaway location" (under the Whitehurst Freeway) lends a sense of discovery that, even with its "long waits" and "dubious service", makes it seem "different, adventurous, fun."

Hinode S
22 ⟧ 18 ⟧ 20 ⟧ $23 ⟧

Bethesda Shopping Ctr., 4914 Hampden Ln. (Arlington Rd.), Bethesda, MD, 301-654-0908
134 Congressional Ln. (Rockville Pike & Jefferson St.), Rockville, MD, 301-816-2190

■ These "family-oriented" Japanese offer "low-fat food", "quick service" and a "calming Zen atmosphere."

Hisago S
22 ⟧ 20 ⟧ 20 ⟧ $39 ⟧

3050 K St., NW (Washington Harbour), 202-944-4181

◪ An across-the-board drop in ratings since our last *Survey* signals local resistance to "outrageous prices for teensy portions" and "brusque" service at this Washington Harbour Japanese; designed for "business-oriented" Japanese, it offers "excellent" sushi and choreographed kaiseki dinners (plus an à la carte menu) in a "lovely", classic setting.

Hogate's S
11 ⟧ 14 ⟧ 13 ⟧ $23 ⟧

800 Water St., SW (bet. 9th St. & Maine Ave.), 202-484-6300

◪ "Retirements" and "rum buns" are the excuses locals give for visiting this Maine Avenue "seafood factory" "inundated" with tour buses; even the "strong" drinks, jazz and river views can't rescue the "mass-production" food and "mechanical" hospitality.

House of
Chinese Gourmet (CLOSED)
20 ⟧ 12 ⟧ 18 ⟧ $16 ⟧

1485 Rockville Pike (1 block north of Congressional Plaza), Rockville, MD, 301-984-9440

■ "Delicious" Peking duck and equally impressive vegetarian possibilities are why Chinese food mavens take this Rockville mainstay seriously; priced for everyday family dining, some think it's the area's "best Chinese."

Houston's S
19 ⟧ 17 ⟧ 18 ⟧ $19 ⟧

1065 Wisconsin Ave., NW (M St.), 202-338-7760
7715 Woodmont Ave. (bet. Cheltenham Dr. & Old Georgetown Rd.), Bethesda, MD, 301-656-9755
12256 Rockville Pike (Montrose Rd.), Rockville, MD, 301-468-3535

◪ The model of what you could "expect from a chain" – a "little style", a "staff that hustles", "great" burgers, ribs and other "simple food prepared remarkably well" with "classy" touches like freshly squeezed juice; factor the "wait and parking hassles" into the "formula."

Hsiang Foong S 18 | 10 | 17 | $15
2919 N. Washington Blvd. (bet. Filmore & Garfield Sts.), Arlington, VA, 703-522-1121

◪ With the exception of "certain dishes", i.e. "ants on the tree" (a pork and noodle dish), some find little reason to "go back" to this "humble" Clarendon Chinese, though fans praise its "creative" fare and say "good when it works."

Hunan Chinatown S 20 | 15 | 18 | $19
624 H St., NW (bet. 6th & 7th Sts.), 202-783-5858

◪ Close to Downtown galleries, one of the few places in Chinatown "with tablecloths" does classy post-opening events (it's where our First Eater, Bill Clinton, celebrated the Chinese New Year); the reliable Hunan and Szechuan fare can be had "old-style" or "stir-fried in broth."

Hunan Lion S 19 | 20 | 19 | $20
2070 Chain Bridge Rd. (Old Courthouse Rd.), Vienna, VA, 703-734-9828

Hunan Lion II
18140 The Galleria (near Tysons II), Tysons Corner, VA, 703-883-1938

◪ Their lordly manner may promise a bit more than these "dependable suburban Chinese" siblings deliver; but for "sit-down" dining near Tysons Corner, they beat the competition cold: "gladly sell my first born for the spare ribs"; N.B. post-*Survey* management changes mean they are no longer connected.

Hunan Number One ◐S 21 | 15 | 19 | $16
3033 Wilson Blvd. (Garfield St.), Arlington, VA, 703-528-1177

◪ It's "very popular", "authentic", inexpensive, kid-proofed ("plastic on the chairs") and open late (after 1 AM), yet you "can always get a table" at this Northern VA Chinese; the weekend dim sum ties up Wilson Boulevard traffic and the Hong Kong–style dishes on the menu are "very good", too.

Hunan Palace S ▽ 20 | 12 | 18 | $19
Shady Grove Ctr., 9011 Gaither Rd. (Shady Grove Rd.), Gaithersburg, MD, 301-977-8600

◪ This Northern Chinese in Gaithersburg specializes in the flavorful cooking of Taiwan and Shanghai; go for the "wonderful" dim sum, then explore the rest of the bilingual menu for some of that area's "best" food.

Ichiban 17 | 17 | 18 | $20
637 N. Frederick Ave. (near Lake Forest Mall), Gaithersburg, MD, 301-670-0560

◪ In Gaithersburg, where locals are "always on the lookout" for sushi and places to entertain a group, "beautiful landscaping" and lots of space draw attention to this Japanese-Korean; while many shrug off its faulty English and "only ok" food, an increasing number complain "food went downhill, prices up."

Il Borgo S   22 | 22 | 22 | $31
1381-A Beverly Rd. (bet. Old Dominion Dr. & Elm St.),
McLean, VA, 703-893-1400
■ At his "happy" Italian in McLean, chef-owner Vittorio
Testa (a "charmer" who "pays a visit to each table") has
turned a plush shopping-strip space into a "great hangout";
he's "justifiably proud" of his "wonderful" "Italian cruise
line food" but is "willing to cook anything you want."

Il Cigno S   ▽ 19 | 17 | 19 | $29
Lake Anne Plaza, 1617 Washington Plaza, Reston, VA,
703-471-0121
◪ "Sitting outdoors" by Lake Anne at this Northern Italian
is one of Reston's summer indulgences; its "consistent"
food and service are good enough to make for a pleasant
"outing", though inside dining may be another story
("better food nearby").

Il Pizzico   23 | 15 | 19 | $20
Suburban Park, 15209 Frederick Rd. (Gude Dr.), Rockville,
MD, 301-309-0610
■ "Good deals" on "quality" Italian food are still to be
found at this "unpretentious" Rockville trattoria – despite
price hikes that pushed it off our Bang for the Buck list; it's
unquestionably the best Italian in the area, with "terrific"
homemade pasta and always "a surprise in store", but it's
so "crowded" (causing service glitches) that "weeknights
are the only time to go."

Il Radicchio S   18 | 16 | 16 | $19
1211 Wisconsin Ave. (M St.), 202-337-2627
1509 17th St., NW (bet. P & Q Sts.), 202-986-2627
223 Pennsylvania Ave. (C St.), 202-547-5114
1801 Clarendon Blvd. (Rhodes St.), Arlington, VA, 703-276-2627
■ At these "amusing" Italians, you can "go cheap and still
get stuffed" or spaghetti, rustic pizzas or "peasant" platters;
Roberto Donna's (Arucola, Galileo, I Matti) "innovative"
format for "affordable" dining is so successful that prime-
time waits (especially at Dupont Circle) draw fire.

Il Ritrovo S   ▽ 22 | 18 | 21 | $30
4838 Rugby Ave. (bet. Woodmont & Auburn Aves.),
Bethesda, MD, 301-986-1447
■ Bethesda's "promising" Pan-Mediterranean earns kudos
for its "broad menu" ("how do they do so many things so
well?"), "attractive" appearance, "experienced personnel"
and "easy parking"; its weak points – "unevenness" and
a few "pedestrian" dishes – don't deter "repeat visits."

I Matti ⑤   22 | 19 | 19 | $30

2436 18th St., NW (bet. Belmont & Columbia Rds.),
202-462-8844

■ DC's "best" surrogate for an "evening in Florence" brings "all the essential tastes of Italy" to Adams Morgan; at this "cosmopolitan", "accessibly priced" trattoria, you'll find rustic pastas and regional dishes, "excellent fish", "knowledgeable waiters" and an "upbeat" ambiance; despite "occasional lapses", it seems "just right."

India Kitchen ⑤   – | – | – | I

Shady Grove Ctr., 9031 Gaither Rd. (Shady Grove Rd.),
Gaithersburg, MD, 301-212-9174

Not yet well known outside of Gaithersburg, this "pleasant" Indian's broad menu reflects that nation's cultural diversity, ranging from the tandooris and biryanis of the meat-loving North to the fiery vegetarian dishes of Southern India's Hindus; the pretty room engenders a "relaxing, get-away-from-it-all atmosphere."

Inn at Glen Echo   18 | 20 | 18 | $29

6119 Tulane Ave. (MacArthur Blvd. & Cabin John Pkwy.),
Glen Echo, MD, 301-229-2280

☑ The "charm potential" of this former roadhouse's "lovely setting" overlooking Glen Echo Park isn't fully realized; despite efforts to upgrade, it remains an "ok neighborhood place" with "spotty" American "nostalgia" food and service; the outdoor deck and Sunday night jazz are bright points.

INN AT LITTLE WASHINGTON ⑤   29 | 29 | 29 | $81

Inn at Little Washington, Middle & Main Sts., Washington,
VA, 540-675-3800

■ Improving on "perfection" isn't easy, yet Patrick O'Connell and Reinhardt Lynch manage it; how else could their Virginia countryside inn (No. 1 for food, service and decor in this *Survey*) meet everyone's stratospheric "expectations"; with flawless Contemporary American food and service as "precise and flowing as modern dance", a meal here is best described by paraphrasing Oscar Wilde – 'my tastes are simple, I only want the best.'

I RICCHI   25 | 23 | 23 | $42

1220 19th St., NW (bet. M & N Sts.), 202-835-0459

☑ "Heartwarming on a dreary day", this popular Northern Italian's "down-to-earth" pastas, risottos and "succulent" grills are a "biz lunch bonanza" and "delightful" for a high-end "celebration"; yes, the "waiters have personality" (which can be tough to take), but "when it's good, its very, very good", though it's best if you're "known."

JALEO ●⑤   22 | 21 | 19 | $25
480 Seventh St., NW (E St.), 202-628-7949

■ A high-energy Downtown setting earns this Spanish tapas bar its name (Jaleo means 'revelry' as well as 'racket'); it's indispensable for biz lunches or a "bite" before or after "Shakespeare"; putting together a meal of the zesty "finger foods" or more substantial plates also can be a "complete evening's" entertainment – but allow for waits.

Jean-Michel ⑤   22 | 19 | 21 | $37
Wildwood Shopping Ctr., 10223 Old Georgetown Rd. (Democracy Blvd.), Bethesda, MD, 301-564-4910

☑ The epitome of an "old French restaurant" thrives in a suburban strip mall, where its "classic" cooking and "personal" cosseting never go out of style; apart from K Street prices, its coterie of fans finds little to fault: "lifesaver for lunches", "safe place to take the in-laws for a lovely meal"; others, however, liken it to "flat champagne."

Jefferson Restaurant ⑤   23 | 24 | 23 | $42
Jefferson Hotel, 1200 16th St., NW (M St.), 202-833-6206

☑ This "intimate", "European"-feeling hotel dining room near the White House is often chosen for "quiet lunches"; long considered one of "DC's premier kitchens", with "incomparable" service, it's undergone "too many changes" at the stove recently, but the post-*Survey* arrival of a new Contemporary American chef bodes well.

JIN-GA ⑤   23 | 25 | 22 | $28
1250 24th St., NW (bet. M & N Sts.), 202-785-5319

■ "'Seoul food' at its best" (plus some Japanese standouts), served in a "gorgeous" space, adds an exciting option to West End dining; most appreciate getting the "Korean royal" treatment at this Asian import but warn that "authentic" doesn't always mean "pleasing to the US palate" and that you should be "prepared to cook for yourself."

JOCKEY CLUB ⑤   24 | 25 | 24 | $46
ITT Luxury Collection, 2100 Massachusetts Ave., NW (21st St.), 202-659-8000

■ This Kennedy-era, "upper-crust" Continental looks more like a hunt club than ever; its "wonderful seafood" and service are legendary and, notwithstanding some cracks ("quiet to the point of coma"), it remains *the* place to "experience Washington"; P.S. "don't miss the bar."

J. Paul's ●⑤   15 | 16 | 16 | $20
3218 M St., NW (bet. Potomac St. & Wisconsin Ave.), 202-333-3450

☑ Its open-to-the-street raw bar with good brews on tap generates good "people-watching" and "pickups", yet this Georgetown watering hole is sometimes considered a "backup pick"; it does an "ok" job with burgers, bar food and brunch and "really buzzes" if you're single.

Kabob Bazaar S
▽ 19 | 12 | 17 | $13

3133 Wilson Blvd. (bet. N. Highland St. & Washington Blvd.), Clarendon, VA, 703-522-8999
■ The enticing smells of grilling kebabs at this Clarendon-area Persian might be "tempting even to vegetarians", but chances are its list of authentic, unusual vegetarian sides and salads would interest them more; although the setting is simple, the staff is "gracious" and the generously portioned food is "outstanding for the price."

Kabul Caravan S
24 | 20 | 20 | $22

Colonial Shopping Ctr., 1725 Wilson Blvd., Arlington, VA, 703-522-8394
■ Don't let the strip mall location deter you – this Arlington Afghan "pioneer" offers "excellent", reasonably priced food in intriguing surroundings; locals insist it's a "cozy getaway" and a comfortable place "to linger"; NYers swear there's "nothing as good in the Big City."

Kawasaki
– | – | – | E

1140 19th St., NW (bet. M & L Sts.), 202-466-3798
Like the motorcycle, this business district Japanese's sushi is precision-made and priced for fast-trackers (i.e. the check can accelerate at "breathtaking" speed); it's also functionally designed and delivers a high-"quality" product, though the international clientele appears to have less trouble with the service department than locals do.

Kazan
23 | 19 | 23 | $27

McLean Shopping Ctr., 6813 Redmond Dr., McLean, VA, 703-734-1960
■ This Northern Virginia storefront is known locally for "wonderful" Turkish cuisine, including "excellent" doner kebab and lamb, and "outstanding" service, which make up for the "tired surroundings" and lack of "privacy."

King Street Blues S
18 | 20 | 18 | $17

112 N. St. Asaph St. (King St.), Alexandria, VA, 703-836-8800
■ "Dominion beer makes the menu" at this "raucous" Old Town fun fair where the colorful "papier-mâché" decor and live entertainment please kids of all ages; highlights of the "good, greasy", cheap, all-American comfort food include the "best cheese fries in creation", "dessert"-sweet BBQ and "meat loaf 'n' mashed potatoes done right."

KINKEAD'S S
27 | 22 | 24 | $40

Red Lion Row, 2000 Pennsylvania Ave., NW (I St., bet. 20th & 21st Sts.), 202-296-7700
■ Bob Kinkead's urban bistro, with its "elegantly casual" two-tier setting, is the most popular in-town eatery in this *Survey*; "no one does fish better" or more "imaginatively" reinterprets regional American dishes and few can resist his "incredible" desserts; most reviewers would go back in a heartbeat despite a few "ups and downs."

Kramerbooks & Afterwords Cafe ◐⑤
15 | 16 | 14 | $17

1517-21 Connecticut Ave., NW (bet. Q St., NW & Dupont Circle), 202-387-1462

◪ Browsing books while "waiting for a table is half the fun" at this '60s-era bookstore/cafe off Dupont Circle – a haven for "bookish" singles, late-night sucrophiles, jazz fiends and artistic types; since the American kitchen is little more than a "closet and a microwave", and service is hardly top-shelf, keep it simple.

Krupin's ⑤
17 | 10 | 15 | $16

4620 Wisconsin Ave., NW (Chesapeake St.), 202-686-1989

◪ "Tacky" and overly "bright", this is a "real NY-style deli where rudeness" is part of the shtick; however, DC deli mavens would prefer their corned beef and pastrami, along with the "best pickled herring", boiled chicken and matzo-ball soup, served without a side of condescension.

La Bergerie
24 | 23 | 23 | $40

218 N. Lee St. (bet. Queen & Cameron Sts.), Alexandria, VA, 703-683-1007

▩ "Every diner is treated like a valued old customer" at this Classic French in Old Town whose "Basque-accented" menu and plush quarters hark back to a more "gracious" era; but this is not a place to go when rushed – everything is done "right", but a bit "slow."

La Bonne Auberge
20 | 21 | 21 | $37

Great Falls Shopping Ctr., 9835 Georgetown Pike (Walker Rd.), Great Falls, VA, 703-759-3877

◪ In contrast to the rusticity of nearby L'Auberge Chez Francois, this "dressy" French in Great Falls provides a formal setting for more "classic" dining; the "romantic" ambiance works well for special occasions, and although the food strikes some as "unexciting", the "raspberry soufflé makes it worth a trip."

La Brasserie ⑤
23 | 20 | 20 | $33

239 Massachusetts Ave., NE (bet. 2nd & 3rd Sts.), 202-546-9154

◪ There is no more "charming" setting for outdoor dining on Capitol Hill than this "once great" French brasserie; the food is still "good" and "hearty", but with the exception of some signature dishes and a notable crème brûleé, it "won't interfere" with your pitch and service can be "awkward and slow"; N.B. Sunday brunch is a buy.

La Chaumiere
22 | 22 | 21 | $35

2813 M St., NW (bet. 28th & 29th Sts.), 202-338-1784

▩ Julia Child's visit to this "cozy" Country French 'cottage' in her old Georgetown neighborhood focused attention on its comforting, "old-fashioned" fare and "warm", welcoming atmosphere; "in winter", cozy up to the fire and dig into the cassoulet (Thursday nights).

La Colline
23 **19** **22** **$35**

400 N. Capitol St., NW (bet. D & E Sts.), 202-737-0400

■ Before the congressional gift ban, this deceptively "dull"-looking French bistro was known for the "best working lunch" on the Hill; but now that fewer pols come to "see pals", surveyors hope that its "consistently" "great", market-driven menu, "excellent" staff and dinner prix fixe ($19.95) will be enough of a draw.

La Cote d'Or Cafe ⑤
23 **21** **22** **$37**

6876 Lee Hwy. (bet. Washington Blvd. & Westmoreland St.), Arlington, VA, 703-538-3033

☑ Falls Church blesses this neighborhood bistro for bringing "Gallic charm and cuisine" to a culinarily deprived area; it may be "pricey for a low-rent district", and the "food can be hit or miss", but "when it's good it's a wonderful asset."

Lafayette ⑤
▽ **26** **29** **27** **$46**

Hay-Adams Hotel, 800 16th St., NW (H St.), 202-638-2570

■ A meal in this "most elegant dining room" is a "true Washington experience" and "as close as most of us will get to dinner at the White House" (across the square); the aura of "power", awesome service and rubbernecking nearly eclipse its "tasty" Contemporary American fare; a svelte cellar wine bar is a site of 'off-the-record' encounters.

La Ferme ⑤
21 **23** **21** **$38**

7101 Brookville Rd. (East-West Hwy. & Western Ave.), Chevy Chase, MD, 301-986-5255

☑ "Enjoyable" if "unimaginative" French food endears this Chevy Chase destination to the "old guard"; although this "pretty" place is often called "romantic", it's a bit too "ladylike" for amour; "no great flair, no great flaws."

La Fourchette ⑤
22 **20** **20** **$27**

2429 18th St., NW (bet. Kalorama St. & Columbia Rd.), 202-332-3077

☑ Charming, "family-run" French bistros casually dishing up escargot, moules and pommes frites "throughout the day" are "basic" in Paris, but not in Adams Morgan, which is why this one is considered a "petit trésor", especially from the vantage point of its "bohemian" sidewalk cafe.

La Lomita ⑤
20 **13** **20** **$17**

1330 Pennsylvania Ave., SE (G St.), 202-546-3109

■ "Hill rats" burrow into this "cheerful" Tex-Mexican for "great margaritas" and "cheap", spicy food; with its "tasty offerings beyond the standards", "no attitude" and low-down, eat-in-a-"garage" appeal, it's a "good place to crash after work."

La Madeleine French Bakery S   17   18   15 $14
3000 M St., NW (30th St., NW), 202-337-6975
500 King St. (Pitt St.), Alexandria, VA, 703-739-2853
5861 Crossroads Ctr., Bailey's Crossroads (Leesburg & Columbia Pikes), Falls Church, VA, 703-379-5551
1833 Fountain Dr. (bet. Baron Cameron & Reston Pkwy.), Reston, VA, 703-707-0704
18330 Fountain Dr. (Reston Pkwy.), Reston, VA, 703-707-0704
1915 C Chain Bridge Rd. (Rte. 7), Tysons Corner, VA, 703-827-8833
7607 Old Georgetown Rd. (Commerce St.), Bethesda, MD, 301-215-9142
Mid-Pike Plaza, 11858 Rockville Pike (Montrose Rd.), Rockville, MD, 301-984-2270

☑ "Vive la quiche" is the motto of these self-serve, French-style cafe/bakeries, although their "phenomenal tomato basil soup" and "fabulous rotisserie chicken" are the big draws; though critics pan "slow fast food", they rise to some occasions as an "unhurried place to have a light bite."

La Miche S   23   21   22 $36
7905 Norfolk Ave. (bet. Wisconsin Ave. & Old Georgetown Rd.), Bethesda, MD, 301-986-0707

☑ Lace curtains in the window tell Bethesda passersby that this "accomplished" French bistro does things in a "traditional" way; it's a "solid" performer with a few highs ("high consistency, high prices", "hit a good night and it's a 10") and a few lows ("cramped", "fusty").

La Mirabelle S   17   17   19 $30
6645 Old Dominion Dr. (McLean Sq.), McLean, VA, 703-893-8484

☑ McLean locals frequent this "very personable" yet "little known" suburban French; aside from "heavy sauces" and "dingy" decor, regulars find it "extremely pleasant."

Landini Brothers S   22   18   20 $28
115 King St. (Union St.), Alexandria, VA, 703-836-8404

☑ At "Old Town's power lunch spot", run by people who "appreciate your business", you can find "everything from a loan to a lawyer at the bar" and old-fashioned ("too much garlic") Italian seafood and pasta in back; it may look like a "dark, scary" tourist trap, but it's not.

La Panetteria S   18   15   19 $21
4921 Cordell Ave. (bet. Old Georgetown Rd. & Norfolk Ave.), Bethesda, MD, 301-951-6433

☑ "Welcoming and friendly", this old-timer's comfortable cooking, garden setting and a "reasonable early bird" keep it competitive in Bethesda's "saturated Italian market"; it's "handy for family Sunday night dinner" or entertaining friends, when it doesn't really matter if the food is "not as good as you expect."

La Tomate 🟦
17 | 18 | 18 | $26

1701 Connecticut Ave., NW (Dupont Circle), 202-667-5505
🔲 Prime people-watching from the patio and window
seats make this popular Italian a great Dupont Circle
hangout, but not necessarily a great place to dine;
reviews run the gamut from "good day-in, day-out choice"
to "inattentive", "pricey", "location is the only good
thing about this place."

L'AUBERGE CHEZ FRANCOIS 🟦
28 | 27 | 27 | $47

*332 Springvale Rd. (2 mi. north of Georgetown Pike), Great
Falls, VA, 703-759-3800*
⬛ Utterly comfortable because it's "not haute anything",
our surveyors' favorite place is set in a rustic "French
farmhouse" that embraces diners in a "warm, friendly
hug", feeds them hearty Country French fare and makes
them feel their money is well spent; a meal here is always
a "charming and unforgettable experience" and, "on a
moonlit night", the garden is "dreamy."

L'AUBERGE PROVENCALE 🟦
26 | 26 | 26 | $57

*L'Auberge Provencale, Rte. 340 (Rte. 50), White Post, VA,
540-837-1375*
⬛ In the Virginia countryside near White Post, Alain Borel
and his charming wife re-create the ambiance of a country
restaurant near his native Avignon, where patrons laze on
the front porch and experience "happiness on a plate"; if
asked whether it's a "little too French for Americans" (i.e.
heavy food, "stuffy" help), most would answer 'mais non.'

Lauriol Plaza 🟦
20 | 17 | 18 | $22

1801 18th St., NW (S St.), 202-387-0035
🔲 Sitting outside, drinking margaritas and eating "too
many chips" amidst the "diverse" Adams Morgan/Dupont
Circle "hubbub" is such "fun" that few mind the "ridiculous"
crowds or waits at this urban Latin (or want to be inside);
popular for fajitas, paella and roast pork, the "reasonably
priced", recently revised menu tilts toward Mexican, with
several Spanish "faves."

Lavandou 🟦
23 | 17 | 20 | $31

*3321 Connecticut Ave., NW (bet. Macomb & Newark Sts.),
202-966-3002*
⬛ The "warmth of Provence" pervades this quintessential
neighborhood bistro in Cleveland Park, where everything
from its flavorful, "affordable" cooking, friendly charm
and "hopelessly cramped" quarters are straight from
a book; while hardly perfect, nearly everyone wishes
"everyone else would please stop going."

LEBANESE TAVERNA S 24 | 18 | 20 | $22
2641 Connecticut Ave. (bet. Calvert St. & Woodley Rd.),
202-265-8681
5900 Washington Blvd. (McKinley Rd.), Arlington, VA,
703-241-8681

LEBANESE TAVERNA MARKET
4400 Old Dominion Dr. (bet. Lee Hwy. & Lorcom Ln.),
Arlington, VA, 703-276-8681
■ Consistently rated a "big yum" for their "impressive
variety of meze" and "many vegetarian" choices served
by waiters who "care if you clean your plate", these
"congenial" Lebanese siblings are "great values for
outstanding food"; enjoy the "family show" (VA) or join
"in the city fun"; no reserving means waits.

Le Bon Cafe 19 | 14 | 13 | $12
210 2nd St., SE (bet. Pennsylvania Ave. & C St., SE),
202-547-7200 S ⌺
1310 Braddock Pl. (West St.), Alexandria, VA, 703-519-1777
▨ Hilltoppers head to the "cutest cafe" on the "uncivilized
House side" to "reward" themselves with "quality" salads,
sandwiches and soup; since it's "crowded, cramped" and
staffed with "good intentions", you can be sure that if the
"food wasn't good they wouldn't go"; the Braddock metro
location (lunch only) is less rewarding.

Le Caprice S (CLOSED) 23 | 19 | 21 | $37
2348 Wisconsin Ave., NW (Calvert St.), 202-337-3394
■ Relocating to Tysons Corner in fall, 1997, where this
charming French bistro will be reborn with an exciting
restaurant/wine bar/wine shop format; diners can order any
wine in stock – at the retail price plus a modest corkage
fee – sample a tasting flight or even take home a meal.

Ledo Pizza S 17 | 10 | 15 | $12
4400 Connecticut Ave., NW (Albemarle St.), 202-244-8109
2420 University Blvd. E. (Westpark Dr.), Adelphi, MD,
301-422-8622
13444 New Hampshire Ave. (Randolph Rd.), Silver Spring,
MD, 301-384-5400 ⌺
7213 Muncaster Mill Rd. (bet. Redland & Shady Grove
Rds.), Rockville, MD, 301-869-7900
Boulevard Shops, 14609 Baltimore Ave. (Rte. 1), Laurel,
MD, 301-498-5336 ⌺
1319-H Rockville Pike (Twinbrook Pkwy.), Rockville, MD,
301-309-8484 ⌺
5425 River Rd. (Kenwood Station), Bethesda, MD,
301-656-5336 ⌺
1035 S. Edgewood (Columbia Pike), Arlington, VA,
703-521-1760

Ledo Pizza (Cont.)
7510 Leesburg Pike (Idlewood Rd.), Falls Church, VA, 703-847-5336
Battlefield Shopping Ctr., 1037 Edwards Ferry Rd. (15 Bypass), Leesburg, VA, 703-777-9500 🕏
▣ "Memories of College Park" whet appetites for the "unique" ("greasy", pie-crusted, "sweet sauced") rectangular pizza at the original location in Adelphi; the franchised operations use the same recipe, "tolerate children very well", have no better decor and are just as "cheap"; yet many think Ledo "lost its soul in the expansion" – it's a "nostalgia thing."

Legal Sea Food S   21 | 18 | 18 | $31
2020 K St., NW (bet. 20th & 21st Sts.), 202-496-1111
Tyson Galleria, 2001 International Dr. (Rte. 123), McLean, VA, 703-827-8900
▣ Calling these up-market fish houses the "best export from Boston since the Babe was traded to the Yankees" overstates the case; but plenty of local fin fanciers cheer their wide selection of "fresh" seafare – if not always the way they cook it, their settings ("expense account" in DC, "mall world" at Tysons Corner), "premium" pricing and no reserving (Tysons); rookie staffers "need full training."

Le Gaulois   23 | 20 | 21 | $30
1106 King St. (bet. Fayette & Henry Sts.), Alexandria, VA, 703-739-9494
▣ Like a "true friend", you can count on this "cozy" Old Town bistro to put you at ease and provide you with "satisfying", well-priced, "unspectacular" French "comfort food"; most lapses are treated with a Gallic shrug ("too crowded, too rushed"), but it's never been forgiven for having "left DC."

LE LION D'OR (CLOSED)   27 | 24 | 26 | $57
1150 Connecticut Ave., NW (bet. 18th & M Sts.), 202-296-7972
▣ Jean-Pierre Goyenvalle, the "accomplished artist" directing this Downtown French classic, is first among his peers and a "superb" dinner in his formal dining room will make a "major impact" on your peers; it's considered Washington's "best" French ("more clearly so" with the post-*Survey* closing of Jean-Louis at The Watergate), yet some find it too "stiff" and in need of a "second wind."

Le Paradis   25 | 14 | 21 | $31
Festival Shopping Ctr., 347 Muddy Branch Rd. (bet. Great Seneca Hwy. & Clopper Rd.), Gaithersburg, MD, 301-208-9493
■ Reports of "city food hiding out" at a "tiny", very plain storefront in Gaithersburg have made this Franco-Asian a very "crowded" find; its French provincial with a "Pacific Rim twist" dishes are "creative" and often successful, but people are starting to notice that they carry a city price tag.

Le Refuge
24 | 20 | 21 | $32 |

*127 N. Washington St. (bet. King & Cameron Sts.),
Alexandria, VA, 703-548-4661*

☑ If this tarted-up Old Town French bistro "were larger" or
less brazen "it would lose its appeal"; as it is, it's the near-
home "bet for most romantic" dining and "very friendly,
too"; most (not all) find it "worth the crowding because
the food's so good."

Le Rivage S
– | – | – | M |

1000 Water St, SW (bet. Maine Ave. & 9th St.), 202-488-8111
"Everyone slips up sometimes", as we did when we left this
French waterfront viewplace off the *Survey*; treasured for
its "affordably priced" seafood and early-bird specials, it
gets ticketholders to the Arena Stage on time and hosts
romantic "sunset" dinners with equal aplomb.

Les Halles ◑S
21 | 18 | 18 | $32 |

1201 Pennsylvania Ave., NW (12th St.), 202-347-6848
☑ From Paris by way of NY, this "Left Bank" steakhouse
with a "breezy Gallic informality" verges on "authentically
rude"; it's the place to come for frites, moules and onglet
steak and to join the tourists, theatergoers and Pennsylvania
Avenue pinstripes on the sidewalk terrace – who are
escaping the cigar smoke inside.

Lespinasse
– | – | – | E |

Sheraton Carlton Hotel, 923 16th St., NW (K St.), 202-879-6900
Dripping with elegance that provides magnificent window
dressing for a deal, and only two blocks from the White
House, this stately, poshly refurbished hotel dining room
reopened October 1996 as an offshoot of NYC's celebrated
French-Asian Lespinasse, with a chef trained at the NYC
original; the question is can its glittering prospects
surmount its daunting prices?

Le Vieux Logis S
22 | 20 | 22 | $38 |

*7925 Old Georgetown Rd. (Auburn Ave.), Bethesda, MD,
301-652-6816*
☑ This agreeably cluttered "French cottage" in Bethesda,
and its "good cooking" and cosseting, "never disappoint"
its discriminating "older crowd"; but its "French food
without all the fuss" approach leaves some younger
diners cold ("boring and traditional", "small, cramped").

Listrani's S
17 | 14 | 16 | $20 |

5100 MacArthur Blvd., NW (Dana Pl.), 202-363-0619
☑ A "good place to grab a bite, with no high hopes" of more
than "average" Italian dining is how surveyors sum up this
MacArthur Boulevard "pizza and salad standby"; despite
perennial complaints about its "tacky" appearance, waits
and "spotty" service, it's "cheerful", comfortable, "satisfies
the pickiest of children" – and there's not much else around.

Lite 'n' Fair
▽ | 18 | 6 | 13 | $16
1018 King St. (bet. Patrick & Henry Sts.), Alexandria, VA, 703-549-3717

Lite 'n' Fair/Belle View Seafood S
Belle View Shopping Ctr., 1510 Belle View Blvd. (Fort Hunt Rd.), Alexandria, VA, 703-660-6085

☑ Offering "high-class" Italian, French or Asian-influenced food at a "low price", including a "super portobello sandwich" and "tarragon chicken salad" you'd love to "replicate", this pocket-sized King Street deli manages to be "very creative in a very small space"; its Belle View sister, a real restaurant specializing in seafood, also "has its charms."

Little Viet Garden S
21 | 16 | 17 | $17
3012 Wilson Blvd. (Garfield Rd.), Arlington, VA, 703-522-9686

☑ More cosmopolitan than its neighbors on "Virginia's Ho Chi Minh Trail" and "very busy", this "funky" Vietnamese does a good ("not the best") job with its specialties and has a "cute garden" which, alas, borders "deafening traffic" and the parking lot; those who love it most "go for lunch."

Los Chorros S
19 | 12 | 17 | $14
2420 Blue Ridge Ave. (Georgia Ave.), Wheaton, MD, 301-933-1066
8401 Snouffer's School Rd. (Center Way), Gaithersburg, MD, 301-840-5894

■ Please "don't tell anyone how good" these "family-run" Salvadorans are, beg reviewers who worry that the remodeling at Wheaton will attract too much trade; as it is, their "good food" and "great value" keep them packed to the max – go for the "papusas" and "shrimp anything."

Louisiana Express Co. S
21 | 9 | 15 | $15
4921 Bethesda Ave. (Arlington Rd.), Bethesda, MD, 301-652-6945

☑ "They know the meaning of Tabasco" at this Bethesda Cajun-Creole "dump" with counter service (loosely speaking) and zip decor; spicy stuff like jambalaya, catfish beignets, "po' boy sandwiches and alligator stew" are "cheap", "greasy" and "good" enough to keep the joint "overcrowded"; "not bad", say natives, if you've "never been to New Orleans."

Luigino S
22 | 20 | 19 | $30
1100 New York Ave., NW (bet. H & 12th Sts.), 202-371-0595

☑ This "slick and smartly done" Northern Italian striver is one of the top biz lunch places near the Convention Center, which could explain the complaints about "unreliable" service and dishes that aren't "up to" their prices; still, "in a city filled with Italian" restaurants, it's "worth going" to and "underappreciated for dinner."

Luna Grill & Diner 🅂   18 | 16 | 17 | $16 |
1301 Connecticut Ave., NW (N St.), 202-835-2280
■ Amid the "bars, chains and carryouts, just south of
Dupont Circle", this spiffy-looking "urban diner" provides
a reality check and some pretty good homestyle food (like
"addictive" sweet potato fries); it's "cheap", "chaotic" and
crowded, but the "chili is reason enough" to go.

Maharaja 🅂   – | – | – | M |
*Cipriano Square Shopping Ctr., 8825 Greenbelt Rd.
(Cipriano Rd.), Greenbelt, MD, 301-552-1600*
The "shortage" of good restaurants in Prince Georges
County is one reason why Greenbelt is "lucky to have" this
Indian; others are its tandoor-baked breads and meats,
savory stews and "good-deal" lunch buffet ($6.95 Tuesday–
Friday); all the above make reports that it's "becoming a
little seedy" unsettling.

Maison Blanche (CLOSED)   24 | 23 | 24 | $46 |
1725 F St., NW (bet. 17th & 18th Sts.), 202-842-0070
☑ It's "staid" and "getting gray" (like its clientele) and has
an aura of "faded glamour", but the food at this "formal"
French "is still quite good", the unflappable service even
better and it's near "lots of offices" and the World Bank
(the White House, too); happy hour is surprisingly active and
the $32.00 prix fixe is an "excellent" pre-concert deal.

MAKOTO 🅂   28 | 25 | 27 | $42 |
4822 MacArthur Blvd., NW (Reservoir Rd.), 202-298-6866
■ An "incredible dining experience", an "immersion in
Japanese culture" – whether you "sit ringside" at the
10-seat sushi bar of this largely "unknown", exquisite
Nipponese "hidden" on MacArthur Boulevard or at one of
the four tables for an "innovative" kaiseki dinner, you're in
for some of the "finest Japanese dining outside of Japan."

Malik 🅂 (CLOSED)   ▽ 23 | 19 | 21 | $17 |
(fka Mali Thai)
1805 18th St., NW (bet. S & T Sts.), 202-986-5124
■ "Suitable for casual" or "romantic" dining, this attractive
Thai is giving nearby Bua "competition" in Dupont Circle
East; if reports that the "waiters couldn't be nicer – so polite
and unobtrusive", and the food (including a long vegetarian
menu) is "wonderful" hold true, it won't be "quiet" long.

Mama Wok & Teriyaki 🅂   ▽ 21 | 5 | 13 | $11 |
*Rockville City Ctr., 595 Hungerford Dr. (N. Washington St.),
Rockville, MD, 301-309-6642*
■ Those who don't "expect much" from "Asian cafeteria
food" may be pleasantly surprised by this "best bargain"
Sino-Japanese off Rockville Pike; it's adept at a mix of
Chinese and Japanese dishes, made with the critters
swimming in the fish tanks (which constitute the decor)
and sold for a pittance.

Mare E Monti ⑤ ▽ 23 | 17 | 19 | $22 |
Freestate Mall, 15554-B Annapolis Rd. (off Hwy. 197),
Bowie, MD, 301-262-9179
☒ Finding "homemade pasta" in a "suburban mall" is
"impressive", particularly in Bowie, where cucina Italiana
alternatives are pizza joints and chains; those who have
discovered this "consistently good, interesting" place wish
the service lived up to the "homey atmosphere" and food.

Market St. Bar & Grill ⑤ 22 | 21 | 22 | $28 |
Hyatt Hotel, 1800 President St. (Market St.), Reston, VA,
703-709-6262
■ One of the highlights of the exurban mix of restaurants,
shops and entertainment in Reston Town Center, this
Contemporary American hotel dining room provides "first-
class food and service in a lively setting"; praise for the
"creative" menu, brunch and weekend jazz is tempered
mostly by concerns about last summer's chef change.

Martin's Tavern ⑤ 17 | 18 | 18 | $21 |
1264 Wisconsin Ave., NW (N St.), 202-333-7370
■ This historic Georgetown tavern, "an island of stability in
a world of change", is as "easy and comfortable" now as in
the days of "FDR and the '40s"; go for an "old-fashioned"
breakfast or "evening snack" of solid American fare and
"feel like Washington is your old hometown."

Matuba ⑤ 22 | 13 | 19 | $21 |
2915 Columbia Pike (Walter Reed St.), Arlington, VA,
703-521-2811
4918 Cordell Ave. (Old Georgetown Rd.), Bethesda, MD,
301-652-7449
■ "Fresh", "friendly", "fast", "no-frills" family sushi stops
that work well for everyday eating when presentation and
surroundings don't matter as much as "reasonable prices"
and "smiles"; "even if you don't eat sushi, there's lots that's
good" – "ask for specials not on the specials board."

Mediterranean Blue ⑤ – | – | – | M |
1910 18th St., NW (bet. T St. & Florida Ave.), 202-483-2583
"Colorful" – that goes for the eponymous exterior, ambiance
and company at this youthful Middle Eastern "fun spot"
below Adams Morgan; write-ins say it has "potential" – after
all, "where else can you listen to the *Laverne & Shirley*
theme while eating shish kebabs", grilled veggies and rice?

Mediterranee ⑤ – | – | – | E |
3520 Lee Hwy. (Monroe St.), Arlington, VA, 703-527-7276
In summer 1996, this warm Mediterranean bistro in Arlington
replaced the similarly named Mediterraneo; although it
also focuses on the sunny cuisine of Southern Europe,
which complements the white-walled, rustic space, the
management and kitchen are new.

Melati   – | – | – | M |
3506 Connecticut Ave., NW (bet. Ordway & Porter Sts.), 202-537-1432

Uptown moviegoers recommend this small Cleveland Park Indonesian-Malaysian for its "intriguing" menu, sidewalk seating and good value, but not for its decor; the staff will be delighted to tell you about dishes you won't find elsewhere.

Melrose   24 | 24 | 24 | $42 |
Park Hyatt Hotel, 24th & M Sts., NW, 202-955-3899

■ Its "urban garden" elegance and hush make this "polished" West End hotel dining room perfect for a biz lunch; diners find "flashes of brilliance" in the Contemporary American kitchen and a sensory cornucopia – a cascading fountain on the sunken patio, museum-quality art, "jumpin'" Saturday night jazz and the "best" wine bar, tea and brunch.

Memphis Bar-B-Q Co. S   – | – | – | I |
Ballston Commons, 4238 Wilson Blvd. (Glebe Rd.), Arlington, VA, 703-875-9883
13067-H Lee Jackson Hwy., Fairfax, VA, 703-449-0500
11804 Baron Cameron Rd. (bet. Reston & Towne Center Pkwys.), Reston, VA, 703-435-5118

Like Red Hot & Blue, these new BBQ joints pay homage to Memphis with wet or dry ribs, pulled pork, chicken, onion straws, sides – and BBQ pizza just in case Elvis drops by; too bad their designer-distressed, mall-based settings are a far cry from down-home pits.

Meskerem ● S   21 | 18 | 18 | $20 |
2434 18th St., NW (Columbia Rd.), 202-462-4100

◪ Adams Morgan Ethiopian serving "really ethnic food" in attractive surroundings; one sits upstairs on hassocks at basketweave tables attended by "beautiful waitresses" and scoops up fiery stews with "sour", sponge-like bread; romantics and vegetarians enjoy it, but novices be warned: it's an "adventure."

Metro Center Grille S   18 | 17 | 18 | $23 |
Marriott at Metro Ctr., 775 12th St., NW (bet. H & J Sts.), 202-737-2200

◪ This "comfortable" Marriott restaurant is making major efforts to upgrade its image – namely, hiring an "ambitious chef" whose "fresh" Contemporary American menu is "worth the price"; but some still think of it as serving "pedestrian business fare" – spillover from its "colorless" appearance and Convention Center location perhaps?

Metro 29 ● S   – | – | – | I |
4711 Lee Hwy. (Glebe Rd.), Arlington, VA, 703-528-2464

Bright and shiny and looking like a diner should, this Arlington entry is a "real" one with "class"; write-ins tell us it has the basics aced with "platter"-sized portions, terrific desserts and "lines out the door" for its "great breakfast."

Mick's S
16 | 16 | 16 | $16 |

2401 Pennsylvania Ave., NW (24th St.), 202-331-9613
Fair Oaks Mall (Junction Rtes. 50 & 66), Fairfax, VA,
703-934-9716
Springfield Mall (Franconia Rd.), Springfield, VA, 703-971-6106

◩ Retro Americana and a "mishmash" menu for mix 'n'
match dining doesn't take these mock saloons much beyond
"TGIF" level now that the "excitement has dimmed";
"convenience counts for something", of course, but so
does "variable" performance.

Mike's American Grill S
21 | 20 | 20 | $20 |

6210 Backlick Rd. (Old Keene Mill Rd.), Springfield, VA,
703-644-7100

◩ "Seating is a major headache" and reviewers, charitably,
"won't comment on the parking situation", yet they jam
this "standard American" warehouse in Springfield "for
what it is" – a place with "fern bar food", "dependable"
prime rib and a "suburban" environment that "tries to be
hip" – and because there isn't much else out there.

Mi Rancho S
21 | 16 | 21 | $18 |

8701 Ramsey Ave. (Fiddler Ln.), Silver Spring, MD,
301-588-4872
19725 Germantown Rd. (Middlebrook Rd.), Germantown,
MD, 301-515-7480

■ Happily, this effort to simulate the Rio Grande Cafe in
Silver Spring (tortilla machine, cement floors, stacked
cartons and all) isn't entirely successful – while its
Tex-Mex menu seems familiar, the atmosphere is less
"frenetic", more genuine; on-site "owners take great
pride in the food – and it shows"; N.B. the new Germantown
branch is unrated.

Miss Saigon S
21 | 15 | 18 | $20 |

1847 Columbia Rd., NW (18th St.), 202-667-1900 **(CLOSED)**
3057 M St. (Thomas Jefferson St.), 202-333-5545

◩ Best liked for its quail and noodle soup, "garden
atmosphere" and "very kind staff", this Adams Morgan
Vietnamese does a brisk takeout trade; eat-in diners
divide: "best cheap Vietnamese in DC" vs. "just ok" –
ergo it may be "inconsistent"; its smashing younger sister
in Georgetown should be a hit.

Miyagi
– | – | – | M |

6719 Curran St. (Old Dominion Dr.), McLean, VA,
703-893-0116

That this pocket-sized Japanese is not well known beyond
its McLean environs is one of its drawing cards; after all,
when one serves "the best sushi in the area, hands down"
and has only eight tables and a sushi bar, the fewer who
vie for a seat, the better.

Mo Bay Cafe ◑ S 16 | 13 | 14 | $18
(fka Montego Cafe)
2437 18th St., NW (bet. Belmont & Columbia Rds.), 202-745-1002
☒ Aside from some of the best sidewalk seats in Adams
Morgan, a "pulsating" reggae beat and a couple of deadly
drinks, fewer are finding this "soft-core Jamaican" joint
fun; it used to have "good Caribbean cuisine" (a few say it
still does), but lately it's been "lackluster all-around."

Moby Dick ⊟ 23 | 6 | 13 | $11
7027 Wisconsin Ave. (Leland St), Bethesda, MD,
301-654-1838 S
Buchanan Mall, 2103 S. Jefferson Davis Hwy. (23rd St.),
Crystal City, VA, 703-413-5100
6864 Old Dominion Dr. (Rte. 123), McLean, VA,
303-448-8448 S
■ Perhaps this area's "best" and most "authentic" Persian
kebabs (making them is an art requiring precise timing and
skillful grilling) can be found at this ramshackle Bethesda
carryout-plus whose "healthy", "delicious", "filling" and
"cheap" versions put it (and its kin) high on our Bang for
the Buck list; they also earn kudos from "kids."

Monocle 15 | 17 | 17 | $29
107 D St., NE (1st St.), 202-546-4488
☒ This "clubby" Senate-side fixture will probably survive
lobbying reform just fine – the 'members' (of congress)
have been bringing their families and staff here for years
for "old-fashioned" (aka "boring") American food in a
"comfortable" setting; besides, no place is as "close to
Senate offices" and handy to the Supreme Court; indeed,
on any given day you could probably get the votes for a
majority decision in the dining room.

Montgomery's Grille S 16 | 17 | 16 | $20
7200 Wisconsin Ave. (Bethesda Ave.), Bethesda, MD,
301-654-3595
☒ While wishing that Bethesda's "we-have-everything"
American had food as "happening as the bar" and that it
didn't treat customers "like herded cows", locals find it
useful for a "no-nonsense bite", "nice Sunday brunch",
outdoor dining, "game watching" and shopping for "Mr.
or Ms. Right" – it's also where "the girls" "do" lunch.

MORRISON-CLARK INN S 25 | 26 | 24 | $39
Morrison-Clark Inn, 1015 L St., NW (bet. 11th St. &
Massachusetts Ave.), 202-898-1200
■ Susan Lindeborg is "back and cooking up a storm" at this
treasured Downtown Victorian, "assuring" its place among
DC's "best" restaurants; her American "home cooking with a
modern flair" is "innovative" yet "understated" and
enhanced by a "lovely" setting and "staff that makes you
feel special"; out-of-town "visitors are enthralled" – though
not by the neighborhood.

MORTON'S OF CHICAGO ⑤   26 | 21 | 23 | $47 |
3251 Prospect St., NW (Wisconsin Ave.), 202-342-6258
1050 Connecticut Ave., NW (L St.), 202-955-5997
8075 Leesburg Pike (Aline Rd.), Tysons Corner, VA, 703-883-0800
■ "In your face – brisk, brusque and noisy", these "top-dollar" cow palaces are a "steak-eater's dream"; their "men's club" atmosphere virtually demands a "porterhouse, martini and a good cigar" (although they serve "great lobster" too); so what if it's "sinful"? – "roll your sleeves up, damn the cholesterol and dig in."

Mr. K's ⑤   23 | 23 | 23 | $39 |
2121 K St., NW (bet. 21st & 22nd Sts.), 202-331-8868
☑ "Fine Chinese dining", as done in Hong Kong, provides an "elegant" backdrop for business dining at this K Street stalwart where the "royal treatment" nearly overwhelms the "outstanding" food; if you're on an expense account, it's quite a "show"; for everyone else, it may be "past its price."

Mrs. Simpson's ⑤   21 | 21 | 21 | $33 |
2915 Connecticut Ave., NW (Cathedral Ave.), 202-332-8300
☑ The romantic theme of the Windsor-Simpson legend casts its spell over this "intimate", slightly "precious" restaurant, its "light", "eclectic, American menu" and "classy" brunch; with few exceptions, it charms Woodley Park and tourists on the way to the zoo; P.S. the "royal memorabilia" is worth a trip to the rest rooms.

Mr. Yung's ●⑤   19 | 11 | 18 | $18 |
740 Sixth St., NW (bet. G & H Sts.), 202-628-1098
■ A choice selection of dim sum is the "good lunch deal" at this Chinatown Cantonese storefront; the "very capable" kitchen does a good job with the "very extensive menu", but be aware of the fact that there may be a "language barrier."

Muer's Seafood (CLOSED)   17 | 18 | 19 | $30 |
1101 Connecticut Ave., NW (L St.), 202-785-4505
☑ "Strictly for business lunches" near Farragut Square, this nautical-themed seafooder stays busy but mostly inspires yawns: "Eastern Shore basic, without the beach", "service and quality spotty"; on weeknights, piano jazz is the bait.

Music City Roadhouse and Doe's Eat Place ⑤   15 | 19 | 17 | $18 |
1050 30th St., NW (bet. M & K Sts.), 202-337-4444
■ "The bigger [and hungrier] the group, the better" at this rollicking Southern roadhouse replica in Georgetown where they pile on the down-home eats (we're talking "serious grease") family-style; upstairs, Doe's Eat Place, an outlet for Greenville Mississippi's legendary hot tamales, gumbo, steak and buttery broiled shrimp, fits right in; plus, there's a "blast" of a Sunday gospel brunch."

Mykonos
| 19 | 18 | 19 | $23 |

1835 K St., NW (19th St.), 202-331-0370

☑ With its "fresh, tasty" fare, staff that "couldn't be nicer" and a K Street setting that evokes its namesake island, this "traditional" Greek is as close to the Aegean "as one can get"; maybe you could find as good or "better" Greek "at lower prices" elsewhere, but it's still a "nice, quiet", reasonable place for dinner or "taking a client to lunch."

Nam's ⑤
| 21 | 16 | 19 | $19 |

11220 Georgia Ave. (University Blvd.), Wheaton, MD, 301-933-2525

Nam's of Bethesda
4928 Cordell Ave. (bet. Woodmont Ave. & Old Georgetown Rd.), Bethesda, MD, 301-652-2635

■ These "high-end" Vietnamese siblings manage to please both the knowledgeable and novices with "refined", French-influenced food, "considerate" help and "relaxing" surroundings (Bethesda is prettier, Wheaton has "better" food); both are "family friendly" and at busy times have a "tendency to rush" ("wham bam, thank you Nam's").

Nam Viet ⑤
| 21 | 14 | 19 | $16 |

1127 N. Hudson St. (Wilson Blvd.), Arlington, VA, 703-522-7110
3419 Connecticut Ave., NW (bet. Porter & Macomb Sts.), 202-237-1015

■ Though it's often a second – or third – choice for Clarendon Vietnamese dining, supporters call this "sleeper" a "diamond in the lemongrass" for its "excellent grilled dishes", "low-stress" atmosphere, "interesting patrons" and "romantic" summer nights on the patio; N.B. its new DC branch is a hit.

Nathan's ⑤
| 17 | 17 | 17 | $28 |

3150 M St., NW (Wisconsin Ave.), 202-338-2000

☑ Lately, this "Center of Georgetown" corner tavern is more of a "popular drinking" and "singles scene" than the "clubby" neighborhood in-spot it once was; the barroom is where preppies munch and mingle, the "cozy" back room is where they take their "parents" for pasta and seafood cooked by chef Giusseppina Alessandrini's daughters.

New Heights ⑤
| 25 | 23 | 23 | $38 |

2317 Calvert St., NW (Connecticut Ave.), 202-234-4110

☑ Matthew Lake, recently honored by *Food & Wine*, is the most recent culinary talent to reach new heights in this New Age American's risk-taking kitchen; set in an "airy", art-filled space overlooking Rock Creek Park, it's "very well-run" (if a bit "joyless") and the food – "fascinating combinations" of seasonal ingredients – can make an ordinary meal an "occasion", but it sometimes veers over the edge.

Nizam's S 21 | 18 | 20 | $27
Village Green Shopping Ctr., 523 Maple Ave. W. (Rte. 123), Vienna, VA, 703-938-8948

▪ The "doner kebab is not to be missed" at this Ottoman outpost in Vienna, but the presence of the local Turkish community means there are other "interesting" dishes to try; it's "friendly", "cramped" and less ornately decorated than nearby compatriot Kazan.

NORA 26 | 24 | 24 | $46
2132 Florida Ave., NW (bet. Connecticut & Massachusetts Aves.), 202-462-5143

▪ Nora Pouillon's pioneering "philosophy" – transforming farm-grown products into a "distinctive", delicious Contemporary American cuisine – has been "realized" so successfully that her "romantic" converted stable is one of the city's most stylish "must go's"; consequently, with the "press", literati and pols competing for the limited seats, expect "waits."

Normandie Farms S 17 | 21 | 19 | $31
10710 Falls Rd. (Democracy Blvd.), Potomac, MD, 301-983-8838

▪ Although this dignified country setting in Potomac has been "improved" since its longtime chef took charge, it hasn't been able to shake its image as a ladies' lunch/ "bountiful brunch"/wedding/popover place – perhaps because the Continental menu and clientele ("blue hair") are largely unchanged.

Notte Luna (CLOSED) 19 | 18 | 18 | $26
809 15th St., NW (bet. H & I Sts.), 202-408-9500

▪ While no longer "the rage", this neon-bright Cal-Ital continues to benefit from its "strategic" location (near offices, the best clubs and National Theatre), sidewalk cafe (decorated by "pretty people") and "trendy" pizza, pasta and calamari menu; noise and "cavalier" attitudes are minor deterrents.

Nova Europa 17 | 15 | 18 | $24
Kemp Mill Shopping Ctr., 1311 Lamberton Dr. (Arcola Dr.), Silver Spring, MD, 301-649-6690

▪ This Silver Spring Continental, "trusted" by the "early-bird set" to provide a "satisfying" meal at an affordable price, is one of the few places hereabouts to try Portuguese specialties like *paelha*, caldo verde and "sardines and wine"; neither its shopping center premises, nor service, impress outsiders, but "when the kitchen is careful, the food can be quite good."

Nulbom S – | – | – | M
4870 Boiling Brook Pkwy. (Nicholson Ln.), Rockville, MD, 301-468-2930
"Consistently well-crafted food", including spicy, grill-your-own BBQ and standard Japanese, can be found at this spartan, Rockville shopping strip Korean that makes few concessions to Western ways; "if you don't mind being regimented", it's a cheap trip to Asia.

OBELISK 27 | 21 | 25 | $46
2029 P St., NW (bet. 20th & 21st Sts.), 202-872-1180
■ Every evening, Peter Pastan cooks dinner for 35 lucky people in his "soigné" boîte off Dupont Circle; his Northern Italian menus "always excite" and are complemented by "perfect bread" and wines and a "knowledgeable staff" that shares his "dedication"; "charming", "exceptional", "a respite" are some of the encomiums he earns as this *Survey*'s top Italian.

Occidental Grill S 22 | 23 | 21 | $35
Willard Complex (Pennsylvania Ave. & 14th St.), 202-783-1475
☑ The sense of history and "Washington power" conveyed at the present reincarnation of this "clubby" Downtown American enhances its updated fare and soothes any "disappointed expectations"; a "stalwart for pre-theater dining", it's been "hard to beat for a business lunch" for nearly a century.

O'Donnell's S 17 | 15 | 18 | $25
8301 Wisconsin Ave. (Battery Ln.), Bethesda, MD, 301-656-6200
☑ For senior citizens and tourists, this "Bethesda landmark" offers a snapshot of the "real" old Washington, its friendliness and the traditional ways seafood was prepared (dripping with butter or "fried"); the rest dismiss it as "mass feeding", yet sneak a rum bun to take home.

OLD ANGLER'S INN S 23 | 24 | 21 | $46
10801 MacArthur Blvd. (1 mi. past Clara Barton Pkwy.), Potomac, MD, 301-365-2425
☑ "One of DC's special places for lovers" offers some of the "best outdoor seating in the area" with "inventive" Contemporary American food "to match"; drinks by the fire are also "romantic", less so the "garret" upstairs; N.B. the chef responsible for the food rating is gone.

OLD EBBITT GRILL ◑ S 19 | 22 | 19 | $26
675 15th St., NW (bet. F & G Sts.), 202-347-4801
■ A "beautiful", bustling, polished wood and brass setting with a "political feel", "well run" and near everything, "steady" American fare and "lots of affordable choices" – it's "easy to see why this restaurant has stood the test of time", is patronized by suits, jeans and "throngs of tourists" and generates relatively few complaints – "it is Washington."

Old Glory BBQ ◐ 🅂   18 | 18 | 18 | $18

3139 M St., NW (bet. Wisconsin Ave. & 31st St.), 202-337-3406
◪ "Serious guy food" (BBQ and buckets of beers) – "cheap
and lots of it" – "good babe watching" (from the open-
window seats), loud music and "'Skins games" make for
"rowdy" times at this "hyper" collegiate happening in
Georgetown; it's so much "fun", who cares if it's "slow"?

Oodles Noodles   21 | 15 | 17 | $16

1120 19th St., NW (bet. L & M Sts.), 202-293-3138
4907 Cordell Ave. (Old Georgetown & Norfolk Rds.),
Bethesda, MD, 301-986-8833 🅂
▰ This compact, attractive noodle house off M Street is
"top rated for value" by just about everyone for its "huge
bowls of spicy soup" and "heaping portions" of "terrific"
noodles that are "well prepared" in many Asian styles;
being "patient" (during long waits) and "packed as tight
as noodles in a box" is included in the "bargain price";
the newer Bethesda locale is also packing them in.

Otello   19 | 15 | 18 | $22

*1329 Connecticut Ave., NW (½ block south of Dupont
Metro Station), 202-429-0209*
◪ A step down from Dupont Circle, this "red-checker-
tablecloth" Italian is a pleasant antidote to trendy pastarias
and chains; it's "dowdy" and "reliable", the food is "nothing
spectacular", yet it's fine for "day-in, day-out" eating – and
"being there makes you feel good."

Outback Steakhouse 🅂   20 | 16 | 19 | $21

*Arlington Forest Shopping Ctr., 4821 N. First St. (off Rte. 50
at Park Dr.), Arlington, VA, 703-527-0063*
*Elden Plaza, 150 Elden St. #100 (Herndon Pkwy.), Herndon,
VA, 703-318-0999*
*Twinbrooke Shopping Ctr., 9579-B Braddock Rd.
(Twinbrooke Dr.), Fairfax, VA, 703-978-6283*
Colonnade, 5702 Union Mill Rd. (Rte. 29), Clifton, VA, 703-818-0804
*Potomac Festival, 14580 Potomac Mills Rd. (Bixby Rd.),
Woodbridge, VA, 703-490-5336*
*Backlick Ctr., 6651 Backlick Rd. (Old Keene Mill Rd.),
Springfield, VA, 703-912-7531*
*Giant Shopping Ctr., 315 Maple Ave. E. (Glyndon St.),
Vienna, VA, 703-242-0460*
*Beacon Mall, 6804 Richmond Hwy. (Rte. 1), Alexandria,
VA, 703-768-1063*
10060 Lee Hwy., Fairfax, VA, 703-352-5000
*7720 Woodmont Ave. (bet. Old Georgetown Rd. &
Wisconsin Ave.), Bethesda, MD, 301-913-0176*
*Germantown Sq., 12609 Wisteria Dr. (Great Seneca Hwy.),
Germantown, MD, 301-353-9499*
*Potomac Run Plaza, 46300 Potomac Run Plaza (Rte. 7),
Sterling, VA, 703-406-3377*
(Continues)

Outback Steakhouse (Cont.)
Hilltop Plaza, 6868 Race Track Rd. (Rte. 450), Bowie, MD,
301-464-5800
☒ "Ersatz" Aussies – strictly for cheapsteaks – "fill the beef craving" with decent steaks, "oversize" appetizers, spicy sides, "frosty beer" and a "welcoming atmosphere" that many find "worth" the "hellacious lines" and "franchise sterility"; grape nuts say the "exceptional Aussie wine values beat the steaks"; open for dinner only.

Oval Room | 23 | 23 | 23 | $37 |
800 Connecticut Ave., NW (H St.), 202-463-8700
■ The bright, young "star on the K Street corridor", with "imaginative" Contemporary American food, "outstanding" service and a "whimsical mural", has become something of a "celebrity" house, earning rave reviews like "wonderfully relaxed", "excellent bar", "chic for business lunches"; "go once and you'll keep returning."

Ozio ▽ | 14 | 19 | 18 | $25 |
1835 K St., NW (19th St.), 202-822-6000
☒ Strictly for lounge lizards and smokers, this slick "cigar and martini" bar on K Street (with trendy nibbles) stocks all the latest quaffs and is reputedly an "after-dinner hot spot"; some go for the "atmosphere, drinks and cigars", the rest "for the secondhand smoke."

Palm, The 🄢 | 23 | 19 | 21 | $42 |
1225 19th St., NW (bet. M & N Sts.), 202-293-9091
☒ At this testosterone-fueled "locker room" for "male dinosaurs", monster steaks and lobsters, "killer martinis", "New York waiters" and "cigar-smoking Republicans are the norm"; you "can always see someone from the Sunday morning TV squad" and it's more fun to "go with a face"; P.S. the food's "first-rate."

Panjshir 🄢 | 24 | 13 | 18 | $19 |
224 W. Maple Ave. (Rte. 123), Vienna, VA, 703-281-4183
924 Broad St. (West St.), Falls Church, VA, 703-536-4566
■ "Modest surroundings belie the wonderful food" and "pleasant" atmosphere at these "Afghan champs" in Northern Virginia; here, you'll find "bold flavors" and "more sophisticated and complex dishes than at most Afghans", yet familiar ingredients (pumpkin, lamb, rice) make them "good places for people squeamish about trying strange food"; N.B. service can be slow.

Paolo's 🄢 | 20 | 19 | 18 | $22 |
1303 Wisconsin Ave., NW (N St.), 202-333-7353 ☯
Reston Town Ctr., Market & Fountain Sts., Reston, VA,
703-318-8920

Paolo's (Cont.)
1801 Rockville Pike, Rockville, MD, 301-984-2211 **(CLOSED)**
☑ "Pop Italians" with the right mix of an action-packed bar scene, outdoor/streetside dining and a pasta/pizza/salad menu to consistently pull crowds (read 'noise'); they hold the middle ground "between pizza and fancy Italian" and are usually enjoyable "despite all the yuppies"; the free tapenade and breadsticks get the rave food reviews.

Pappa-Razzi S
17 | 21 | 17 | $23

1066 Wisconsin Ave., NW (M St.), 202-298-8000
☑ This Georgetown "movie-set" Italian makes "dramatic" use of a landmark firehouse and its "medium-priced" menu "covers the staples well" (pastas, pizzas and grills), making it easy to "eat light"; some warn of "formulaic" food and others find it "too franchisey."

Paradise S
19 | 15 | 17 | $22

7141 Wisconsin Ave. (Montgomery Ave.), Bethesda, MD, 301-907-7500
■ A few knowledgeable foodies recommend this "pleasant" Bethesdan for some of the "best Iranian food around"; its picture-book menu introduces many "interesting" Persian and Afghan dishes and its lunch ($7.95) and dinner ($11.95 M–F, weekends $2 more) buffets are a "good buy of taste treats."

Parioli S
19 | 18 | 18 | $28

4800 Elm St. (Wisconsin Ave.), Bethesda, MD, 301-951-8600
☑ Packed with suburbanites who "know 10 other people eating there", this Bethesda Italian "rec room" was also known for its pastas, seafood and "great pricing scheme" (all pastas are one price); as of fall '97, there's new management and a new chef, making it a new ball game.

Parkway Deli S
19 | 8 | 17 | $14

Rock Creek Shopping Ctr., 8317 Grubb Rd. (bet. 16th St. & Connecticut Ave.), Silver Spring, MD, 301-587-1427
■ It's "a guaranteed favorite for New York transplants"—this "plain, old" Silver Spring Jewish deli pays homage to the 'deli greats' with their photos on the wall, a "great pickle bar", "best matzo-ball soup" and all the other edible trappings of the real thing; the back dining room is the neighborhood "meeting place" for breakfast.

Pasha Cafe S
22 | 17 | 21 | $19

Cherrydale Shopping Ctr., 2109 N. Pollard St. (Military Rd.), Arlington, VA, 703-528-2126
■ Explore "Egyptian variations on Middle Eastern" classics at this simple but "very appealing" room in Cherrydale, where "gracious" hospitality, "good food" and great value are rewarding it with many friends; a selection of "wonderful appetizers" (hummus, falafel) could be the centerpiece of a "delightful" meal.

Pasta Plus ⑤   ▽ 21 | 14 | 19 | $20
Center Plaza, 209 Gorman Ave. (bet. Rtes. 1 & 198E),
Laurel, MD, 301-498-5100

■ "Great surprise – Laurel has a good restaurant now"; any neighborhood would be proud of this attractive, family- run Italian with "homemade food", "fabulous wood-fired pizza" and "very good pasta" and prices; it "smells so good" almost anyone would be willing to "wait in line."

PATISSERIE CAFE DIDIER ⑤   26 | 16 | 18 | $15
3206 Grace St., NW (bet. M & K Sts.), 202-342-9083

■ "World-class" pâtissier Didier Schoner's "sublime" confections, "fantastic soups, soufflés" and light entrees are showcased at this "charming" Georgetown bistro; it's a "warm", "very European" place to have breakfast or tea and "a lovely lunch stop – it feels like you're miles away"; N.B. Monsieur Didier also teaches at NYC's prestigious French Culinary Institute and may eventually leave this place.

PEKING GOURMET INN ⑤   25 | 15 | 21 | $24
Culmore Shopping Ctr., 6029 Leesburg Pike (Glen Carlin St.),
Falls Church, VA, 703-671-8088

☑ The specialty of the house, Peking duck, along with "delicious" garlic sprouts and other custom-grown produce are the reasons this Falls Church perennial wins Top Chinese honors; the "chaos" and lack of "creature comforts" (and hanging "too many Republicans on the wall") are not.

Perry's ⑤   18 | 21 | 15 | $24
1811 Columbia Rd., NW (18th St.), 202-234-6218

■ On DC's "best", "hippest" roof deck, it's sushi "as entertainment" – and it's quite "a scene"; right now the food is fusion, the interior is "lime green, patent leather and red" and on Sundays there's a drag show brunch; but with an owner "addicted to change", who knows what's next?; it "can be exceptional or mundane" – but always over the top.

Persepolis ⑤ (CLOSED)   17 | 12 | 16 | $20
7130 Wisconsin Ave. (bet. Bethesda & Miller Aves.),
Bethesda, MD, 301-656-9339

☑ Most agree this Bethesda Iranian's popular buffet (lunch $6.95, dinner $11.95) offers a "good-value" sampler of Persian cuisine, but perceptions of quality range from "wonderful for large groups" to "not all that good"; plus it's "dark", "disorganized" and not always "helpful."

Pesce ⑤   25 | 15 | 19 | $30
2016 P St., NW (bet. Dupont Circle & 20th St.), 202-466-FISH

■ "DC's best seafood restaurant", an "intimate" Dupont Circle "bistro with style", is "fresh, "imaginative", "congenial" and "thoroughly professional"; the "originality and excellence" of its food belie its "simple" storefront surroundings, not to mention its "reasonable prices"; all told "we need more restaurants like this."

Petitto's S　　　　　–|–|–| M |
2653 Connecticut Ave., NW (Calvert St.), 202-667-5350
On Woodley Park's restaurant row, this sprightly Connecticut Avenue "neighborhood" Italian has "fresh pasta" and enough pizzazz to pull tourists; there's weekend opera (with "singers better than the food") and cappuccino and desserts in Dolce Finale below; plan to spend "an evening."

Phillips Flagship S　　　15 | 15 | 15 | $23 |
900 Water St., SW (9th St.), 202-488-8515
Phillips Seafood Grill S
American Ctr./Signet Bank Bldg., 8330 Boone Blvd. (bet. Rtes. 7 & 23), Tysons Corner, VA, 703-442-0400
◪ "Uninspired" seafood spreads and "nearly invisible" help don't impress locals at these Ocean City imports "made for the tourist trade" visiting the DC and Baltimore waterfronts; there's a great piano bar in Baltimore and an à la carte menu and happy-hour raw bar in Tysons Corner.

Pho S (CLOSED)　　　▽ 22 | 11 | 19 | $14 |
615 Ash St. (H St., bet. 6th & 7th Sts.), 202-789-0211
■ You can find "everything you'd want in a pho" restaurant at this Chinatown Vietnamese, i.e. "cheap", "wholesome", meal-sized bowls of flavorful noodle soup and a selection of unusual garnishes; if "so much soup" becomes a "bore", its "interesting non-pho dishes" are mighty "tasty", too.

Pho Cali S　　　　　▽ 21 | 12 | 16 | $16 |
1621 S. Walter Reed Dr. (Rte. 395, Glebe Rd. exit), Arlington, VA, 703-920-9500
■ This Arlington Vietnamese "treasure" is prized for its "great handling of seafood" as much as its "terrific" soups – ask for clams in black bean sauce, crispy whole fish or seafood fondue; inside is simple but cheery, in summer there's a "nice outdoor terrace", and year-round, "lots of expensive cars out front."

Pho 95 S (CLOSED)　　　21 | 10 | 18 | $12 |
Ritchie Shopping Ctr., 595 Rockville Pike (near Rockville Metro Station), Rockville, MD, 301-294-9391
■ As the name implies, this tidy Rockville pho house opened in '95, joining the growing number of Vietnamese places where you can get a "low-cal filling meal" for a few bucks; although there's a full menu, most go for the "fantastic", "incendiary" soup – not the "inept" service.

Pho 75 S⇗　　　　　21 | 8 | 15 | $10 |
1510 University Blvd. E. (bet. N. Glebe Rd. & Pershing Dr.), Langley Park, MD, 301-434-7844
771 Hungerford Dr., Rockville, MD, 301-309-8873
3103 Graham Rd. (Rte. 50), Falls Church, VA, 703-204-1490
(Continues)

Pho 75 (Cont.)

1711 Wilson Blvd. (Quinn St.), Arlington, VA, 703-525-7355
■ The concept behind these "cheap", "communal", "good-for-the-soul" Vietnamese soup kitchens is "very simple" – eating "great noodle soup while sitting at long, camplike tables" and letting smiles smooth "tough communications"; they're the area's first pho restaurants and still "an exceptional value."

Pier 7 S   14 | 15 | 16 | $25 |

Channel Inn, 650 Water St., SW (bet. 7th St. & Maine Ave.), 202-554-2500
☑ DC's long-running "office party" for pols and feds working near the SW waterfront (Arena Stage convenience brings in the rest of its local trade); though this seafooder is often dismissed as a "high-priced Ho Jo's" with "nice water views", too much tourist traffic and not enough in the way of food and service, we hear it's bobbing up.

Pilin Thai S   25 | 18 | 22 | $17 |

116 W. Broad St. (Rte. 29), Falls Church, VA, 703-241-5850
■ A "contender for Virginia's top Thai" sums up patron praise for this "inviting" Falls Church storefront whose "delightful owners" pile on enough "excellent" food for "$10 to feed three starving students" or a family of four – it "seems to get better each time."

Pines of Florence S   15 | 9 | 15 | $16 |

2053 Wilson Blvd. (Courthouse Rd.), Arlington, VA, 703-243-7463 ·
Foxchase Shopping Ctr., 4603 Duke St. (Seminary Rd.), Alexandria, VA, 703-370-6383
7151 Lee Hwy. (bet. Graham Rd. & Annandale Rd.), Falls Church, VA, 703-533-0024
2100 Connecticut Ave. (California Ave., 2 blocks from Hilton Hotel), 202-332-8233
☑ Most go to this "true, non-yuppie Italian" in Arlington (with saplings elsewhere) "because it's cheap" and treats families well, "not because it's good"; while devoid of "atmosphere", the "home cooking" is nostalgic – "like being back in 1963."

Pines of Rome S   18 | 10 | 16 | $18 |

4709 Hampden Ln. (Wisconsin Ave.), Bethesda, MD, 301-657-8775
☑ A "cheap eats" evergreen that looks "crummy", cooks red-sauce Italian, acts "rude" and is beloved by Bethesda families who don't want to spend money or cook at home; dissenters chop it down: "they get away with it because they're an institution", "overrated by the beatnik trust fund set."

Pirandello 🅂 (CLOSED) 19 | 17 | 19 | $24
4922 Cordell Ave. (Old Georgetown Rd.), Bethesda, MD, 301-718-0800
☑ "When the Italian mood strikes" in Bethesda, you "can usually get in" here and (less consistently) "leave feeling good and full"; outdoor seating and "step-up-from-red-sauce" menu and decor give it an "adult" edge over "like-sounding restaurants" in the area; N.B. don't expect too much and you won't be disappointed.

Pizza de Resistance 18 | 18 | 16 | $17
Courthouse Plaza, 2300 Clarendon Blvd. (bet. Barton St. & Courthouse Rd.), Arlington, VA, 703-351-5680
☑ "Immense efforts" to distinguish itself from other pizza/pastarias with unique crusts, "bizarre" toppings, "artsy" presentations and "quality sarcasm" at the bar get a mixed verdict at Courthouse Plaza: "interesting dishes not always pulled off", "harried staff", "guilty of great food."

PIZZERIA PARADISO 🅂 25 | 17 | 18 | $18
2029 P St., NW (bet. 20th & 21st Sts.), 202-223-1245
■ "Best pizza anywhere, bar none" – Obelisk offshoot's "heavenly" hearth-baked pizzas merit near unanimous acclaim; crisp-crusted, with just the right amount of primo toppings, they have "lots of character" – like the place; this "celestial sphere is a little crowded, so expect to wait."

Planet Hollywood ◗🅂 12 | 22 | 15 | $19
1101 Pennsylvania Ave., NW (11th St.), 202-783-7827
☑ Filled with props and glitter, movie memorabilia and Hollywood fantasy decor, this Downtown "amusement park" near the Mall is "rated NA-17" (no adult over 17 unaccompanied by "kids or foreign friends"); it's "way too commercial" and the $8 burgers and bar food are "not worth" the fuss, but film buffs have a "lot of fun."

Planet X ◗🅂 ∇ 16 | 19 | 14 | $13
7422 Baltimore Ave. (Regence Dr. & College Ave.), College Park, MD, 301-779-8451
☑ A green light for veggie alternative rock types in College Park; "'90s food meets '60s coffeehouse chic" over "cheap veggie" fare, "good desserts if you hit it right", herbal "smart drinks" (to sharpen your mental edge) and "beat poetry"; if that's not your universe, you'll find "bad-tempered granola types" and not much service.

Polly's Cafe ◗🅂 18 | 17 | 16 | $16
1342 U St., NW (bet. 13th & 14th Sts.), 202-265-8385
☑ New U "mainstay" where locals soak up the log cabin atmosphere over "winter suppers" and nurse hangovers at brunch; visitors enjoy the burgers, the bartenders and the vibes, but warn that the "strange combinations" on the specials go a bit too close to the "frontier."

Positano ⑤   18 | 18 | 19 | $27 |
4940 Fairmont Ave. (Old Georgetown Rd.), Bethesda, MD, 301-654-1717

☑ "Sitting outside under the grape arbor" at this "trusty" Bethesda Southern Italian is always a pleasure and the fact that the food "hardly ever changes" heightens its appeal; the feeling that it's "not as good as it was" (though "still ok") may reflect, in part, its "expansion" as well as changing tastes ("can't compete with DC Italians" at the price).

Potowmack Landing ⑤   15 | 22 | 16 | $24 |
Washington Sailing Marina, George Washington Pkwy. (1½ mi. south of National Airport), Alexandria, VA, 703-548-0001

☑ This rustic Park Service American near National Airport has never had food and service to match its "wonderful river setting" and fascinating runway views; hence, customers complain about the waits and "government-issue food" and go for the "ambiance."

PRIME RIB   26 | 25 | 25 | $45 |
2020 K St., NW (bet. 20th & 21st Sts.), 202-466-8811

■ Decked (and deco-ed) out like a *"Guys and Dolls"* stage set lined with "celebrities", lawyers, lobbyists and "lovelies", this "decadent-feeling" Downtown American supper club is unequaled for "business or pleasure"; it's one of the "best-run" restaurants in town and a bargain at lunch, with DC's definitive prime rib and crab imperial; "a step back in time, but oh what a time."

Primi Piatti   22 | 20 | 20 | $32 |
2013 I St., NW (bet. 20th & 21st Sts.), 202-223-3600 ⑤
8045 Leesburg Pike (Gallows Rd.), Tysons Corner, VA, 703-893-0300

■ These "very sophisticated", "very Italian" trattorias offer "excellent pasta", "fine fish and breads", "too little room" and too much noise; they're best enjoyed by those who "love the snotty waiters", sidewalk seating (DC) and "private dining in the wine rooms."

PROVENCE ⑤   25 | 24 | 20 | $48 |
2401 Pennsylvania Ave., NW (L St.), 202-296-1166

■ The "charm and beauty" of Provence is "on the plate" as well as in the setting of Yannick Cam's West Ender; when it's "on" (as it mostly is) the dishes "dazzle", but the restaurant suffers from "superstar" success – it gets "pressured" and "too loud" during busy times.

Queen Bee ⑤   22 | 12 | 18 | $17 |
3181 Wilson Blvd. (Washington Blvd.), Arlington, VA, 703-527-3444

☑ It's nearly "impossible to have a bad meal or spend much more than $15" at this "homely" Clarendon Vietnamese; its spring rolls and grilled meats shine, yet some can't "tune out" the waits and "hurried" service.

RABIENG S
25 | 19 | 23 | $21

Glen Forest Shopping Ctr., 5892 Leesburg Pike (bet. Glen Forest Dr. & Payne St.), Falls Church, VA, 703-671-4222
■ Surprisingly edging out its showy cousin Duangrat's as the *Survey's* top Thai, this "understated", "often overlooked" sib focuses on food; here, one can explore the diversity of "regional Thai cooking" in a "quiet setting" where the "sparse decor and dismissive service don't matter" once the vivid, "spicy" tastes explode in your mouth.

Radio Free Italy S
15 | 12 | 14 | $17

The Torpedo Factory, 5 Cameron St. (Union St.), Alexandria, VA, 703-683-0361
▧ This entrepreneurial Old Towner bids for your frequency with Potomac views from outdoor tables, lotsa inexpensive Italian food, a $10 wine list and thoughtful touches like giving kids pizza dough to play with and letting them eat at a discount (or Wednesday after 5 PM for free); the consensus is "variable-quality food, consistently great views."

Raku ◑ S
– | – | – | I

1900 Q St., NW (19th St.), 202-265-7258
7240 Woodmont Ave., Bethesda, MD, 301-718-8681
Jammed from day one, Mark Miller's Asian street food cafe concept is shaking down in the DC area before being syndicated nationwide"; it's a New Wave "wow" with pre-fab food – a mix 'n' match of noodles, salads, skewers and dumplings prepared off-site – and a "tiny tab"; early reports are "promising" provided you "stick with the staff's" advice.

Red Hot & Blue S
20 | 15 | 17 | $17

1120 19th St., NW (bet. L & M Sts.), 202-466-6731 **(CLOSED)**
1600 Wilson Blvd. (Pierce St.), Arlington, VA, 703-276-7427
Canterbury Ctr., 8637 Sudley Rd. (bet. Rtes. 234 & 28), Manassas, VA, 703-330-4847 **(CLOSED)**
3014 Wilson Blvd. (Highland St.), Arlington, VA, 703-243-1510 (carryout only)
208 Elden St. (near Herndon Pkwy.), Herndon, VA, 703-318-7427
16811 Crabbs Branch Way (Shady Grove Rd.), Gaithersburg, MD, 301-948-7333
677 Main St. (Rte. 216), Laurel, MD, 301-953-1943
■ "Elvis eats here" . . . well, if he could, chances are he'd find that the "excellent" Memphis-style ribs, rings and sides ("those baked beans!") dished out at these too-popular, "picnic"-like BBQ joints meet a Tennessean's "high standard" at a "great price"; he'd even enjoy the sounds.

Red River Grill S
10 | 13 | 13 | $18

201 Massachusetts Ave., NE (bet. 2nd & 3rd Sts.), 202-546-7200
▧ An after-work scrum for "preppy congressional aides", its Southwestern aspirations are more evident in the stagey decor and "exotic"-sounding specials than what's slapped on the plate; most call it "mediocre" and best if you stick to the Tex-Mex basics and beer.

RED SAGE S   22 | 26 | 20 | $36
605 14th St., NW (F St.), 202-638-4444

More than 1,100 surveyors attest to the long burn of Mark Miller's megamillion-dollar chili palace; whether upstairs for casual, more affordable snacking and a "great bar scene" or a "treat-yourself evening" in the Disneyesque dining room downstairs, his showmanship and imagination "bring excitement" to SW cuisine; that the portions are "measly", the help occasionally "arrogant" or that everything is "spicy" hasn't diminished the heavy traffic.

Red Sea ◐S   20 | 14 | 18 | $18
2463 18th St., NW (Kalorama Rd.), 202-483-5000

In nice weather, this Adams Morgan Ethiopian's outdoor seating gives it an edge over nearby compatriots; the food isn't for timid palates, but "you can't beat the price" and "eating with your hands can be fun" with the right group.

Red Tomato Cafe S   21 | 19 | 19 | $19
4910 St. Elmo Ave. (bet. Old Georgetown & Norfolk Rds.), Bethesda, MD, 301-652-4499
2030 M St., NW (bet. 20th & 21st Sts.), 202-463-9030

With its "adorable" brick-oven pizzas, sampler platters, "trendy" wine bar and "down-to-earth" attitude, this "cute", "casual", "low-cost" Bethesda Cal-Ital is so "promising" it just grew a DC branch, which is unrated.

Renato S   19 | 18 | 19 | $27
10120 River Rd. (Potomac Pl.), Potomac, MD, 301-365-1900

Potomac's "perfect" osteria – "overpriced but charming" – with great pizza, pasta, seafood and notable tiramisu; it "can't grow fast enough" to suit a neighborhood willing to suffer "knee-to-knee" dining and being elbowed out by "important walk-ins."

RIO GRANDE CAFE S   21 | 18 | 18 | $20
4301 N. Fairfax Dr. (Glebe Rd.), Arlington, VA, 703-528-3131
Reston Town Ctr., 1827 Library St. (Reston Pkwy.), Reston, VA, 703-904-0703
4919 Fairmont Ave. (Old Georgetown Rd.), Bethesda, MD, 301-656-2981

It's always party time at these Tex-Mex "theme parks"; the menu is "limited to the great stuff" (fajitas, quesadillas, cabrito), they consistently "do well" and you "can't get a better deal"; were it not for the "painful" queue and clatter, people would eat here "three times a week."

Ristorante Capri S (CLOSED)   16 | 17 | 17 | $27
4871 Cordell Ave. (Norfolk Ave.), Bethesda, MD, 301-654-8333

Though this Italian is welcomed for "casually refined" patio dining and an accommodating, Mediterranean-feeling room, it's rapped for inconsistency and inability to cope with the "Bethesda crush"; a new, ambitious chef and manager (post-*Survey*) is good news.

RITZ-CARLTON, THE GRILL S   24 | 25 | 25 | $40

Ritz-Carlton at Pentagon City, 1250 South Hayes St. (bet. 15th St. & Army Navy Dr.), Arlington, VA, 703-415-5000

■ "Dining in the grand manner" at this luxury hotel's "gorgeous" Contemporary American dining room, with "lots of space for conversation" and "excellent food", is a great way to "conduct business" and even better for "special occasions"; the "languorous elegance" of afternoon tea is the perfect antidote to a Pentagon City shopping spree.

RITZ-CARLTON, THE RESTAURANT S   23 | 25 | 24 | $38

Ritz-Carlton at Tysons II, 1700 Tysons Blvd. (Galleria, International Blvd.), McLean, VA, 703-506-4300x7488

■ "An oasis in VA . . . or anywhere", this hunt-clubby hotel dining room epitomizes "quiet elegance" with the "finest service" and "beautifully presented" Continental food; the Friday night seafood spread and Sunday brunch buffet are "special occasion" treats – as is the "best English tea."

River Club S **(CLOSED)**   19 | 22 | 19 | $40

3223 K St, NW (bet. Wisconsin Ave. & 32nd St.), 202-333-8118

☑ Dust off your dancing shoes, dress to the nines and head for deco glamour, champagne and caviar in Georgetown; known mainly for dancing, and for 'backside of 40' romancing, this "classy" supper club's Continental fare "can surprise" – and it's still the "best place to seduce your wife."

Rockland's S   22 | 12 | 16 | $15

2418 Wisconsin Ave., NW (Calvert St.), 202-333-2558
4000 Fairfax Dr. (Quincy St.), Arlington, VA, 703-528-9663

■ "Perfect" BBQ ribs, chicken, meats and veggies, "surprisingly tender grilled fish", "great sides", "free nuts" and the world's largest collection of hot sauces are all reasons to frequent this Glover Park carryout and eat-in counter; at its Arlington locale, you can even sit down.

Roof Terrace Kennedy Center S   17 | 22 | 18 | $38

Kennedy Ctr., 2700 F St. (New Hampshire Ave.), 202-416-8555

☑ Ticketholders "can't beat the convenience or the view" (or the curtain-timed service) at this Kennedy Center rooftop dining room; so word that "a new chef" is "improving" the Contemporary American food gets a round of applause; its "leisurely" Sunday brunch has always been a hit.

Royal Dragon S   ▽ 17 | 12 | 17 | $17

(fka Moshe Dragon)
Randolph Hills Shopping Ctr., 4840 Bollingbrook Pkwy. (Nicholson Ln.), Rockville, MD, 301-468-1922

☑ "When you need kosher Chinese", this uninviting Rockville eatery is probably your only choice; its certified kitchen woks out kosher versions of Chinese and American menu staples; until the staff cleans up its "sloppy" act, however, many carry out.

R.T.'s 🖪
24 | 15 | 21 | $27 |

3804 Mt. Vernon Ave. (Glebe Rd.), Alexandria, VA,
703-684-6010

■ This neighborly pub in a "grubby" Alexandria 'hood serves some of the "best, unhealthy" New Orleans–style seafood around; it's "great for a casual evening" and, given the "high quality" fare, "a great buy."

R.T.'s Seafood Kitchen 🖪
18 | 15 | 18 | $23 |

Courthouse Plaza, 2300 Clarendon Blvd. (bet. Barton St. &
Courthouse Rd.), Arlington, VA, 703-841-0100

■ "Cholesterol never tasted so good" except, of course, at the original Alexandria R.T.'s; this Courthouse Plaza copy, with its "faux New Orleans" look, "pleasant" patio and "similar" Creole-Cajun menu, "falls short" of its parent foodwise, but it's "convenient."

RUPPERTS
26 | 21 | 25 | $40 |

1017 7th St., NW (bet. New York Ave. & L St.),
202-783-0699

■ "Just showing up" at this "cutting-edge" Contemporary American "confirms that you are a true DC insider"; it's doing some of the "best serious" cooking in town and everything from the "sparse, romantic room" to the "helpful" if overly "enthusiastic" staff is pretty much "just as it should be" (and priced accordingly) – that is, until one hits the not yet completely gentrified street.

Ruth's Chris Steak House 🖪
24 | 21 | 22 | $39 |

1801 Connecticut Ave., NW (S St.), 202-797-0033
7315 Wisconsin Ave. (Elm St.), Bethesda, MD, 301-652-7877
2231 Crystal Dr. (23rd St.), Crystal City, VA, 703-979-7275

☑ A safe bet for an "outstanding steak", this franchise's "sizzlicious", butter-drenched beef is top quality and "they know how to treat customers like no one else"; although they lack the "personality" of comparable steakhouses like Morton's or The Palm (notwithstanding Crystal City's "superb view"), they're "consistently good at what they do."

Sabang 🖪
20 | 17 | 19 | $21 |

2504 Ennalls Ave. (Georgia Ave.), Wheaton, MD,
301-942-7859

☑ Novices find Indonesian food "interesting, like a cross between Indian and Chinese", a bit "oily" and more than a bit hot; if that sounds appealing, try this "attractive", "modest" "jewel hidden in a Wheaton strip mall"; but note that some find the "rice table [sampler] disappointing."

Saigon Gourmet 🖪
22 | 16 | 21 | $19 |

2635 Connecticut Ave., NW (Calvert St.), 202-265-1360

☑ Surveyors debate whether this Woodley Park Vietnamese is DC's "best" (when you know what to order, i.e. shrimp rolls, fish) or merely very good (and boosted by "superior service"); either way, you get a "pleasant, inexpensive" meal.

Saigon Inn ⑤   20 | 14 | 19 | $15
2614 Connecticut Ave. (Calvert St), 202-483-8400
2928 M St. (30th St), 202-337-5588

■ The 'four dishes for $4.50' lunch specials at these "eager" Vietnamese places in Georgetown and Woodley Park give tourists on budgets a break; they're "small" and "simple", with some good plates (spring rolls, caramel pork) and prices that are "worth the wait."

Saigonnais ⑤   20 | 16 | 18 | $22
2307 18th St., NW (Belmont Rd.), 202-232-5300

■ This "tranquil" Vietnamese on Adams Morgan's main drag is "treasured" for its "lovely atmosphere and exquisite cuisine" served "with balletic grace"; but be aware that the pace is andante and it's "more expensive than most."

Sala Thai ⑤   21 | 15 | 19 | $19
2016 P St., NW (20th St., near Dupont Circle), 202-872-1144

◪ Many find the pungent Thai standards as "tasteful" as the "lavender" decor at this "efficient lunch stop" in an "unassuming basement" off Dupont Circle; it seems like "they work hard to do things better than necessary" – though possibly less so lately.

Sam & Harry's   24 | 23 | 24 | $41
1200 19th St., NW (bet. M & N Sts.), 202-296-4333

■ "Honesty compels high marks" for this "polished" Dupont Circle steakhouse with top-notch beef, a "great prime rib and wine selection" and a "more diverse menu" than most; its power-dining patrons go for the "clubby ambiance", but a few enjoy themselves elsewhere more.

Sam Woo ⑤   20 | 16 | 18 | $20
1054 Rockville Pike (Edmonds St.), Rockville, MD, 301-424-0495

◪ "Luscious California rolls" draw Rockville workers to this commodious Korean-Japanese's lunch buffet ($7.40); as for the extensive Korean menu, "you don't always know what you're going to get" – but it's likely to be "quick", "spicy" and "good", if a bit "pricey."

Santa Fe East ⑤   20 | 21 | 19 | $26
110 S. Pitt St. (bet. King & Prince Sts.), Alexandria, VA, 703-548-6900

◪ With its secluded courtyard, intimate rooms and "great fireplace", this historic Alexandria building "is a setting you'd mistake for Santa Fe"; but the departure of chef Alison Swope has left reviewers less certain about the Southwestern fare: "food and service by Jekyll and Hyde."

Sarinah Satay House ⑤   18 | 19 | 17 | $22
1338 Wisconsin Ave., NW (bet. N & O Sts.), 202-337-2955

■ Rainforest-inspired greenery and a cozy fireplace lend romance to a leisurely Indonesian meal at this Georgetown hideaway; it's an unusual place with "interesting" cuisine where one goes for the ambiance more than for the food.

Savory S   17 | 20 | 14 | $11
7071 Carroll Ave. (Columbia Ave.), Takoma Park, MD,
301-270-2233
▟ A budding 'hood "haunt" with big, comfy couches to sink
into while enjoying "big coffee drinks", homemade desserts,
sandwiches and heated-up bistro fare; as a "limited"
operation (counter service/precooked food) it's "good", but
Takoma Park still "needs a real restaurant."

Sea Catch   21 | 21 | 20 | $34
Canal Sq., 1054 31st St., NW (M St.), 202-337-8855
▟ The "best tables on the canal", "marvelous" mussels at
the raw bar, booths by the fire and "high-quality" seafood –
this Georgetowner has "so much potential"; yet it feels "a
bit industrial and impersonal"; still, with the canal awash
this "watering hole" may fill up.

SEASONS S   27 | 26 | 26 | $49
Four Seasons Hotel, 2800 Pennsylvania Ave., NW
(29th St.), 202-944-2000
▮ The city's "best hotel restaurant", a "stylish retreat" in
Georgetown, wows a "sophisticated clientele" with its
"light" Contemporary American food and "extremely
knowledgeable" staff; respondents rave: "as close to
perfect as can be", "in heaven they serve the Sunday
brunch seven days a week."

Sequoia ◑S   17 | 24 | 17 | $28
3000 K St., NW (Washington Harbour), 202-944-4200
▟ "Major drink scene" doesn't begin to describe the bedlam
on the panoramic terrace of this Washington Harbour
American on a warm summer night; and since one of DC's
most "spectacular" settings has pressured help and a
kitchen geared for "factory line production", it works best
for "gazing", grazing and brunch.

Sesto Senso S   19 | 18 | 17 | $28
1214 18th St., NW (bet. M St. & Jefferson Pl.), 202-785-9525
▟ A "real Italian restaurant" near Dupont Circle with "real
Italians" serving "sensibly priced", "authentic food" in a
"European atmosphere" at lunch or dinner; "after 11 PM", it
becomes a "flashy", "smoky", "Euro-hip", "nightlife" scene;
the one constant is that it's "uneven."

701 S   24 | 24 | 23 | $36
701 Pennsylvania Ave., NW (7th St.), 202-393-0701
▮ It all comes together at this "most civilized", "elegant"
Downtown New American, where its "memorable" service
and "imaginative" fare complement the "lovely", "spacious"
room; hundreds of "grown-ups" have fallen in "love" with
the "night views" from the terrace, the "power" buzz at
lunch, the "cool green" champagne bar, "the way its run"
and, especially, the fact that it's "not overpriced."

Seven Seas S   20   12   17 $19
*Federal Plaza, 1776 E. Jefferson St. (bet. Montrose &
Rollins Aves.), Rockville, MD, 301-770-5020*
◪ It's "not worth going all the way" to this "dingy" Rockville
Chinese to "order egg foo young"; but if you're looking for
some of the area's "best, freshest seafood" prepared in
"unusual, interesting" ways, ask this Taiwanese about the
specials on its Chinese menu.

1789 S   25   26   24 $46
1226 36th St., NW (Prospect St.), 202-965-1789
◼ Old Washington "charm amid the hustle and bustle of
Georgetown" – this historic townhouse has always had
"atmosphere and then some", and now that chef Ris
Lacoste (ex Kinkead's) "has done her magic", the regional
American cuisine is "even better than it was before"; in a
place where "excellence is the norm", a "most romantic,
delicious dinner is guaranteed."

Shamshiry S   ▽ 21   15   17 $18
*8607 Westwood Ctr. Dr. (Leesburg Pike), Vienna, VA,
703-448-8883*
◪ "An incredible find – if you can find" this Persian hidden
in a Vienna shopping strip; its "wonderful" flavored rice
dishes and "fabulous" kebabs are "great for quick takeout"
or you can join local Iranians and "enthusiastic" staff in
the simple, decorative room; either way, you'll get a "huge
amount of food for the buck."

Shelly's Woodroast S   18   23   20 $21
*Congressional Shopping Ctr., 1699 Rockville Pike
(Halpine Rd.), Rockville, MD, 301-984-3300*
◪ Decorated like "the Northwoods brought in from the
cold", this showpiece lodge on Rockville Pike generates
long lines and mixed reviews; its "novel" menu of wood-
roasted ("smoky") meats and fish is definitely "high
gravity" (lumberjack "heavy") and short of a pricey,
"full-blown dinner", some find little to eat; others are
pleased by "surprisingly good food" and service "in a
casual, woodsy setting."

Shiney's Kabab House S⊘   ▽ 18   8   14 $12
(fka Asian Kabab House)
1108 K St., NW (bet. 11th & 12th Sts.), 202-637-9770
◼ "Recommended by cab drivers" for "satisfying" kebabs
wrapped in "wonderful" baked-to-order flatbreads, this
Downtown Formica dive defines "cheap, cheap eats";
new management post-*Survey* has spiced up the deal
with an all-you-can-eat Pakistani buffet ($4.95 for lunch,
$5.95 for dinner).

Shiro-ya S   ▽ 24 | 16 | 20 | $23 |
2512 L St. (bet. 25th St. & Pennsylvania Ave.), 202-659-9449
☑ This "peaceful retreat" with "superfresh sushi" and
an authentic Japanese menu is something of a West
End neighborhood secret – aficionados swear it "blows
away" the competition.

Silverado S   – | – | – | M |
*Magruder's Shopping Ctr., 7052 Columbia Pike (Evergreen Ln.),
Annandale, VA, 703-354-4560*
In Annandale (replacing Fritzbie's), the Great American
Restaurants group has corralled another crowd-pleaser –
an open-range, cowboy-themed bistro that adds SW
spicing to a please-all, Contemporary American menu.

Silver Diner ◑ S   14 | 16 | 16 | $13 |
*11806 Rockville Pike (bet. Montrose & Old Georgetown Rds.),
Rockville, MD, 301-770-2828*
14550 Baltimore Ave. (Cherry Ln.), Laurel, MD, 301-470-6080
12251 Fair Lakes Pkwy. (W. Ox Rd.), Fairfax, VA, 703-359-5999
8101 Fletcher St. (International Dr.), McLean, VA, 703-821-5666
*Potomac Mills Mall, 14375 Smoketown Rd., Dale City, VA,
703-491-7376*
*11951 Killingsworth Ave. (Barron Cameron/Reston Pkwy.),
Reston, VA, 703-742-0801*
*Springfield Mall, 6592 Springfield Mall, Springfield, VA,
703-924-1701*
8150 Porter Rd. (Gallows Rd.), Fairfax, VA, 703-204-0812
*3200 Wilson Blvd. (Clarendon & Washington Blvds.),
Arlington, VA, 703-812-8600*
☑ Almost everyone likes the "modern diner concept" –
"homestyle" cooking, "lots of menu choices", late
hours and a noisy ambiance that distracts "toddlers";
these '50s "flashbacks" are a fair (not great) substitute
for the "real thing."

Skewers/Cafe Luna S   19 | 15 | 18 | $17 |
1633 P St., NW (bet. 16th & 17th Sts.), 202-387-7400
■ Dupont Circle East Mediterranean offering just what the
neighborhood wants – cheap, healthy, "hot grub when you
need it"; while its upstairs Middle Eastern restaurant and
downstairs informal cafe have "separate" identities, they
function in tandem as an artistic and literary hub.

Slade's S   15 | 14 | 16 | $18 |
*7201 Wisconsin Ave. (Willow Ave.), Bethesda, MD,
301-951-8541* **(CLOSED)**
*Montgomery Mall, 7101 Democracy Blvd. (Rte. 270),
Bethesda, MD, 301-469-0690*
*Tysons I, 7943-B Tysons Corner Ctr. (Rtes. 7 & 123), Tysons
Corner, VA, 703-760-9030*

Slade's (Cont.)
*Ballston Commons, 4238 N. Wilson Blvd. (N. Glebe Rd.),
Arlington, VA, 703-243-8830* **(CLOSED)**
☑ Though some say these "shopping mall" eateries "define mediocrity", they're "ok in a pinch" for a burger and beer, grilled chicken salad, "pretty good" ribs or other "standard" American fare; patron enthusiasm depends on what else is available ("visit only if the food court is full").

Southside 815 🅂 | 18 | 17 | 18 | $19 |
*815 S. Washington St. (bet. Franklin & Green Sts.),
Alexandria, VA, 703-836-6222*
◼ "Cholesterol à la carte", but how "comforting" it is to dig into low-country shortcake (cornbread, roast chicken, oysters, mashed potatoes and succotash gravy) and similar "delicious", over-the-top, "Southern-style" dishes at this "homey" Alexandria bar off the Old Town beaten track; minority reports of "inconsistent food" and service are a downside.

Spices 🅂 | 20 | 15 | 17 | $20 |
*3333-A Connecticut Ave., NW (bet. Macomb &
Newark Sts.), 202-686-3833*
◼ In "tight" Cleveland Park quarters, this Pan-Asian does a "good job" at the seemingly "impossible task" of reproducing the "street food" of a "panoply" of distinctive cuisines (including sushi); since its dark, "Tokyo"-like premises get "crowded" and "service can be slow", consider takeout or delivery.

Stage Door 🅂 **(CLOSED)** ▽ | 14 | 13 | 16 | $19 |
1433 P St., NW (bet. 14th & 15th Sts.), 202-234-4050
◼ "Definitely downscale", but welcome in a gritty DC area with lots of exciting theaters and few places to eat; this "friendly" American bistro has a lively "burgers and bar scene", stays open late on weekends and "tries hard to please" – bravo!

Starke's Head Hog BBQ 🅂 | 19 | 10 | 18 | $15 |
(nka Head Hog)
*11410 Rockville Pke. (bet. Security Blvd. & Nicolson Ln.),
Rockville, MD, 301-881-7195*
◼ Even if you're not a 'Skins fan, you gotta love the hog-sized portions of "lean" juicy ribs, pulled pork and "good" sides dished up by George and company in what looks like a cross between a sports bar and his kitchen; but, as you'd expect, a Dallas contingent doesn't agree: "George tries hard, but he'll eat anything."

Star of Siam 🅢
18 | 14 | 17 | $19

2446 18th St., NW (Columbia Rd.), 202-986-4133
1136 19th St., NW (bet. L & M Sts.), 202-785-2838
International Pl., 1735 N. Lynn St. (N. 19th St.), Rosslyn,
VA, 703-524-1208

◪ These "upmarket" Thais are known for "boldly" spiced curries and not much else; one has the "best rooftop in Adams Morgan" ("food doesn't match"), Rosslyn has a "nice atmosphere", and Downtown DC's most "redeeming quality" is the chance to "sit outside" for an inexpensive lunch.

State of the Union
13 | 17 | 14 | $14

1357 U St. (bet. 13th & 14th Sts.), 202-588-8810

◪ "Hang out in front with Gen X intellectuals or shake your booty in the back with DC's best DJs" at this "hip, happening" New U place; however, most advise skipping the Russian "gulag fare" and settling for "cool jazz" and other live sounds, "many vodkas" and "funky decor."

Stella's 🅢
18 | 20 | 18 | $22

1725 Duke St. (across from King St. Metro Station),
Alexandria, VA, 703-519-1946

◼ Southwestern and Contemporary American cooking provides a lively contrast to the '40s memorabilia at this "W.W.II canteen" in Alexandria; however, the departure of chef Alison Swope, who introduced the menu, and the "slow" service make the "fun decor" and pleasant outdoor dining the best reasons to go.

St. Elmos Cafe 🅢 (CLOSED)
15 | 15 | 15 | $25

7820 Norfolk Ave. (St. Elmos St.), Bethesda, MD, 301-657-1607

◪ While this "nondescript" French bistro in Bethesda "sometimes succeeds" in offering a "pleasant", "relaxing" meal, it's often "more expensive than you would think" appropriate for "undistinguished" food and service; the "nice sidewalk cafe" is inviting, inside is "very beige."

Stone Manor 🅢
▽ 25 | 27 | 27 | $54

5820 Carroll Boyer Rd., Middletown, MD, 301-473-5454

◼ Celebrating an occasion at this historic stone house outside Frederick is "very special"; its "lovely", set-price Contemporary American menus are crafted with "imagination" and matched with fine wines and service; the setting itself – a blazing fire in an elegant dining room – is premium, as is the price.

Straits of Malaya 🅢
21 | 17 | 18 | $22

1836 18th St., NW (T St.), 202-483-1483

◪ On a moonlit night, the romance of this Adams Morgan Malaysian's rooftop terrace and the "exotic flavors and textures" of its food can transport you to the Far East; most other nights, you'll "eat well" if you "follow the waiter's recommendation" and are prepared for a few glitches – that goes for the pace and the taste; "when it's good, it's great."

Sunny Garden S   19 | 9 | 15 | $15

1302 E. Gude Dr. (S. Law Rd.), Rockville, MD, 301-762-7477
350 Fortune Ter., Potomac, MD, 301-294-4578 **(CLOSED)**

☑ "Don't judge a book by its cover" or a Chinese restaurant by its overly "bright" appearance and "out-of-the-way" Rockville location; this Taiwanese, which has been a local "premier Chinese" for years, insists that new owners haven't changed anything; if you "order from the Chinese menu with help from a waitress" you can judge for yourself.

Sushi Chalet S   20 | 13 | 19 | $22

Festival Shopping Ctr., 323 Muddy Branch Rd. (Great Seneca Hwy.), Gaithersburg, MD, 301-945-7373
4910 Fairmont Ave. (Old Georgetown Rd.), Bethesda, MD, 301-652-7733

■ When a Korean sushi shop in a Gaithersburg mall is SRO at 2:30 PM on Saturday, it's an indication that the buffet is a "real bargain" – and it is, offering some 20 kinds of sushi, salads, soups and Korean dishes for $6.96 at lunch, $14.95 at dinner; sure, it's "fast food" and the "wrong atmosphere for sushi, but what a deal"; ditto in Bethesda.

Sushi-Ko S   24 | 15 | 20 | $27

2307 Wisconsin Ave., NW (south of Calvert St.), 202-333-4187

■ "DC's best sushi" comes with "typical lack of ambiance" (just like in Tokyo) in Glover Park; it's "very fresh, expertly prepared" and "innovative", as are the "East meets West appetizers", daily specials and classic noodle soups; rather than choose, the area's top chefs simply put themselves in Kaz's (chef Kazuhiro Okochi) hands – you should too.

Szechuan Gallery S   ▽ 21 | 11 | 18 | $19

617 H St., NW (bet. 6th & 7th Sts.), 202-898-1180

■ "Go for the green Taiwanese menu" at this Chinatown Chinese and you "won't get hurt"; the Szechuan dishes are "tasty" too, offering "value for the price."

Tabard Inn S   22 | 22 | 20 | $29

Tabard Inn, 1739 N St., NW (bet. 17th & 18th Sts.), 202-833-2668

■ "For years", this "endearingly worn" hotel off Dupont Circle has charmed DC with its "down-at-the-heels" demeanor and "good", "simple" (albeit somewhat "pricey" and "inconsistent") Eclectic food; there's no place like it for "cocktails by the fire" or a left-wing "power lunch."

TABERNA DEL ALABARDERO   25 | 26 | 25 | $44

1776 I St., NW (18th St.), 202-429-2200

■ The Spanish traditions of "la buena mesa" (the good table) and "gracious dining" come to life at this "elegant" K Street Madrileño; it's a "dazzling" setting for sampling the regional delights of an earthy yet refined cuisine, for pampering by "DC's most courteous waiters" and for spying "who's who in close quarters" – "if price is no object."

TACHIBANA 🅂   25 | 15 | 19 | $26
6715 Lowell Ave. (Emerson Ave.), McLean, VA, 703-847-1771
■ "Generous slices" of very fresh fish at its "top-notch
sushi bar", extremely "light tempura", "excellent udon"
and sukiyaki, all "reasonably priced" and served in a
welcoming atmosphere – the area's "best" Japanese
"really has everything" it does down pat; and now that its
McLean relocation (post-*Survey*) gives it "facilities" it
lacked, there are "high hopes" for it to do even more.

Taipei/Tokyo Cafe 🅂⊅   21 | 7 | 11 | $12
*Metro Ctr. Plaza, 11510-A Rockville Pike (Nicholson Ln.),
Rockville, MD, 301-881-8388*
■ "Arrive hungry, leave stuffed" – it's no wonder Rockville
"lives" at this Sino-Japanese storefront; everything from
"Hiro's fresh sushi" to the "huge" bowls of noodle soup to
veggie stir-fries are "made from scratch" and a "tremendous
bargain"; service (at least on the Chinese "side") and decor
are definitely not why it's "always packed."

Tako Grill 🅂   23 | 15 | 18 | $23
*7756 Wisconsin Ave. (Cheltenham Rd.), Bethesda, MD,
301-652-7030*
■ While this stylish Japanese slices some of Bethesda's
"best" sushi, its selling point is the variety of "little stuff"
(grilled fish and vegetables) along with soba and other
noodle dishes that encourage sampler meals; hopefully, its
post-*Survey* remodeling will ease the crowding and
pressure on the sometimes "harried" help.

Tara Thai 🅂   24 | 22 | 20 | $22
*4828 Bethesda Ave. (bet. Arlington Rd. & Wisconsin Ave.),
Bethesda, MD, 301-657-0488*
*226 Maple Ave. W. (bet. Lawyer's Rd. & Nutley St.),
Vienna, VA, 703-255-2467*
*7501-E Leesburg Pike (Pimmit Dr.), Falls Church, VA,
703-506-9788*
■ These "aquatic"-themed "Asians with atmosphere"
provide a "nice meal at an affordable price" in the suburbs –
a commodity so prized that "reservations are a must"; their
"fresh" fish, boldly accented Thai dishes and "competent"
crew live up to the "exciting" high-tech decor.

TASTE OF SAIGON 🅂   26 | 20 | 22 | $20
410 Hungerford Dr. (Beall Ave.), Rockville, MD, 301-424-7222
*8201 Greensboro Dr. (International Dr.), Tysons Corner,
703-790-0700*
■ The area's "No. 1 Vietnamese meets all criteria" – the
"extensive menu has many, many hits", the "pleasant"
Rockville dining room is run by a "family" of pros and,
although Grandmother Ma Tu has retired from the kitchen,
the "black pepper dishes and appetizers" are still major
reasons why it's way too "hard to get in"; there's a new
sib in Tysons Corner.

Taste Of Thai S   _|_|_| I |

Fairfax Circle Plaza, 9534 Arlington Blvd. (½ mi. south of Fairfax Circle), Fairfax, VA, 703-352-4494

Those willing to forgo the glossy decor of nearby Tara Thai will find the food at least "as good" and at "better prices" at this attractive, "gracious", family-run restaurant in Fairfax; we're told it has the "best pad Thai on earth", but be sure to ask about the charcoal-baked fish and other specialties.

Taverna Cretekou S   21 | 20 | 20 | $26 |

818 King St. (bet. Alfred & Columbus Sts.), Alexandria, VA, 703-548-8688

■ This "pretty" Greek taverna is "sometimes too small for the people who love it" – especially for festive weekend dinners or "brunch al fresco" in the arbored Old Town courtyard; credit its convincing 'opa' ambiance, with "dancing and singing by waiters", hearty homestyle cooking and a welcome that says "come hungry and don't hurry."

Teaism S   _|_|_| M |

2009 R St., NW (Connecticut Ave.), 202-667-3827

Steeped in ancient tradition, this beautifully handcrafted Asian teahouse provides a soothing contrast to Dupont Circle coffee bars and bustle; its extensive selection of teas, made-to-order tandoori breads, kebabs, salads, sandwiches, stir-fries and luscious American desserts can be paired for an anytime snack or meal, eaten in its handsome upstairs lounge or taken home.

Tel Aviv Cafe S   16 | 16 | 16 | $21 |

4869 Cordell Ave. (Norfolk Ave.), Bethesda, MD, 301-718-9068

■ At the epicenter of Bethesda's "maddening crowds" is this Middle Eastern, which started out as an "open-air" cafe/carryout with "good falafel", appetizers and kosher grills; now it's action central for "Jewish singles" (Thursday night) and a place for "well-dressed suburbanites" to "be seen"; eating is no longer the point, although one Zionist quips that it all tastes like a "Palestinian plot to discredit Israeli food."

Tempo S   22 | 15 | 21 | $30 |

4231 Duke St. (N. Gordon St.), Alexandria, VA, 703-370-7900

☑ "An odd place" refers to the locale, "a converted Alexandria gas station", as well as the "blend of California, Italy" and the Southwest that the "different chefs" (usually the "friendly owners") bring to the menu; given the "tight space" on weekends, the neighbors are just as happy that a few surveyors think their "gem" is "just ok."

Terramar S (CLOSED)　　　20 | 20 | 19 | $28
7800 Wisconsin Ave. (Cheltenham Dr.), Bethesda, MD,
301-654-0888

☑ The tapas served at this "congenial" Bethesda Latin are
"fun to play with", "varied enough to warrant frequent visits"
and supplemented by "tasty" entrees; the "airy, open",
Spanish-feeling setting encourages conversation and
turns lively with "entertainment on weekends"; however,
some find it merely "pleasant, that's all."

T.G.I. Friday's ◑S　　　14 | 14 | 15 | $15
2100 Pennsylvania Ave. (21st St., NW), 202-872-4344
1201 Pennsylvania Ave., NW (1 block north of Federal
Triangle Metro Station), 202-628-8443
7401 Sudley Rd. (Nicholson St.), Manassas, VA,
703-330-8333
13071 Worldgate Dr. (Elden St.), Herndon, VA, 703-787-9630
4650 King St. (N. Beauregard St.), Alexandria, VA, 703-931-4101
2070 Chain Bridge Rd. (Old Courthouse Rd.), Tysons
Corner, VA, 703-556-6160
13225 Worth Ave. (across from Potomac Mills),
Woodbridge, VA, 703-492-0090
12147 Rockville Pike (Twinbrook Pkwy.), Rockville, MD
301-231-9048
6460 Capitol Dr. (Greenbelt Rd.), Greenbelt, MD,
301-345-2503
14600 Baltimore Ave. (Cherry Ln.), Laurel, MD,
301-498-8443

☑ You know "what you're going to get" at these "kid-and-
carnivore-friendly" fern bars – "nothing special" eats like
burgers, salads and "finger food" plus "spotty service" from
aggressively "cheerful" help; they're a "relatively cheap
place to take relatives" (and secretaries) to lunch, though
"on the Fifth Day, God didn't create them."

T.H.A.I. S　　　22 | 24 | 22 | $21
Village at Shirlington, 4029 S. 28th St. (Randolph St.),
Arlington, VA, 703-931-3203

■ With its "handsome and inviting" interior, "jazzy" cuisine
interpretations and attractively plated fare, Shirlington's
Thai is a "beautiful presentation" of a restaurant; most are
delighted to have an ethnic eatery with "real decor" and are
hopeful that start-up food and service glitches "will improve."

Thai Flavor S　　　▽ 21 | 14 | 21 | $21
2605 Connecticut Ave. (Calvert St.), 202-745-2000

■ Some of its customers lost track of this "very good" Thai
when it moved to a bigger space with a sidewalk cafe in
Woodley Park; they're missing out on flavorful, Chinese-
influenced food, an "excellent buffet" and the "nice
people" who run it.

Thai Garden S **(CLOSED)**   15 | 13 | 15 | $17
(fka Bangkok Orchid)
301 Massachusetts Ave., NE (3rd St.), 202-546-5900
☑ Congressional staffers "desperate for Thai on the Hill"
and a cheap lunch buffet vote both ways on the food:
"competent fare at a good price" and "eager to please" vs.
"horrible" and "service is often rude"; takeout, delivery or
eating on the patio is advised to avoid the "cheesy decor."

Thai Kingdom S   22 | 17 | 21 | $20
2021 K St., NW (bet. 20th & 21st Sts.), 202-835-1700
☑ Business-class K Street Thai with "solid" virtues, i.e.
"quick", "efficient", "reasonable" and "dependable", a
large menu of "well-spiced" dishes and an authentically
"overdecorated" room; assessments range from "superb"
to "average", with a median of "good."

That's Amore S   19 | 16 | 18 | $21
5225 Wisconsin Ave., NW (Jennifer St.), 202-237-7800
Danor Plaza, 150 Branch Rd. (Rte. 123), Vienna, VA,
703-281-7777
Potomac Run Shopping Ctr., 46300 Potomac Run Plaza
(Cascades Pkwy. & Leesburg Pike), Sterling, VA, 703-406-4900
15201 Shady Grove Rd. (Research Blvd.), Rockville, MD,
301-670-9666
☑ The family-style dining "gimmick" at these "bulk Italians"
works only when you "go with a big appetite, a big crowd"
and "every piece of Tupperware in the house for leftovers";
even then, everyone better love garlicky, heavy-duty food
and a raucous "'50s atmosphere – in short, this deal is
"not for everyone."

Thyme Square S   – | – | – | M
4735 Bethesda Ave. (Woodmont Ave.), Bethesda, MD,
301-657-9077
Chalk up another "promising" venture to Mark Caraluzzi
(American Cafe, Bistro Bistro), whose well-designed formats
for everyday eats set trends; his latest, in Bethesda,
combines "healthy" dining with a "bright Pottery Barn"
setting, adaptations of favorite vegetable and fish dishes
from all over the world and some sinfully delicious desserts.

Tia Queta S   19 | 16 | 20 | $22
8009 Norfolk Ave. (Old Georgetown Rd.), Bethesda, MD,
301-654-4443
■ Somewhat off the Bethesda beaten track (and looking
"tired"), this "real" Mexican is worth finding for "authentic"
fish dishes, "terrific tortilla soup", "classic" mole and a
very "pleasant patio"; it's also worth mentioning that the
"accommodating" staff has been there "forever", is
"understanding" about "messy" kids and is willing to
"custom-cook anything" – but it's relatively pricey.

Tiberio (CLOSED)　　　| 22 | 22 | 20 | $42 |
1915 K St., NW (bet. 19th & 20th Sts.), 202-452-1915
◪ Time has faded the roses at this K Street Northern Italian "grande dame", but the kitchen experiences "flashes of its former glory" (notably with pastas) and the dining room was just gussied up; still, an increasing number find its "old-fashioned" luxury "overpriced" even now that prices have supposedly been lowered to 1976 levels.

Tivoli　　　　　　　| 22 | 21 | 22 | $31 |
1700 N. Moore St. (19th St.), Rosslyn, VA, 703-524-8900
■ "Everything's right" about this "consistently excellent" Continental – "fine" food, "living room" comfort, "wonderful service" and "very impressive desserts" – only its Rosslyn "location" holds it back; nevertheless, knowledgeable party planners count on its "professionalism", good prices and parking for pre-theater, quiet business, private events and "that special dinner" for two.

Tokyo Lighthouse ⑤　　| – | – | – | M |
Diamond Sq. Shopping Ctr., 22 Bureau Dr. (bet. Clopper Rd. & Quince Orchard Rd.), Gaithersburg, MD, 301-977-0988
Watching tableside chefs slicing and dicing their way through your teppanyaki dinner is "great entertainment"; equally appealing is a quiet sushi lunch; in Gaithersburg, where there's a shortage of comfortable, commodious restaurants, this Japanese is a beacon.

Tomato Tango ⑤　　　| – | – | – | I |
Olney Towne Ctr., 18115 Towne Ctr. Dr. (Spartan Rd. & Rte. 108), Olney, MD, 301-570-5247
Even though this Cal-Ital pizza and pasta place sometimes gets "crowded" and "rushed", it meets the need for casual family and business dining in Olney with "tons of pasta" at "unbelievably" low prices.

Tom Tom ⑤　　　　| 17 | 19 | 16 | $21 |
2333 18th St., NW (bet. Belmont St. & Kalorama Rd.), 202-588-1300
◪ In Adams Morgan, you can't beat this "electric" summer rooftop with its "hip" help, "trendy" tapas, artists at work "before your eyes", relentless music and "good beer on tap"; in winter, the action moves indoors, where it's both "artsy" and "too Melrose Place" – anyone over 30 will experience "sensory overload."

Tony & Joe's Seafood Place ⑤　| 16 | 19 | 16 | $28 |
Washington Harbour, 3000 K St., NW (30th St.), 202-944-4545
◪ Sweeping Potomac views and a waterfront bar "mob scene" that rivals Sequoia's are the bankable assets of this Washington Harbour seafooder; the "typical" food and service are "not as impressive" as the vista, but this doesn't detract when one is "sitting outside" for an "enjoyable" brunch or a solo lunch at the bar (inside is less "fun").

Tony Cheng's Mongolian S
19 14 17 $20

Tony Cheng's Seafood S
619 H St., NW (bet. 6th & 7th Sts.), 202-842-TONY

☑ "A reliable address in Chinatown" to take tourists or teens for an "all-you-can-eat", "build-your-own" Mongolian BBQ (choose ingredients to be stir-fried, grilled or steeped tableside in hot pots); local Sinophiles who find the "novelty has worn off" head upstairs for "excellent dim sum" and Taiwanese food.

Tragara S
23 22 21 $41

4935 Cordell Ave. (bet. Old Georgetown Rd. & Norfolk Ave.), Bethesda, MD, 301-951-4935

■ It's "elegant" and a "bit formal", yet Bethesda's "big-bucks Northern Italian" makes "you feel like you're in Italy" and ready to enjoy "a long meal"; that's due, in part, to the "pleasant" waiters, but mostly to chef Michel Laudier's "well-prepared", "attractively presented" food – look for his breads, lobster dishes and unusual frozen sweets.

Trattoria da Franco S
▽ 22 19 19 $29

305 S. Washington St. (Duke St.), Alexandria, VA, 703-548-9338

☑ One of several "cozy" restaurants that preserve Old Town's "neighborhood" feel, but either you take to its "warm, hokey atmosphere", pastas with pesto and "inspired veal" or it will seem like a "poor excuse for Italian"; it's very much owner Franco Abbruzzetti's place – he even holds opera nights so he can sing.

Trattu (CLOSED)
21 16 21 $26

1823 Jefferson Pl., NW (bet. Connecticut Ave. & 19th St.), 202-466-4570

■ "Thank goodness" this "sweet" Dupont Circle Italian is "still small, still good and still a [relative] secret" – it's "crowded" enough at lunch already and if the garlicky food were "better, portions bigger" and it got a "face-lift", the price might no longer be "right."

Trumpets S
23 19 21 $28

1603 17th St., NW (Q St.), 202-232-4141

■ Chef David Hagedorn's gay following is proud to share the "highest-quality New American cuisine east of Dupont Circle" with everyone; just go past the bar to the "dark", "funky" back dining room where his wittily presented, "creative, delicious food" comes at a "good price"; Sunday brunch ($12.95) with unlimited champagne is a good intro.

Tsukiji S
– – – M

Ritchie Shopping Ctr., 785-K Rockville Pike, Rockville, MD, 301-294-9160

Walk in the door of this tiny Rockville retreat and visit Japan; it's an understated, "wonderful place for sushi and other Japanese food delights" run by a lovely "family" who will bring you tea and make you feel at home.

Tuscana West   18 | 19 | 17 | $28
1350 I St., NW (bet. 13th & 14th Sts.), 202-289-7300
☑ Weekday biz lunches at this "flashy" Downtown neo-Tuscan are "often quite good", which means the food is "not [too] exciting . . . not [too] distracting" and not marred by the "indifferent, sometimes arrogant service" one can sometimes encounter here; those who go at night for happy hour, opera night (Thursdays) and dancing and dining (weekends) have more fun.

219 S   20 | 22 | 21 | $31
219 King St. (Fairfax St.), Alexandria, VA, 703-549-1141
■ On one of Old Town's busiest dining streets, this "picturesque" replica of "'50s New Orleans" entices passersby; here, "good Creole cooking" can be eaten in a "romantic dungeon", a "perfect" period parlor or a people-watching heated terrace; it's also a "great jazz place" and the "best bar" in town.

Two Quail S   21 | 24 | 21 | $30
320 Massachusetts Ave., NE (bet. 3rd & 4th Sts.), 202-543-8030
☑ The "table in the window" of this Capitol Hill Victorian is the "ultimate for romance" (and it's not just the privacy or the view); there's something seductive about this eatery's "quirky", decorative mix of Laura Ashley and "your crazy aunt's" attic, its equally quirky American food (albeit "not as outrageous" lately) and "solicitous" staff; very few disagree.

Udupi Palace S   – | – | – | I
1329 University Blvd. E. (New Hampshire Ave.), Langley Park, MD, 301-434-1531
Southern India's extensive vegetarian cuisine offers a myriad of "unusual" taste sensations even though it's prepared without meat, fish or eggs; in Langley Park, this exemplar's long menu of "cheap, fabulous" dishes makes it "paradise" for anyone with a serious interest in food; no booze or decor.

Union Street Public House S   18 | 19 | 18 | $20
121 S. Union St. (bet. King & Prince Sts.), Alexandria, VA, 703-548-1785
☑ Don't be fooled by the weekend "Gen X" free-for-all at the bar (and resulting "scatterbrained" service); this "model American pub" sets a "standard for decent food at decent prices" in "pleasant surroundings" with the "best steak sandwich", oyster bar and "homemade butterscotch sundaes" in town, "good tap beers" and Southern-influenced cooking – bring "out-of-towners."

Uptown Cafe 🅂 (CLOSED)　　14 | 12 | 15 | $17
*3311 Connecticut Ave., NW (bet. Macomb & Newark Sts.),
202-966-7462*
☑ What you see is what you get at this open-to-the-street,
"cheap French bistro" in Cleveland Park; it has a drop-by
neighborhood bar, worn surroundings and old-fashioned
"cafe fare" (crêpes, quiche, "french fries with everything")
with enough "good dishes" to make the early-bird special
worthwhile; "better than expected" if you "don't expect
much" is the bottom line.

U-topia 🅂　　17 | 19 | 19 | $21
1418 U St., NW (bet. 14th & 15th Sts.), 202-483-7669
☑ The New U's "neighborhood" restaurant is "primarily a
bar" with live music that happens to serve "interesting"
Eclectic food; the "crowd", original art and "old bike
pictures" displayed against subdued modern walls are
major decorative elements.

Vegetable Garden 🅂　　19 | 15 | 18 | $18
*11618 Rockville Pike (Old Georgetown Rd. &
Nicholson Ln.), Rockville, MD, 301-468-9301*
☑ This "alternative" Chinese in Rockville makes a "good
effort" at presenting "healthy", "inexpensive" vegetarian
food in "relaxing" surroundings; since there are "so few
vegetarian eateries", it seems churlish to complain about
one of the area's best and most "creative", but "some
dishes taste distressingly the same" – "bland."

Veneziano 🅂　　21 | 17 | 20 | $30
2305 18th St., NW (Kalorama Rd.), 202-483-9300
■ "Fresh", authentically prepared food and "professional
service" keep patrons "happy" at this "middling" Northern
Italian; it's "relatively unknown" outside Adams Morgan
(largely due to the parking hassle), but its $13.95 early-bird/
late-supper menu, pasta and fagioli soup at lunch and more
than 200 grappas reward a visit.

VIDALIA 🅂　　25 | 22 | 23 | $40
1990 M St., NW (bet. 19th & 20th Sts.), 202-659-1990
☑ Whether DC is "still a Southern town" is debatable, but it
certainly has an appetite for contemporary Dixie-accented
food in sophisticated, business-oriented surroundings;
possibly the "best" of the "sorta-Southern" contingent
has settled into a "well-appointed", "attentively" run, step-
down space on M Street "where what they do with onions"
(and "the check") "will bring tears to your eyes."

Vienna's Grille ●⬛ ▽ 19 14 15 $18
146 Maple Ave. E. (bet. Park & Center Sts.), Vienna, VA, 703-255-0800
⬛ Cajun-Creole food plus live music and a dance floor sounds like a winning combo for this 'New Orleans in Vienna' complex; throw in an impressive list of beers, a kitchen that has the "spice level" right (if not the "side dishes"), lots of discounts and nice people, and it adds up to a place that surveyors hope "stays open."

Vietnam ⬛ ▽ 22 13 21 $19
4924 St. Elmos St. (Carter Ave.), Bethesda, MD, 301-656-2280
⬛ One of several new Vietnamese options in Bethesda comes in a "plain" wrapper and does a "very good" job with a long menu of grills, rice dishes, curries and pho; recommended choices include the "outrageous" special pancake, soups and appetizers.

Village Bistro ⬛ 24 16 20 $25
Colonial Village, 1723 Wilson Blvd. (Quinn St.), Arlington, VA, 703-522-0284
⬛ A "gem", a "sleeper", a "surprise on Wilson Boulevard" – only our savvy surveyors would've found this "outstanding" French bistro in a "nondescript strip mall" (which houses several other worthwhile eateries); the "food has DC sophistication, but the restaurant has local warmth and prices"; ergo it's often "packed."

Vincenzo (CLOSED) 21 20 19 $35
(fka Trattoria "al Sole")
1606 20th St., NW (bet. Q St. & Connecticut Ave.), 202-667-0047
⬛ Recasting "the best of Old Vincenzo's at reasonable prices", one of DC's top Italians is now a "gracious, refined" setting for "exceptional seafood", delicate housemade noodles and regional pastas and entrees; there's also a "divine" private dining room that hosts classy events; within those parameters, V. keeps fine tuning its format.

Virginia Beverage Co. ⬛ – – – M
607 King St. (bet. St. Asaph & S. Washington Sts.), Alexandria, VA, 703-684-5397
There's a "wild and woolly beer selection" at Old Town's "fine new microbrewery" – an "upscale" King Street attraction that "feels like Seattle" (home of pioneering brewpubs); early reports suggest that diners stick with basics, like the "great club sandwich and homemade potato chips", since the "hot" stuff can "leave you cold"; P.S. check out the single-malt scotch and bourbon list.

Vivace Enoteca S (CLOSED)   18 | 16 | 19 | $23
2311 M St., NW (bet. 23rd & 24th Sts.), 202-833-3227

☑ This enterprising West End Italian has many interesting "concepts" – it's a "wine bar", a "sports bar", an after-work hangout featuring Italian tapas (half-portion entrees and "appetizers ordered as a meal") and a staff that "really makes an effort" to mix "service and speed"; but its ideas "need to be developed" and aren't helped by the "post-Armageddon decor."

Vox Populi   21 | 19 | 19 | $19
800 Connecticut Ave., NW (H St.), 202-835-2233

☑ Along with breakfast cappuccino, "great" salads and light French fare, there are "good celebrity-gazing possibilities" at this near-the-White-House, "daytime cafe/buffet"; the tone (politics and biz) is "quite likable", the servers "super friendly and helpful" – and the price "a bit too expensive" for what it is.

Warehouse Bar & Grill S   22 | 20 | 21 | $26
214 King St. (bet. Fairfax & Lee Sts.), Alexandria, VA, 703-683-6868

■ "One of Old Town's best" cooks Creole-Cajun seafood and steaks, looks like its parent (the "original" R.T.'s as "rendered by Disney") and has one of the neatest piano bars around; its "loyal following" (whose caricatures are on the wall) has no problem with the menu's "predictable twists", the "noise" or "waits" when ensconced in a "window table."

West End Cafe S   20 | 19 | 19 | $29
1 Washington Circle Hotel, NW (bet. New Hampshire Ave. & 23rd St.), 202-293-5390

■ Prized for "business lunches" and before or after Kennedy Center, this gardenlike West End room's hostess ("always a laugh") and the "best piano player in town" make it "*the* place to go" for dinner after the show; an "inventive" Contemporary American menu, a Ken-Cen shuttle and an antipasto lunch buffet ($8.50) are further recommendations.

WILLARD ROOM S   23 | 27 | 24 | $46
Willard Hotel, 1401 Pennsylvania Ave., NW (bet. 14th & 15th Sts.), 202-637-7440

■ A "great room", restored to its former Beaux Arts glory, where "one expects Teddy Roosevelt to come striding in"; now, as then, it's DC's premier "big event" setting, with "excellent" Contemporary French food and exemplary service; try the "innovative tasting menu with perfect wines to match" or go for "high tea."

Willow Grove Inn S   ▽ 23 | 23 | 24 | $40

Willow Grove Inn, 14079 Plantation Way (off Rte. 15, 1 mi. north of Orange), Orange, VA, 540-672-5982

■ When visiting Charlottesville and Monticello, this "romantic" antebellum mansion is a lovely stop; its Regional American "country home cooking", "natural" garden setting, "nice" manners – even the "scraped paint" and occasional misses – lend it a "quaint" charm.

Woo Lae Oak S   24 | 17 | 19 | $24

River House, 1500 S. Joyce St., Arlington, VA, 703-521-3706

◪ As "in Seoul", this Arlington Korean offers a range of "authentic", fiery eating possibilities – "cook your own" BBQ, bi bim bap (grilled meat and vegetables), noodle dishes, casseroles and real kimchi; one fares best in this "remote", "Hot Shoppes"–like location "with Korean friends for guides" since English is not always "spoken here."

Wurzburg-Haus   20 | 16 | 18 | $22

Red Mill Shopping Ctr., 7236 Mancaster Mill Rd. (Shady Grove Rd.), Rockville, MD, 301-330-0402

■ The wholesome, "hearty" food and rollicking "rathskeller" atmosphere at this Rockville German could fit a "cold winter night" mood; it's not the best (and not nearby), but "you could do a lot wurst" – and, for a relatively modest tab, you'll eat more than your fill.

Xing Kuba S (CLOSED)   21 | 21 | 21 | $31

2218 Wisconsin Ave., NW (Calvert St.), 202-965-0665

◪ In a great-looking, neo-deco Glover Park setting, diners "test pilot" a "clever menu" of fusion food inspired by Asian, Latino and Southwestern "flavors" and techniques.

Yin Yang S (CLOSED)   – | – | – | I

2323 18th St., NW (bet. Kalorama & Belmont Rds.), 202-319-1111

This Adams Morgan Pan-Asian noodle house is cheap, fast, tasty and light; the salads and noodle bowls come in an industrial-feeling space.

Yosaku S   21 | 14 | 20 | $25

4712 Wisconsin Ave., NW (Davenport St.), 202-363-4453

■ Near movies and shopping, this trusty Upper Northwest Japanese "never fails" to provide "fine", "fresh" sushi and "delicious" noodle soups and cooked dishes along with a sense of "peace"; it's a "good value" ("especially t lunch") – try it once, you'll "go a lot."

Zed's S   19 | 11 | 17 | $18

3318 M St., NW (bet. 33rd & 34th Sts.), 202-333-4710

◪ Many consider this "shabby" Ethiopian storefront in Georgetown (near the Key Bridge) to be "peerless"; reputedly "used by the embassy" for official dining, it makes "authentic injera" (using the proper grain, "teff") and "better seasoned dishes" with many vegetarian choices; "if you like" spicy finger food, it's "cheap eats."

Indexes to Washington, D.C. Restaurants

Special Features and Appeals

TYPES OF CUISINE

Afghan
Kabul Caravan
Panjshir
Paradise

African
Meskerem
Red Sea
Zed's

American (Contemporary)
American Grill
Aquarelle
Bistro
Bistro Bistro
Bistro 2015
Bleu Rock Inn
Cafe Bethesda
Cafe on M
Cafe Promenade
Calasia
Carlyle Grand Cafe
Cashion's Eat Place
Chardonnay
Cities
Coeur de Lion
Dean & DeLuca
Elysium
Eye St. Cafe
Felix
Fern St. Bistro
Flint Hill Public Hse.
4 & 20 Blackbirds
Greenwood's
Inn/Little Wash.
Jefferson
Lafayette
Market St. B&G
Melrose
Metro Center Grille
Morrison-Clark Inn
Mrs. Simpson's
New Heights
Nora
Occidental Grill
Old Angler's Inn
Oval Room
Perry's
Pesce
R.C., The Grill
Roof Terrace
Ruppers
Seasons
701
1789
Silverado
Stage Door
Stella's
Stone Manor
Tabard Inn
Thyme Square
Trumpets

Two Quail
Vidalia
West End Cafe
Willard Room
Willow Grove Inn

American (Regional)
America
Crisfield
Georgia Brown's
Inn/Little Wash.
Kinkead's
Morrison-Clark Inn
O'Donnell's
Old Angler's Inn
1789
Shelly's Woodroast
Stone Manor
Vidalia
Virginia Bev. Co.
Willow Grove Inn

American (Traditional)
America
Artie's
B & C
Bardo Rodeo
Belmont Kitchen
Bilbo Baggins
Bistro Bistro
Cafe Deluxe
Calvert Grille
Capitol City Brewing
Carlyle Grand Cafe
Cashion's Eat Place
Cedar Knoll Inn
Chadwick's
Chart House
Cheesecake Factory
Clyde's
Cowboy Cafe
Dixie Grill
Easby's Buffet
Evans Farm Inn
Fedora Cafe
Fleetwood's
Gadsby's Tavern
Garrett Park Cafe
Gulf Coast Kitchen
Hard Rock Cafe
Hard Times Cafe
Herb's
Hogate's
Houston's
Inn at Glen Echo
J. Paul's
King Street Blues
Kramerbooks
Legal Sea Food
Luna Grill
Martin's Tavern
Metro 29

Mick's
Mike's American
Monocle
Montgomery's Grille
Music City Roadhouse
Nathan's
O'Donnell's
Old Ebbitt Grill
Old Glory BBQ
Phillips Flagship
Phillips Seafood
Pier 7
Planet Hollywood
Polly's Cafe
Potowmack Landing
R.C., The Restaurant
Red Hot & Blue
Roof Terrace
Savory
Sequoia
Shelly's Woodroast
Silver Diner
Slade's
Southside 815
T.G.I. Friday's
Union St. Public Hse.
Virginia Bev. Co.
Warehouse B&G

Bakeries
Firehook Bakery
La Madeleine
Patisserie Cafe Didier

Bar-B-Q
Chicken Place
Crisp & Juicy
El Pollo Rico
Granja de Oro
Houston's
King Street Blues
Memphis Bar-B-Q
Old Glory BBQ
Red Hot & Blue
Rockland's
Starke's
Tony Cheng's Mongolian

Brazilian
Cafe Atlantico
Coco Loco
Grill from Ipanema

Brewpubs
Bardo Rodeo
Blue & Gold
Capitol City Brewing
Virginia Bev. Co.

Cajun/Creole
Blue & Gold
Cajun Bangkok
Fatt Daddy's
Gulf Coast Kitchen
Louisiana Express
R.T.'s
R.T.'s Seafood

219
Vienna's Grille
Warehouse B&G

Caribbean
Cafe Atlantico
Hibiscus Cafe
Mo Bay Cafe
Xing Kuba

Chili
Hard Times Cafe
Red Sage

Chinese
Charlie Chiang's
China Canteen
China Chef
China Inn
City Lights of China
Dynasty
Eat First
Foong Lin
Fortune
Four Rivers
Full Kee
Full Key
Good Fortune
House of Chinese
Hsiang Foong
Hunan Chinatown
Hunan Lion
Hunan Lion II
Hunan Number One
Hunan Palace
Mama Wok
Mr. K's
Mr. Yung's
Peking Gourmet Inn
Royal Dragon
Seven Seas
Sunny Garden
Szechuan Gallery
Taipei/Tokyo Cafe
Tony Cheng's Mongolian
Tony Cheng's Seafood
Vegetable Garden

Coffeehouses
Dean & DeLuca
Firehook Bakery
Kramerbooks
Le Bon Cafe
Planet X
Savory
Vox Populi

Coffee Shops/Diners
Bob & Edith's Diner
C.F. Folks
Florida Ave. Grill
Luna Grill
Metro 29
Silver Diner

Continental

Baron's
Bilbo Baggins
Eurogrill
Falls Landing
Jockey Club
Lafayette
Lite 'n' Fair
Lite 'n' Fair/BV
Normandie Farms
Nova Europa
R.C., The Grill
R.C., The Restaurant
River Club
Tivoli
Two Quail

Cuban

Havana Cafe

Delis

Cafe Mozart
Krupin's
Lite 'n' Fair
Lite 'n' Fair/BV
Parkway Deli

Dim Sum

China Chef
China Inn
Fortune
Four Rivers
Good Fortune
Hunan Lion II
Hunan Number One
Mr. Yung's
Sunny Garden
Tony Cheng's Seafood

Eclectic

C.F. Folks
Cities
Fern St. Bistro
Greenwood's
Planet X
Savory
State of the Union
Tabard Inn
Tempo
Thyme Square
Trumpets
Two Quail
U-topia
Xing Kuba

Ethiopian

Meskerem
Red Sea
Zed's

French

Au Pied du Cochon
Bistro Francais
Bistrot Lepic
Cafe Parisien
Cafe Riviera
Gerard's Place
Jean-Michel
La Bergerie
La Bonne Auberge
La Brasserie
La Chaumiere
La Colline
La Cote d'Or Cafe
La Ferme
La Fourchette
La Madeleine
La Miche
La Mirabelle
L'Auberge Chez Francois
L'Auberge Provencale
Lavandou
Le Caprice
Le Gaulois
Le Lion D'Or
Le Paradis
Le Refuge
Le Rivage
Lespinasse
Le Vieux Logis
Maison Blanche
Provence
St. Elmos Cafe
Willard Room

French Bistro

Au Pied du Cochon
Bistro Francais
Bistro Le Monde
Bistrot Lepic
Cafe Parisien
Cafe Riviera
Gerard's Place
La Brasserie
La Chaumiere
La Colline
La Cote d'Or Cafe
La Fourchette
La Madeleine
La Miche
Lavandou
Le Bon Cafe
Le Caprice
Le Gaulois
Le Paradis
Le Refuge
Les Halles
Patisserie Cafe Didier
St. Elmos Cafe
Uptown Cafe

Village Bistro
Vox Populi

French (Contemporary)
Citronelle
Gerard's Place
Jean-Michel
Le Caprice
Le Refuge
Lespinasse
Maison Blanche
Provence
Willard Room

German
Cafe Berlin
Cafe Mozart
Wurzburg-Haus

Greek
Aegean Taverna
Ambrosia
Athenian Plaka
Mykonos
Taverna Cretekou

Hamburgers
Artie's
Capitol City Brewing
Carlyle Grand Cafe
Chadwick's
Clyde's
Cowboy Cafe
Hard Rock Cafe
Herb's
Houston's
J. Paul's
Martin's Tavern
Mick's
Mike's American
Montgomery's Grille
Nathan's
Old Ebbitt Grill
Planet Hollywood
Polly's Cafe
Slade's
Stage Door
T.G.I. Friday's
Union St. Public Hse.
Virginia Bev. Co.

Indian/Pakistani
Aangan
Aaranthi
Aditi
Aroma
Bombay Bistro
Bombay Club
Bombay Dining
Bombay Palace
Cafe New Delhi
Cafe Taj
Connaught Place
Delhi Dhaba
Food Factory
Haandi
India Kitchen

Maharaja
Shiney's Kabab House
Udupi Palace

Indonesian
Melati
Sabang
Sarinah Satay House

Italian
(N=Northern; S=Southern;
N&S=Includes both)
Arucola (N&S)
BeDuCi (N&S)
Bei Tempi (N)
Bertolini's (N&S)
Bertucci's (N&S)
Bice (N)
Buon Giorno (N&S)
Cafe Milano (N)
Cafe Mileto (S)
Café Oggi (N&S)
"Ciao baby" Cucina (N&S)
Da Domenico (N&S)
Donatello (N&S)
Duca Di Milano (N)
Ecco Cafe (N&S)
Faccia Luna (N&S)
Filomena Ristorante (N&S)
Galileo (N)
Generous George's (N&S)
Geranio (N&S)
Goldoni (N)
Il Borgo (N&S)
Il Cigno (N)
Il Pizzico (N&S)
Il Radicchio (N&S)
Il Ritrovo (N&S)
I Matti (N&S)
I Ricchi (N)
Landini Brothers (N&S)
La Panetteria (N&S)
La Tomate (N&S)
Listrani's (N&S)
Luigino (N)
Mare E Monti (N&S)
Nathan's (N)
Notte Luna (N&S)
Obelisk (N&S)
Otello (N&S)
Paolo's (N&S)
Pappa-Razzi (N&S)
Parioli (N&S)
Pasta Plus (N&S)
Petitto's (N&S)
Pines of Florence (N&S)
Pines of Rome (N&S)
Pirandello (N&S)
Pizza de Resistance (N&S)
Positano (S)
Primi Piatti (N&S)
Radio Free Italy (N&S)
Red Tomato Cafe (N&S)
Renato (N&S)
Ristorante Capri (N&S)

Palm, The
Prime Rib
Ruth's Chris
Sam & Harry's

Sushi

Appetizer Plus
Atami
Benkay
Cafe Asia
Genji
Ginza's
Hinode
Hisago
Kawasaki
Makoto
Mama Wok
Matuba
Miyagi
Perry's
Sam Woo
Shiro-ya
Spices
Sushi Chalet
Sushi-Ko
Tachibana
Taipei/Tokyo Cafe
Tako Grill
Tokyo Lighthouse
Tsukiji
Yosaku

Tapas

Gabriel
Jaleo
Taberna del Alabardero
Terramar
Tom Tom

Tex-Mex

Alamo
Alamo/VA
Arizona
Austin Grill
Burrito Brothers
Burro
Cactus Cantina
California Tortilla
Cowboy Cafe
Guapo's
La Lomita
Mi Rancho
Red River Grill
Rio Grande Cafe
South Austin Grill

Thai

Bangkok St. Grill
Bangkok Vientiane
Benjarong
Bua
Busara
Cajun Bangkok
Crystal Thai
Duangrat's
Dusit
49 Twelve Thai
Haad Thai
Malik
Pilin Thai
Rabieng
Sala Thai
Star of Siam
Tara Thai
Taste Of Thai
T.H.A.I.
Thai Flavor
Thai Garden
Thai Kingdom

Turkish

Kazan
Nizam's

Vegetarian

Greenwood's
Kabob Bazaar
Malik
Planet X
Thyme Square
Udupi Palace
Vegetable Garden

Vietnamese

Cafe Dalat
Cafe Saigon
Chesapeake Seafood
Galaxy
Little Viet Garden
Miss Saigon
Nam's
Nam Viet
Pho
Pho Cali
Pho 95
Pho 75
Queen Bee
Saigon Gourmet
Saigon Inn
Saigonnais
Taste of Saigon
Vietnam

NEIGHBORHOOD LOCATIONS

WASHINGTON, D.C.

NEARBY MARYLAND

Rockville

Ambrosia
Andalucia
Benjarong
Bombay Bistro
Cafe Bethesda
China Canteen
Crisp & Juicy
Easby's Buffet
Four Rivers
Garrett Park Cafe
Hard Times Cafe
Hautam Kebobs
House of Chinese
Houston's
Il Pizzico
La Madeleine
Ledo Pizza
Mama Wok
Nulbom
Paolo's
Pho 95
Pho 75
Royal Dragon
Sam Woo
Seven Seas
Shelly's Woodroast
Silver Diner
Starke's
Sunny Garden
Taipei/Tokyo Cafe
Taste of Saigon
T.G.I. Friday's
That's Amore
Tsukiji
Vegetable Garden
Wurzburg-Haus

Silver Spring/Wheaton/ Langley Park/Laurel/ Landover

Chicken Place
China Chef
Crisfield
Crisp & Juicy
Dusit
Dynasty
El Gavilan
El Pollo Rico
Food Factory
Full Key
Good Fortune
Ledo Pizza
Los Chorros
Maharaja
Mare E Monti
Mi Rancho
Nam's
Nova Europa
Outback Steakhouse
Parkway Deli
Pasta Plus
Pho 75
Planet X
Red Hot & Blue
Sabang
Savory
Silver Diner
T.G.I. Friday's
Udupi Palace

Columbia

Clyde's

NEARBY VIRGINIA

Alexandria

Alamo/VA
Bilbo Baggins
Blue Point Grill
Cajun Bangkok
Calif. Pizza Kit.
Calvert Grille
Cedar Knoll Inn
Chadwick's
Charlie Chiang's
Chart House
Cowboy Cafe
Ecco Cafe
Elysium
Firehook Bakery
Fleetwood's
Gadsby's Tavern
Generous George's
Geranio
Hard Times Cafe
King Street Blues
La Bergerie
La Madeleine

Landini Brothers
Le Bon Cafe
Le Gaulois
Le Refuge
Lite 'n' Fair
Lite 'n' Fair/BV
Outback Steakhouse
Pines of Florence
Potowmack Landing
Radio Free Italy
R.T.'s
Santa Fe East
South Austin Grill
Southside 815
Stella's
Taverna Cretekou
Tempo
T.G.I. Friday's
Trattoria da Franco
219
Union St. Public Hse.
Virginia Bev. Co.
Warehouse B&G

SPECIAL FEATURES AND APPEALS

Breakfast
(All major hotels
and the following)
Au Pied du Cochon
B & C
Bob & Edith's Diner
Cafe Parisien
Dean & DeLuca
Firehook Bakery
Kramerbooks
Krupin's
La Brasserie
La Colline
La Madeleine
Le Bon Cafe
Louisiana Express
Martin's Tavern
Old Ebbitt Grill
Parkway Deli
Patisserie Cafe Didier
Pho Cali
Silver Diner
Teaism

Brunch
(Best of many)
America
Aquarelle
Artie's
Austin Grill
Belmont Kitchen
Bilbo Baggins
Bistro
Bistro Bistro
Bistro 2015
Bleu Rock Inn
Bombay Club
B. Smith's
Calvert Grille
Carlyle Grand Cafe
Cashion's Eat Place
Cedar Knoll Inn
Citronelle
Clyde's
Coppi's
Felix
Filomena Ristorante
Flint Hill Public Hse.
4 & 20 Blackbirds
Gabriel
Gadsby's Tavern
Georgia Brown's
Inn at Glen Echo
Jaleo
Kinkead's
Kramerbooks
Mediterranean Blue
Melrose
Mike's American
Morrison-Clark Inn
Mrs. Simpson's

New Heights
Old Angler's Inn
Paolo's
Pappa-Razzi
Polly's Cafe
R.C., The Grill
R.C., The Restaurant
Roof Terrace
Santa Fe East
Seasons
Sequoia
Tabard Inn
Taverna Cretekou
Trumpets
Union St. Public Hse.
West End Cafe

Buffet Served
(B = brunch; L = lunch;
D = dinner)
Aangan (L)
Aaranthi (L)
Aroma (B)
Athenian Plaka (B)
Balalayka (L)
Benkay (L)
Bistro 2015 (B)
Bombay Bistro (B,L)
Bombay Club (B)
Bombay Dining (L)
Cafe Dalat (L)
Cafe Mileto (L)
Cafe New Delhi (B)
Cafe Promenade (B)
Cafe Taj (L)
"Ciao baby" Cucina (L)
Cintra (B)
Coco Loco (L)
Connaught Place (L)
Delhi Dhaba (B)
Easby's Buffet (L,D)
El Tamarindo (L)
Evans Farm Inn (L)
Fedora Cafe (B)
Filomena Ristorante (B,L)
Gabriel (L)
Gangplank (B)
Generous George's (L)
Georgia Brown's (B)
Guapo's (L)
Hogate's (B,L)
India Kitchen (B,L)
Maharaja (L)
Metro Center Grille (L)
Normandie Farms (B)
Persepolis (L)
Phillips Flagship (B,L,D)
Phillips Seafood (B)
Radio Free Italy (L)
R.C., The Grill (B,L)
R.C., The Restaurant (L)

Coco Loco (D/bands)
Coeur de Lion (jazz/piano)
Cowboy Cafe (bands)
Da Domenico (opera)
Dar Es Salaam (belly dancing)
Dixie Grill (jazz)
Duangrat's (Thai dance)
Duca Di Milano (D/bands)
El Caribe (guitar)
Elysium (piano)
Evans Farm Inn (piano)
Fatt Daddy's (jazz)
Felix (D/DJ/varies)
Fleetwood's (varies)
Fran O'Brien's (piano)
Gadsby's Tavern (lute/violin)
Galaxy (Vietnamese band)
Hard Rock Cafe (bands)
Havana Cafe (DJ/guitar)
Herb's (singing)
I Matti (comedy)
Jefferson (piano/jazz)
King Street Blues (blues/jazz)
Kinkead's (piano)
Melrose (D/varies)
Muer's Seafood (jazz/piano)
Normandie Farms (D/piano)
Ozio (D/DJ)
Paolo's (jazz)
Pappa-Razzi (jazz/opera)
Petitto's (opera)
Planet X (varies)
R.C., The Grill (piano)
R.C., The Restaurant (D/jazz)
River Club (D)
State of the Union (varies)
Terramar (Latin guitar)
Thai Flavor (varies)
Tony & Joe's (varies)
Trattoria da Franco (piano)
219 (jazz)
U-topia (blues/Brazilian jazz)
Vivace Enoteca (opera)
West End Cafe (piano)
Willard Room (piano)
Yin Yang (D/DJ)

Delivers*/Takeout

(Nearly all Asians, coffee
shops, delis, diners &
pizzerias deliver or do
takeout; here are some best
bets; D = delivery, T = takeout)
Aangan (D,T)
Aaranthi (T)
Aditi (T)
Aegean Taverna (T)
Alamo (T)
Ambrosia (T)
America (T)
Appetizer Plus (T)
Aroma (T)
Asia Nora (T)
Athenian Plaka (T)

Austin Grill (T)
Bacchus (T)
Balalayka (D,T)
Bangkok St. Grill (T)
Bei Tempi (T)
Belmont Kitchen (D,T)
Benkay (T)
Bertucci's (T)
Bice (T)
Bistro Bistro (D,T)
Bistro Francais (T)
Bistro Le Monde (T)
Bistrot Lepic (T)
Blue & Gold (T)
Blue Point Grill (T)
Bombay Bistro (T)
Bombay Club (T)
Bombay Dining (T)
Bombay Palace (T)
Burro (D,T)
Cactus Cantina (T)
Cafe Asia (D,T)
Cafe Bethesda (T)
Cafe Deluxe (T)
Cafe Mozart (D,T)
Cafe New Delhi (D,T)
Café Oggi (T)
Cafe Parisien (T)
Cafe Rose (D,T)
Cafe Taj (D,T)
Cheesecake Factory (T)
Chicken Place (T)
Clyde's (T)
Connaught Place (T)
Cottonwood Cafe (T)
Cowboy Cafe (D,T)
Crisfield (D,T)
Da Domenico (T)
Dar Es Salaam (T)
Dean & DeLuca (D,T)
Duca Di Milano (T)
Enriqueta's (D,T)
Evans Farm Inn (T)
Falls Landing (T)
Fedora Cafe (T)
Felix (D,T)
Fern St. Bistro (T)
Filomena Ristorante (T)
Fran O'Brien's (T)
Gabriel (T)
Georgetown Seafood (T)
Georgia Brown's (T)
Germaine's (T)
Greenwood's (T)
Haandi (T)
Hard Times Cafe (T)
Hibiscus Cafe (T)
Hinode (T)
Hogate's (T)
Ichiban (T)
Il Borgo (T)
Il Pizzico (T)
Il Ritrovo (D,T)
India Kitchen (D,T)

Kabob Bazaar (T)
Kabul Caravan (T)
King Street Blues (D,T)
La Chaumiere (T)
La Ferme (T)
Lebanese Taverna (T)
Legal Sea Food (T)
Le Gaulois (T)
Lite 'n' Fair (T)
Los Chorros (T)
Louisiana Express (D,T)
Luigino (T)
Martin's Tavern (T)
Matuba (T)
Mediteranean Blue (T)
Memphis Bar-B-Q (D,T)
Meskerem (D,T)
Muer's Seafood (T)
Music City Roadhouse (T)
Mykonos (D)
Nizam's (T)
Nova Europa (T)
Old Ebbitt Grill (T)
Oodles Noodles (T)
Otello (T)
Outback Steakhouse (T)
Ozio (T)
Panjshir (T)
Parioli (T)
Pasha Cafe (T)
Pasta Plus (T)
Perry's (T)
Persepolis (D,T)
Pesce (T)
Phillips Flagship (T)
Phillips Seafood (T)
Pirandello (T)
Planet X (T)
Raku (T)
Red Hot & Blue (D,T)
Red Sea (D,T)
Renato (T)
Rockland's (T)
R.T.'s (T)
R.T.'s Seafood (T)
Ruth's Chris (T)
Saigonnais (T)
Shelly's Woodroast (T)
Shiro-ya (D,T)
Skewers/Cafe Luna (T)
South Austin Grill (T)
Southside 815 (T)
Spices (D,T)
Stage Door (T)
Starke's (T)
Stella's (T)
Straits of Malaya (T)
Sushi Chalet (T)
Sushi-Ko (T)
Tako Grill (T)
Taste of Saigon (T)
Taverna Cretekou (T)
Teaism (D,T)
Tel Aviv Cafe (T)

Tempo (T)
Terramar (T)
That's Amore (T)
Tokyo Lighthouse (T)
Tony & Joe's (T)
Trumpets (T)
219 (T)
Veneziano (T)
Vidalia (T)
Warehouse B&G (T)
Xing Kuba (T)
Yin Yang (T)
Yosaku (T)
Zed's (T)
(*Call to check range and charges, if any)

Dessert & Ice Cream

(Besides Baskin-Robbins, Ben & Jerry's, Bob's Famous, Haagen-Dazs, Jeffrey's, Steve's, Thomas Sweet, Swensen's, I Can't Believe It's Yogurt)
Bice
Cheesecake Factory
Dean & DeLuca
Firehook Bakery
Galileo
Kinkead's
Morrison-Clark Inn
Obelisk
Patisserie Cafe Didier
Roof Terrace
Rupperts
1789
Thyme Square
Tivoli
Tragara
Vidalia

Dining Alone

(Other than hotels)
Bistro Bistro
Blue & Gold
B. Smith's
Carlyle Grand Cafe
C.F. Folks
Clyde's
Coco Loco
Gabriel
Georgetown Seafood
Il Radicchio
I Matti
Jaleo
Kinkead's
Kramerbooks
La Madeleine
Luigino
Makoto
Melrose
Morrison-Clark Inn
Music City Roadhouse
Notte Luna

Perry's
Pesce
Pizzeria Paradiso
Raku
Red Sage
701
Sushi-Ko
Tachibana
Vivace Enoteca
Vox Populi

Family Style
Arucola
Evans Farm Inn
Music City Roadhouse
That's Amore

Fireplaces
Bilbo Baggins
Bleu Rock Inn
Chadwick's
Chart House
Dixie Grill
Elysium
Evans Farm Inn
Falls Landing
4 & 20 Blackbirds
Gangplank
Geranio
Inn/Little Wash.
Jefferson
La Chaumiere
La Ferme
La Madeleine
La Mirabelle
L'Auberge Chez Francois
L'Auberge Provencale
Le Gaulois
Mike's American
Monocle
Normandie Farms
Old Angler's Inn
Polly's Cafe
Potowmack Landing
R.C., The Grill
Red Sage
Ruth's Chris
Santa Fe East
Sea Catch
1789
219
Willow Grove Inn

Health/Spa Menus
(Most places cook to order to
meet any dietary request; call
in advance to check; almost
all health-food spots, Chinese,
Indian and other ethnics have
health-conscious meals, as
do the following)
Asia Nora
Bistro 2015
Cashion's Eat Place
Greenwood's

Melrose
Morrison-Clark Inn
Nora
Old Angler's Inn
Planet X
Seasons
Thyme Square
Trumpets
Vegetable Garden
Zed's

Historic Interest
(Year Opened)
1750 Alamo/VA*
1753 L'Auberge Provencale
1778 Willow Grove Inn
1792 Gadsby's Tavern*
1800 Bilbo Baggins
1800 Santa Fe East
1817 Pappa-Razzi*
1856 Music City Roadhouse
1860 Old Angler's Inn
1860 1789*
1865 Morrison-Clark Inn*
1867 Martin's Tavern*
1887 Tabard Inn
1890 Rupperts
1904 Two Quail
1910 4 & 20 Blackbirds
1931 Normandie Farms
(* Building)

Hotel Dining
ANA Hotel
  Bistro
Capitol Hilton
  Fran O'Brien's
Carlton
  Lespinasse
Channel Inn
  Pier 7
Doubletree Park Terr. Hotel
  Chardonnay
Embassy Row Hotel
  Bistro 2015
Four Seasons Hotel
  Seasons
Georgetown Inn
  Cafe Riviera
Hay-Adams Hotel
  Lafayette
Henley Park Hotel
  Coeur de Lion
Holiday Inn/Governor's House
  Herb's
Hyatt/Reston
  Market St. B&G
Inn at Little Washington
  Inn/Little Wash.
ITT Luxury Collection
  Jockey Club
Jefferson Hotel
  Jefferson
Latham Hotel
  Citronelle
L'Auberge Provencale
  L'Auberge Provencale

"In" Places

Bistro Francais
Cafe Atlantico
Cafe Milano
Cashion's Eat Place
Coco Loco
Felix
Germaine's
Jaleo
Rupperts
Sesto Sento
Sushi-Ko
Tel Aviv Cafe

Jacket Required

Baron's
Jockey Club
Lafayette
L'Auberge Chez Francois
L'Auberge Provencale
River Club
1789
Tragara

Late Late – After 12:30

(All hours are AM)
Ambrosia (2)
Au Pied du Cochon (24 hrs.)
Bistro Francais (4)
Bob & Edith's Diner (24 hrs.)
Burrito Brothers (3)*
Cafe Rose (1)
Carlyle Grand Cafe (1)
Chadwick's (1)

Coppi's (1)
Dynasty (1:30)
El Gavilan (1)
El Tamarindo (3)*
Full Kee (3)
Full Key (2)
Good Fortune (2)
Hard Rock Cafe (1)
Hunan Number One (1:45)
Il Ritrovo (2)
Kramerbooks (24 hrs.)
Meskerem (2)
Metro 29 (3)
Mo Bay Cafe (5:30)
Mr. Yung's (1)
Music City Roadhouse (1)
Old Ebbitt Grill (1)
Planet Hollywood (1)
Planet X (1)
Polly's Cafe (2)
Raku (2)
Sequoia (1)
Seven Seas (1)
Sunny Garden (1)
Tel Aviv Cafe (1)
T.G.I. Friday's (1)
Thai Flavor (3)
Vienna's Grille (1)
Virginia Bev. Co. (1)
(* Check locations and nights)

Meet for a Drink

America
Artie's
Bistro Bistro
Blue & Gold
Bombay Bistro
B. Smith's
Cafe Atlantico
Cafe Milano
Capitol City Brewing
Carlyle Grand Cafe
"Ciao baby" Cucina
Clyde's
Coco Loco
Fedora Cafe
Gabriel
Georgia Brown's
Gulf Coast Kitchen
Jaleo
Jockey Club
Kinkead's
Lespinasse
Montgomery's Grille
Old Ebbitt Grill
Oval Room
701
Trumpets
West End Cafe

Noteworthy Newcomers

Bangkok St. Grill
Bertolini's

Bistro Lepic
Bombay Bistro
Bombay Curry Co.
Bugaloo Creek
Cafe Atlantico
Cafe Deluxe
Cafe Mileto
Cafe Riviera
Calasia
Cashion's Eat Place
Cintra
Fatt Daddy's
Felix
Fran O'Brien's
Galaxy
Goldoni
Greenwood
Grillfish
Il Ritrovo
Jin-ga
Lespinasse
Luna Grill
Malik
Mediterranee
Memphis BBQ
Oodles Noodles
Ozio
Raku
Red River Grill
Ristoranti Capri
Shelly's Woodroast
Silverado
Stage Door
Sushi Chalet
Teaism
Tel Aviv Cafe
T.H.A.I.
Thyme Square
Uptown Cafe
Virginia Bev. Co.
Vivace Enoteca
Yin Yang

Offbeat
Au Pied du Cochon
Bistro Francais
Bob & Edith's Diner
C.F. Folks
Cowboy Cafe
Florida Ave. Grill
Hibiscus Cafe
Trumpets

Outdoor Dining
(G = Garden; P = Patio;
R = Rooftop; S = Sidewalk;
T = Terrace; W = Waterside)
Aangan (P)
Aegean Taverna (P)
America (S)*
Argentine Grill (S)
Aroma (P)
Arucola (P)
Athenian Plaka (P)
Bacchus (P)*

BeDuCi (S)
Belmont Kitchen (P)
Bertolini's (S)*
Bice (P)
Bistro (G)
Bistro Bistro (P,S)*
Bistro 2015 (P)
Bleu Rock Inn (T)
Blue Point Grill (P)
Bombay Bistro (P)*
Bombay Club (P)
Bua (P)
Busara (G)
Cactus Cantina (S)
Cafe Berlin (P)
Cafe Bethesda (P)
Cafe Deluxe (P)
Cafe Milano (P)
Cafe Mileto (P)
Cafe New Delhi (P)
Cafe Parisien (S)
Cafe Taj (P)
Capitol City Brewing (T)*
Carlyle Grand Cafe (P)
Cashion's Eat Place (S)
C.F. Folks (P)
Chadwick's (P)*
Chardonnay (G)
Chart House (P)
Chesapeake Seafood (P)
Clyde's (P,W)*
Coco Loco (P)
Cottonwood Cafe (P)
Crystal Thai (T)
Dean & DeLuca (P)*
Donatello (T)
Duangrat's (P)
Duca Di Milano (T)
Evans Farm Inn (G)
Faccia Luna (P)*
Falls Landing (P)
Fatt Daddy's (P)
Fern St. Bistro (P)
Fleetwood's (P)
Flint Hill Public Hse. (T)
Gabriel (T)
Gadsby's Tavern (P)
Galileo (G)
Gangplank (P)
Gerard's Place (S)
Grill from Ipanema (T)
Guapo's (P)*
Gulf Coast Kitchen (R,T)
Havana Cafe (S)
Herb's (P)
Hibiscus Cafe (P)
Hisago (P)
Hogate's (P)
Il Ritrovo (S)
Inn at Glen Echo (P)
Inn/Little Wash. (G)
Kabul Caravan (T)
Kinkead's (P)
Kramerbooks (S)

Outstanding Views

Parking

(L = Parking Lot;
V = Valet Parking;
CP = Validated Parking;
$ = Discount Parking;
* = Suburban locations;
** = Check locations)

R.C., The Restaurant (L,V)
Red Hot & Blue (L)
Red River Grill (L)
Red Tomato Cafe (L,V)
Renato (L)
Rio Grande Cafe (L)*
Ristorante Capri (V)
River Club (V)
Rockland's (L)
Roof Terrace (L)
Royal Dragon (L)
R.T.'s Seafood (L)
Rupperts (L)
Ruth's Chris (V)
Sabang (L)
Saigon Gourmet (L)
Sam & Harry's (V)
Sam Woo (L)
Santa Fe East (CP,$)
Savory (L)
Sea Catch (L,CP)
Seasons (L,V)
Sesto Sento (V)
701 (V)
Seven Seas (L)
1789 (L)
Shamshiry (L)
Shelly's Woodroast (L)
Silverado (L)
Silver Diner (L)
Slade's (L)
Southside 815 (L)
Spices (L)
Star of Siam (L)
Stella's (L)
St. Elmos Cafe (V)
Stone Manor (L)
Sushi Chalet (L)
Sushi-Ko (V)
Taberna del Alabardero (L,V)
Tachibana (L)
Taipei/Tokyo Cafe (L)
Tako Grill (L)
Tara Thai (L)
Taste of Saigon (L)
Taste Of Thai (L)
Tel Aviv Cafe (V)
Tempo (L)
Terramar (V)
T.G.I. Friday's (L,CP)**
T.H.A.I. (L)
Thai Flavor (L,CP)
Thai Kingdom (L)
That's Amore (L)
Tia Queta (V)
Tiberio (V)
Tivoli (L)
Tokyo Lighthouse (L)
Tomato Tango (L)
Tragara (V)
Tsukiji (L)
Tuscana West (L,V)
U-topia (L)
Vegetable Garden (L)

Veneziano (L)
Vidalia (V)
Vienna's Grille (L)
Vietnam (L)
Village Bistro (L)
Vox Populi (L)
Warehouse B&G (L,CP)
West End Cafe (CP)
Willard Room (L,V)
Willow Grove Inn (L)
Woo Lae Oak (L)
Wurzburg-Haus (L)
Xing Kuba (V)
Yin Yang (L,$)

Parties & Private Rooms

(Any nightclub or restaurant charges less at off hours; * indicates private rooms available; best of many, excluding hotels)

Alamo*
America*
Bacchus*
Bice*
Bilbo Baggins*
Bistro Le Monde*
Bleu Rock Inn*
Blue & Gold*
B. Smith's*
Busara*
Cactus Cantina*
Cafe Milano*
Capital Grille*
Carlyle Grand Cafe
Chadwick's*
Chardonnay*
"Ciao baby" Cucina*
Cintra*
Cities*
Citronelle*
Clyde's*
Coco Loco*
Coeur de Lion*
Cowboy Cafe*
Da Domenico*
Dar Es Salaam*
Duangrat's*
Duca Di Milano*
Ecco Cafe*
Enriqueta's*
Evans Farm Inn*
Falls Landing*
Felix*
Fleetwood's*
Fortune*
4 & 20 Blackbirds*
Gabriel*
Galaxy*
Galileo*
Gangplank
Generous George's*
Geranio*
Germaine's

141

People-Watching

Power Scenes

Taberna del Alabardero
Vidalia
Willard Room

Pre-Theater Menus

(Call to check prices,
days and times;
best of many)
Artie's
Bistro Bistro
Bistro Francais
Bombay Club
Citronelle
Clyde's
Donatello
Felix
Lafayette
Luigino
Maison Blanche
Old Ebbitt Grill
701
1789
St. Elmos Cafe
Tivoli
Uptown Cafe
West End Cafe

Post-Theater Menus

(Call to check prices,
days and times)
Bistro Bistro
Bistro Francais
Clyde's
Donatello
Gangplank
Mrs. Simpson's
Old Ebbitt Grill
Paolo's
Uptown Cafe
Virginia Bev. Co.

Prix Fixe Menus

(Call to check prices,
days and times)
American Grill
Asia Nora
Au Pied du Cochon
Bacchus
Bei Tempi
Bistro Francais
Bistro 2015
Bombay Club
Cafe Berlin
Cafe Bethesda
Citronelle
Coco Loco
Cottonwood Cafe
Crisfield
Crystal Thai
Dar Es Salaam
Donatello
Duca Di Milano
Elysium
Felix
Grill from Ipanema

Hibiscus Cafe
India Kitchen
Jin-ga
La Panetteria
L'Auberge Chez Francois
L'Auberge Provencale
Le Caprice
Le Rivage
Maison Blanche
Makoto
Market St. B&G
Melrose
Obelisk
Oval Room
Pho Cali
Red River Grill
Ruppers
701
1789
St. Elmos Cafe
Stone Manor
Taberna del Alabardero
Tivoli
Trattu
Uptown Cafe
West End Cafe
Willard Room
Willow Grove Inn
Yosaku

Pubs

Blue & Gold
Chadwick's
Clyde's
Houston's
Inn at Glen Echo
J. Paul's
King Street Blues
Martin's Tavern
Nathan's
Old Ebbitt Grill
Polly's Cafe
R.T.'s
Southside 815
Union St. Public Hse.

Quiet Conversation

Bombay Club
Chardonnay
Coeur de Lion
Elysium
Jefferson
Lafayette
Le Caprice
Melrose
Morrison-Clark Inn
Obelisk
R.C., The Grill
R.C., The Restaurant
Seasons
1789
Tivoli
Vincenzo
Willard Room

Raw Bars
Chart House
Clyde's
Georgetown Seafood
J. Paul's
Kinkead's
Legal Sea Food
Old Ebbitt Grill
Perry's
Sea Catch

Reservations Essential
Calasia
Citronelle
Coeur de Lion
Duca Di Milano
Geranio
Gerard's Place
Germaine's
La Bergerie
La Bonne Auberge
Lafayette
L'Auberge Chez Francois
L'Auberge Provencale
Le Lion D'Or
Maison Blanche
Morton's of Chicago
Nora
Palm, The
Prime Rib
Provence
R.C., The Restaurant
Rupperts
Saigonnais
Stone Manor
Taberna del Alabardero

Reservations Not Accepted
(Check for larger parties)
Alamo/VA
Ambrosia
Arucola
Austin Grill
Bangkok St. Grill
Bertucci's
Bilbo Baggins
Bombay Bistro
Bugaboo Creek
Cafe Deluxe
Calif. Pizza Kit.
Calvert Grille
Capitol City Brewing
Chadwick's
Clyde's
Crisfield
Dixie Grill
Enriqueta's
Fatt Daddy's
4 & 20 Blackbirds
Generous George's
Georgetown Seafood
Hard Rock Cafe
Hard Times Cafe
Havana Cafe

Hibiscus Cafe
King Street Blues
Luna Grill
Mare E Monti
Mick's
Outback Steakhouse
Ozio
Paolo's
Pasha Cafe
Perry's
Persepolis
Pesce
Pho Cali
Radio Free Italy
R.T.'s Seafood
Saigon Gourmet
Shamshiry
South Austin Grill
Southside 815
Tel Aviv Cafe
T.G.I. Friday's
That's Amore
Tomato Tango
Tony Cheng's Mongolian
Uptown Cafe
Wurzburg-Haus

Romantic Spots
Bleu Rock Inn
Bombay Club
Chardonnay
Citronelle
Coeur de Lion
Inn/Little Wash.
L'Auberge Chez Francois
Le Refuge
Provence
River Club
Saigonnais
Stone Manor
Two Quail

Saturday Dining
(B = brunch; L = lunch; best of many)
Aangan (L)
Aaranthi (L)
Aditi (L)
Alamo/VA (L)
Ambrosia (L)
America (B,L)
American Grill (L)
Aroma (B)
Artie's (L)
Arucola (L)
Atami (L)
Athenian Plaka (L)
Au Pied du Cochon (L)
Austin Grill (B)
Balalayka (L)
Bangkok Vientiane (L)
Bei Tempi (L)
Belmont Kitchen (B)
Benjarong (L)
Bertolini's (L)

Taste Of Thai (L)
Taverna Cretekou (L)
Teaism (L)
Tel Aviv Cafe (L)
T.G.I. Friday's (B,L)
T.H.A.I. (L)
Thai Flavor (L)
Thai Garden (L)
Thai Kingdom (L)
Thyme Square (L)
Tia Queta (L)
Tiberio (L)
Tokyo Lighthouse (L)
Tomato Tango (L)
Tony & Joe's (L)
Tony Cheng's Mongolian (L)
Trattoria da Franco (L)
Tsukiji (L)
219 (L)
Union St. Public Hse. (L)
Uptown Cafe (L)
U-topia (B)
Vegetable Garden (L)
Veneziano (L)
Vienna's Grille (L)
Vietnam (L)
Virginia Bev. Co. (B,L)
Warehouse B&G (L)
West End Cafe (L)
Woo Lae Oak (L)
Wurzburg-Haus (L)
Xing Kuba (B)
Zed's (L)

Sunday Dining

(B = brunch; L = lunch;
D = dinner; plus all hotels
and most Asians)
Aangan (B,D)
Aaranthi (D)
Aditi (L,D)
Aegean Taverna (L,D)
Alamo/VA (L,D)
America (B,L,D)
Andalucia (D)
Appetizer Plus (D)
Argentine Grill (B,D)
Aroma (B,D)
Artie's (B,D)
Atami (D)
Athenian Plaka (B,L,D)
Au Pied du Cochon (L,D)
Austin Grill (B,D)
Bacchus (D)
Balalayka (L,D)
Bangkok St. Grill (L,D)
Bangkok Vientiane (L,D)
Bei Tempi (D)
Belmont Kitchen (B,D)
Bertucci's (L,D)
Bice (D)
Bilbo Baggins (B,L,D)
Bistro Bistro (B,D)
Bistro Francais (B,L,D)

Bistrot Lepic (L,D)
Bleu Rock Inn (B,D)
Blue & Gold (B,D)
Blue Point Grill (B,L,D)
Bombay Bistro (B,D)
Bombay Club (B,D)
Bombay Dining (L,D)
Bombay Palace (L,D)
Bua (L,D)
Bugaboo Creek (L,D)
Burma (D)
Burrito Brothers (D)
Burro (L,D)
Busara (L,D)
Cactus Cantina (B,L,D)
Cafe Asia (L,D)
Cafe Berlin (D)
Cafe Bethesda (D)
Cafe Dalat (L,D)
Cafe Deluxe (B,L,D)
Cafe Milano (L,D)
Cafe Mileto (D)
Cafe Mozart (B,L,D)
Cafe New Delhi (B,D)
Café Oggi (D)
Cafe Riviera (L,D)
Cafe Saigon (L,D)
Cafe Taj (L,D)
Cajun Bangkok (D)
Calasia (D)
Capitol City Brewing (L,D)
Capital Grille (D)
Carlyle Grand Cafe (B,L,D)
Cashion's Eat Place (B,D)
Cedar Knoll Inn (L,D)
Chadwick's (L,D)
Chart House (B,D)
Cheesecake Factory (L,D)
Chesapeake Seafood (L,D)
Chicken Place (L,D)
Cintra (B,D)
Cities (D)
Clyde's (B,D)
Connaught Place (B,L,D)
Cottonwood Cafe (D)
Cowboy Cafe (B,L,D)
Crisfield (L,D)
Dar Es Salaam (D)
Dean & DeLuca (B,L,D)
Delhi Dhaba (B,L,D)
Dixie Grill (D)
Donatello (D)
Duangrat's (L,D)
Dusit (L,D)
Easby's Buffet (B,L,D)
El Caribe (L,D)
El Gavilan (L,D)
El Pollo Rico (L,D)
El Tamarindo (L,D)
Enriqueta's (D)
Evans Farm Inn (B,L,D)
Fatt Daddy's (B,L,D)
Fedora Cafe (B,D)
Felix (B,D)

Singles Scenes

Sleepers

(Good to excellent food, but
little known)

149

Pho 75
Pizzeria Paradiso
Planet X
Queen Bee
Rabieng
Raku
Red Tomato Cafe
Renato
Rockland's
Roof Terrace
R.T.'s Seafood
Sabang
Saigon Inn
Sala Thai
Sam Woo
Shamshiry
Stone Manor
Sushi Chalet
Tachibana
Taipei/Tokyo Cafe
Tako Grill
Tara Thai
Teaism
Terramar
T.G.I. Friday's
Thyme Square
Tia Queta
Tomato Tango
Tragara
Tsukiji
Vegetable Garden

Teas
(See also *Coffeehouses* &
Dessert Indexes)
Aquarelle
Cafe Promenade
Coeur de Lion
Elysium
Jefferson
Lafayette
Lespinasse
Melrose
Morrison-Clark Inn
Patisserie Cafe Didier
R.C., The Grill
R.C., The Restaurant
Seasons
Teaism
Willard Room

Transporting Experiences
Bombay Club
Dar Es Salaam
Duangrat's
Gadsby's Tavern
Hisago
Inn/Little Wash.
Jin-ga
Morrison-Clark Inn
Sarinah Satay House
Shelly's Woodroast
Taverna Cretekou

Visitors on Expense Accounts
Aquarelle
Asia Nora
Bice
Bombay Club
Capital Grille
Citronelle
Elysium
Galileo
Gerard's Place
Hisago
Inn/Little Wash.
Jefferson
Jockey Club
Kinkead's
La Bergerie
Lafayette
L'Auberge Chez Francois
Le Lion D'Or
Lespinasse
Makoto
Melrose
Morrison-Clarke Inn
Morton's of Chicago
New Heights
Nora
Obelisk
Old Angler's Inn
Oval Room
Palm, The
Prime Rib
Primi Piatti
Provence
R.C., The Grill
R.C., The Restaurant
Red Sage
Rupperts
Ruth's Chris
Sam & Harry's
Seasons
701
1789
Stone Manor
Taberna del Alabardero
Vidalia
Willard Room

Wheelchair Access
(Check for bathroom access;
almost all hotels and chains
plus the following best bets)
America
Andalucia
Artie's
Athenian Plaka
Bacchus*
B & C
Bei Tempi
Bilbo Baggins
Bistro Bistro
Bleu Rock Inn
Blue & Gold
Blue Point Grill

151

Peking Gourmet Inn
Pesce
Phillips Flagship
Phillips Seafood
Pier 7
Planet Hollywood
Planet X
Prime Rib
Primi Piatti
Provence
Radio Free Italy
Raku
Red Hot & Blue
Red Sage
Red Tomato Cafe
Renato
Roof Terrace
R.T.'s
R.T.'s Seafood
Rupperts
Ruth's Chris
Sam & Harry's
Sea Catch
701
Shelly's Woodroast
Silver Diner
South Austin Grill
Southside 815
Stella's
St. Elmos Cafe
Stone Manor
Straits of Malaya
Sunny Garden
Sushi Chalet
Taberna del Alabardero
Tako Grill
Taste of Saigon
Taste Of Thai
Taverna Cretekou
Tel Aviv Cafe
Terramar
T.H.A.I.
Thai Flavor
Thai Kingdom
That's Amore
Thyme Square
Tia Queta
Tiberio
Tivoli
Tokyo Lighthouse
Tomato Tango
Tom Tom
Tony & Joe's
Tragara
Trattoria da Franco
Trumpets
Tuscana West
Vegetable Garden
Vidalia
Village Bistro
Virginia Bev. Co.
Vox Populi
Warehouse B&G

West End Cafe
Woo Lae Oak
(*Check location)

Wine & Beer Only

Ambrosia
Atami
Balalayka
Bombay Bistro
Cafe Asia
Cafe Bethesda
Cafe Parisien
Cafe Rose
Cafe Saigon
Calasia
Calif. Pizza Kit.
Cambodian
China Canteen
Crisfield
Dean & DeLuca
Delhi Dhaba
Eat First
Eye St. Cafe
Fern St. Bistro
Generous George's
Hard Times Cafe
Hinode
Il Pizzico
India Kitchen
Kabob Bazaar
Krupin's
La Madeleine
Lebanese Taverna
Le Bon Cafe
Ledo Pizza
Le Paradis
Lite 'n' Fair
Maharaja
Mama Wok
Parkway Deli
Queen Bee
Raku
Red River Grill
Red Tomato Cafe
Renato
Silver Diner
Sushi Chalet
Thyme Square
Tokyo Lighthouse
Vegetable Garden
Vietnam
Vivace Enoteca
Vox Populi

Winning Wine Lists

Bilbo Baggins
Cafe Mozart
Chardonnay
Citronelle
Gabriel
Galileo
Gerard's Place
Inn/Little Wash.
I Ricchi
La Colline

L'Auberge Chez Francois
Le Caprice
Le Lion D'Or
Melrose
Morton's of Chicago
Obelisk
Prime Rib
Provence
Sam & Harry's
Seasons
1789
Stone Manor
Taberna del Alabardero
Trumpets
Willard Room

Worth a Trip

MARYLAND
Potomac
   Old Angler's Inn
Middletown
   Stone Manor
VIRGINIA
Flint Hill
   4 & 20 Blackbirds
   Flint Hill Public Hse.
Great Falls
   L'Auberge Chez Francois
Washington
   Bleu Rock Inn
   Inn/Little Wash.
White Post
   L'Auberge Provencale

Young Children

(Besides the normal fast-food places; * indicates children's menu available)
Austin Grill*

Cactus Cantina*
Cafe Deluxe*
Cafe Promenade*
Calvert Grille*
Chart House*
Clyde's*
Crisfield*
Evans Farm Inn*
Faccia Luna
Generous George's*
Guapo's
Hard Rock Cafe
Hard Times Cafe*
La Lomita*
Lebanese Taverna
Ledo Pizza*
Mare E Monti*
Mick's*
Music City Roadhouse
Normandie Farms*
Old Glory BBQ
Outback Steakhouse*
Paolo's*
Phillips Flagship*
Phillips Seafood*
Radio Free Italy*
Red Hot & Blue*
Rio Grande Cafe
Roof Terrace
Shelly's Woodroast*
Silver Diner*
South Austin Grill*
T.G.I. Friday's*
Tokyo Lighthouse*

Baltimore

Baltimore's Favorites

Finksburg

83

Loch Raven Reservoir

Bel Air

Miles
0   10

Brooklandville

Owings Mills

Towson

95

Pikesville

Baltimore

695

70

Ellicott City

MARYLAND

95

Detail Below

Francis Scott Key Bridge

Indicates home to one or more of the top 40 most popular restaurants

Chesapeake Bay

Washington D.C.

Annapolis

50

St. Michaels

Jeannier's

Polo Grill

Hampden

Cafe Hon

Johns Hopkins University

Donna's at the BMA

Baltimore Museum of Art

Harford Rd.

Charles St.

Calvert St.

Greenmount Ave.

Central Baltimore

83

North Ave.

Spike & Charlie's

Broadway

Champagne Tony's/ Owl Bar

Prime Rib

Chase St.

Brass Elephant

The Helmand

Henninger's Tavern

Donna's

Bombay Grill

40

Tio Pepe

Franklin St.

Ikaros

Mulberry St.

Marconi's

Da Mimmo

Haussner's

Pratt St.

Ruth's Chris

Sabatino's

Eastern Ave.

Paolo's

Pierpoint

Hampton's

Inner Harbor

Little Italy

Fells Pt.

Wild Mushroom

Joy America

Boccaccio

Savannah

Canton

Miles
0   1

156

Baltimore's Favorite Restaurants

Each of our reviewers has been asked to name his or her five favorite restaurants. The 40 spots most frequently named, in order of their popularity, are:

1. Tio Pepe	21. Chart House
2. Prime Rib	22. Wild Mushroom
3. Polo Grill	23. Peerce's Plantation
4. Linwood's	24. Champagne Tony's
5. Hampton's	25. Puffin's
6. Brass Elephant	26. Cafe Troia
7. Helmand	27. Due
8. Haussner's	28. Henninger's Tavern
9. Spike & Charlie's	29. Northwoods/A
10. Ruth's Chris	30. Donna's
11. Joy America	31. California Pizza Kitchen
12. Boccaccio	32. Red Hot & Blue
13. Outback Steakhouse	33. Ikaros
14. Pierpoint	34. Paolo's
15. Tersiguel's	35. Da Mimmo
16. Donna's at BMA	36. Cafe Hon
17. Marconi's	37. Bombay Grill
18. Savannah	38. Inn at Perry Cabin/A
19. Rudys' 2900	39. Stone Mill Bakery & Ecole
20. Jeannier's	40. Sabatino's

It's obvious that most of the restaurants on the above list are among the most expensive, but Baltimore diners love a bargain. Were popularity calibrated to price, we suspect that a number of other restaurants would join the above ranks. Thus, we have listed over 140 "Best Buys" on pages 162 and 163.

A = Annapolis/Eastern Shore.

Top Ratings*

Top 40 Food Ranking

28	Prime Rib		Treaty of Paris/A
27	Inn at Perry Cabin/A		Due
	Rudys' 2900		Purple Orchid
	Hampton's		Antrim 1844
	Northwoods/A		Matsuri
	Linwood's		Spike & Charlie's
26	Tio Pepe		Szechuan Best
	Polo Grill		Ruth's Chris
	Pierpoint		Da Mimmo
25	Tersiguel's		Banjara
	Joy America	23	Wild Mushroom
	Boccaccio		Stone Mill Bakery/Ecole
	Helmand		Jeannier's
	Henninger's Tavern		Cafe Troia
	Savannah		Thai Landing
24	La Piccola Roma/A		Narrows/A
	Brass Elephant		Puffin's
	Josef's Country Inn		Thai
	Orchard Market/Cafe		Bombay Grill
	Peter's Inn		King's Contrivance

Top Spots by Cuisine

Top Additions
- Black Olive
- Brewer's Art
- Le Bistro Midi
- M. Gettier's Orchard Inn
- San Sushi

Top American
- 24 Treaty of Paris/A
- 23 Narrows/A
- Marconi's
- 21 Harryman House
- 20 Reynold's Tavern/A

Top American (New)
- 27 Hampton's
- Linwood's
- 26 Polo Grill
- Pierpoint
- 25 Joy America

Top Breakfast†
- 23 Cafe Normandie/A
- 21 Morning Edition
- Donna's
- 18 Cafe Hon
- Woman's Ind. Exchange

Top Brunch
- 27 Hampton's
- 26 Polo Grill
- Pierpoint
- 25 Savannah
- 24 Treaty of Paris/A

Top Business Lunch
- 27 Linwood's
- 26 Polo Grill
- 25 Savannah
- 24 La Piccola Roma/A
- Brass Elephant

---

* Excluding restaurants with low voting.

† Other than hotels.

A = Annapolis/Eastern Shore.

Top Chinese
24 Szechuan Best
23 Jumbo Seafood
22 Hunan Manor
Joey Chiu's
Szechuan

Top Continental
27 Inn at Perry Cabin/A
Rudys' 2900
Northwoods/A
26 Tio Pepe
24 Brass Elephant

Top Crab Houses
21 Cantler's Riverside/A
Crab Claw/A
Harris' Crab Hse./A
20 Gunning's (Dorsey Rd.)
Jimmy's Famous Seafood

Top Family Dining
21 Cantler's Riverside/A
20 Red Hot & Blue
19 Tomato Palace
18 Loco Hombre
Friendly Farms

Top French
25 Tersiguel's
23 Jeannier's
Cafe Normandie/A
21 Martick's
— Le Bistro Midi

Top Hotel Dining
27 Hampton's/
Harbor Court Hotel
26 Polo Grill/
Inn at the Colonnade
24 Treaty of Paris/
Maryland Inn/A
21 Windows/
Renaissance Harborpl.
19 Berry & Elliot's/
Hyatt Regency

Top Indian
24 Banjara
23 Bombay Grill
22 Mughal Garden
20 Akbar

Top Italian
25 Boccaccio
24 La Piccolo Roma/A
Due
Da Mimmo
23 Cafe Troia

Top Japanese
24 Matsuri
21 Jpn.
Kawasaki
Nichi Bei Kai
Sushi-Ya

Top Seafood
26 Pierpoint
23 Narrows/A
O'Leary's/A
22 Faidley's
21 Hoang's

Top Steakhouses
28 Prime Rib
24 Ruth's Chris
22 McCafferty's
20 Outback Steakhouse
— Lewnes' Steakhouse/A

Top Vegetarian
23 Wild Mushroom
Puffin's
Thai
21 Margaret's Cafe
18 One World Cafe

Top Worth a Trip
28 208 Talbot/
St. Michaels, MD
27 Inn at Perry Cabin/
St. Michaels, MD
Imperial Hotel/
Chestertown, MD
24 Antrim 1844/
Taneytown, MD
— Tilghman Island Inn/
Tilghman Island, MD

Top Yearlings/Rated
25 Joy America
Savannah
23 Wild Mushroom
21 Cafe Zen
19 Nacho Mama's

Top Yearlings/Unrated
OPA
Ruby Lounge
Saigon
Sotto Sopra
Holy Frijole

Top 40 Decor Ranking

29 Inn at Perry Cabin/A
Hampton's
28 Antrim 1884
27 Brass Elephant
26 Linwood's
25 Prime Rib
Champagne Tony's
Polo Grill
Pavilion at the Walters
Joy America
Treaty of Paris/A
Haussner's
24 King's Contrivance
Windows
Tersiguel's
Peerce's Plantation
Boccaccio
23 Narrows/A
Savannah
Rudys' 2900

Carrol's Creek Cafe/A
Tio Pepe
22 Donna's at BMA
Harry Browne's/A
Joey Chiu's
Due
Henninger's Tavern
Northwoods/A
Berry & Elliot's
Helmand
21 Middleton Tavern/A
Chart House
One World Cafe
Ruth's Chris
Windows on the Bay
Rusty Scupper
Cafe Normandie
La Piccola Roma/A
McCafferty's
Margaret's Cafe

Top Outdoor

Bay Cafe
Cantler's Riverside/A
Carrol's Creek Cafe/A
Chart House
Cheesecake Factory
Donna's at BMA
J. Leonard's Waterside
Lista's

McGarvey's/A
Middleton Tavern/A
Paolo's
Peerce's Plantation
River Watch
Rusty Scupper
Sanders' Corner
Victor's

Top Rooms

Antrim 1884
Brass Elephant
Champagne Tony's
Donna's at BMA
Hampton's
Haussner's

Inn at Perry Cabin/A
Linwood's
Lista's
Pavilion at the Walters
Polo Grill
Prime Rib

Top Views

Bamboo House (Harborplace)
Bay Cafe
Berry & Elliot's
Carrol's Creek Cafe/A
Chart House
Hampton's
Inn at Perry Cabin/A

J. Leonard's Waterside
Joy America
Michael Rork's/A
Peerce's Plantation
Piccolo's
Victor's
Windows

Top 40 Service Ranking

28	Hampton's		Treaty of Paris/A
27	Prime Rib	22	Helmand
26	Inn at Perry Cabin/A		Orchard Market/Cafe
25	Rudys' 2900		King's Contrivance
	Linwood's		Due
	Northwoods/A		La Piccola Roma/A
	Antrim 1844		Haussner's
24	Polo Grill		Hunan Manor
	Tersiguel's		Ruth's Chris
	Boccaccio		Sushi-Ya
23	Marconi's	21	Pierpoint
	Brass Elephant		Thai Landing
	Banjara		Jeannier's
	Peerce's Plantation		Joey Chiu's
	Savannah		Narrows/A
	Tio Pepe		Windows
	Joy America		Henninger's Tavern
	Harry Browne's/A		Bombay Grill
	Woman's Ind. Exchange		Orchid
	Da Mimmo		Joseph's Country Inn

Best Buys

Top 100 Bangs For The Buck

This list reflects the best dining values in our *Survey*. It is produced by dividing the cost of a meal into the combined ratings for food, decor and service.

1. One World Cafe
2. Woman's Ind. Exchange
3. Jimmy's (Fells Pt.)
4. GlasZ Cafe
5. Ethel & Ramone's
6. Desert Cafe
7. Adrian's Book Cafe
8. Canopy
9. Chick & Ruth's Delly/A
10. Margaret's Cafe
11. Peter's Inn
12. Attman's Delicatessen
13. Faidley's
14. Cafe Hon
15. Baugher's
16. PaperMoon Diner
17. Nacho Mama's
18. Duda's
19. Double T Diner
20. Banjara
21. Cafe Zen
22. Bel-Loc Diner
23. Field's Pharmacy
24. New Towne Diner
25. Morning Edition Cafe
26. Al Pacino Cafe
27. Louie's Bookstore Cafe
28. Orchard Market/Cafe
29. Ledo Pizza
30. Helmand
31. Szechuan Best
32. Hunan Manor
33. Bombay Grill
34. Cafe Manet
35. Bill Bateman's Bistro
36. Silver Diner
37. Gunning's (Dorsey Rd.)
38. Sanders' Corner
39. Ban Thai
40. Mughal Garden
41. Szechuan
42. Cafe Tattoo
43. Thai
44. Tomato Palace
45. Jumbo Seafood
46. Donna's
47. Akbar
48. Crease
49. Bangkok Place
50. Thai Landing
51. Peerce's Gourmet
52. Alonso's
53. Friendly Farms
54. Wharf Rat
55. Bandaloops
56. Wild Mushroom
57. Matsuri
58. Kisling's
59. Amicci's
60. Tully's
61. Metropol
62. John Steven
63. Bertucci's
64. Adam's Rib/A
65. Red Hot & Blue
66. Ikaros
67. Pavilion at the Walters
68. Hull St. Blues
69. Bare Bones
70. Hunt Valley Szechuan
71. Sushi-Ya
72. Bamboo House
73. Ralphie's Diner
74. Regi's
75. California Pizza Kitchen
76. Strapazza
77. Charred Rib
78. Joey Chiu's
79. Mama Lucia
80. Donna's at BMA
81. Ransome's Harbor Hill Cafe
82. Bertha's
83. No Way Jose
84. Great Amer. Melting Pot
85. Loco Hombre
86. Jerry D's Saloon
87. Mick's
88. Burke's
89. Haussner's
90. Corner Stable
91. McGarvey's/A
92. Acropolis
93. Griffin's/A
94. T.G.I. Friday's
95. Jilly's
96. Swallow at the Hollow
97. Puffin's
98. River Watch
99. Henninger's Tavern
100. Kawasaki

A = Annapolis/Eastern Shore.

Additional Good Values
(A bit more expensive, but worth every penny)

Anne Arundel Seafood

Angler/A

Blue Moon Cafe

Bowman

Braznell's

Broadway Grill

Cafe Bretton

Cafe du Vin/A

Cafe Sophie/A

Ciao Bella

Claddagh Pub

El Salvador

El Taquito Mexicano

Fazzini's

Frazier's

Giolitti/A

Grand Palace

Hampton Tea Room

Hoang's

Holly's/A

Jenning's

J. Patrick's

Kelly's

Kelsey's

Luigi Petti

Mai Thai

Mamie's

Matthew's

Nam Kang

New No Da Ji

OPA

Perring Place

Purim Oak

Rams Head/A

Riordan's/A

Rotisseria

Saigon

Saigon Palace/A

Samos

San Sushi

Schultz's Crab House

Silver Spring Mining Co.

Sunset

Surfin' Bull

Sushi Cafe

Sushi Chalet

Tenosix

Thai Orient

Vito's Cafe

Wing Wah

Winterling's

Yianni Cafe

Ze Mean Bean

Zorba's

Baltimore, Annapolis and the Eastern Shore 1998 Additions

```
      R  = Recommendation Ratings
  ††††  = Don't Miss
   †††  = Very Good Bet
    ††  = Worth a Try, Not a Detour
     †  = Interesting, But No Big Deal
```

Baltimore

R | **C**

Anne Arundel Seafood 🆂   † | I
230 Mountain Rd. (Solley Rd.), Pasadena, 410-255-3344
Line up with local fishermen and boaters, biz lunchers, bikers
and families with kids at this seafooder-cum-retail store
where some of the freshest fish in the Pasadena area is
steamed, fried or served raw bar style; there's an on-the-
way-to-the-beach feel about this informal, self-service place.

Bahama Mamas 🆂   † | M
*601 Wise Ave. (bet. North Point Rd. & Merritt Blvd.),
Dundalk, 410-477-1261*
While there is steak on the menu, many local seafood
mavens believe that this cobbled together Dundalk
roadhouse steams (or fries) some of the plumpest, meatiest
mountains of crabs found anywhere – so stick to the
crustaceans at this quintessentially 'Balmer' waterside spot.

Black Olive 🆂   ††† | M
814 S. Bond St. (Shakespeare St.), 410-276-7141
Classic Greek simplicity shines through in the charcoal-
grilled fish and lamb and beautiful displays of fresh
fruit at this appealing brick, wood and brilliant blue Fells
Point renovation; but the good news – that it does most
things well – is also the bad news since it's small, serves
dinner only (Tuesday–Sunday) and just about everyone
wants to get in.

Blue Moon Cafe 🆂   †† | I
*1621 Aliceanna St. (bet. Bond St. & Broadway),
410-522-3940*
A countrified Fells Point cottage that celebrates American
classics like cinnamon rolls, biscuits, fluffy eggs and
creamed chipped beef with an all-day breakfast menu,
which is supplemented by sandwiches and irresistible
desserts; it's run by surrogate moms who serve breakfast
and lunch weekdays (7 AM–3 PM) and, on weekends, provide
sustenance all night long (11 PM–3 PM).

Blue Nile S   † | ⌐|
2101 N. Charles St. (bet. 20th & 21st Sts.), 410-783-0982
This Uptown Ethiopian is for adventuresome diners – not
only is the cuisine exotic, but the place itself is hard to find
(entrance on 21st Street) and nighttime caution is advised;
nevertheless, if you're primed for scooping up highly spiced
stews with pieces of spongy flatbread while sitting on
traditional low stools, it's an inexpensive trip to another world.

Brewer's Art ◑S   †† | M
1106 N. Charles St. (Biddle & Chase Sts.), 410-547-6925
Artfully designed for quiet lunches, afternoon chitchats
and trendy evenings, the faded grandeur of this revamped
Edwardian townhouse hardly resembles a '90s brewpub
cliché; however, it does have the requisite house-made
brews, roster of international beers and wines, au courant
American menu and raucous late-night scene.

Broadway Theater & Grill S (CLOSED)   † | M
*509-513 S. Broadway (bet. Eastern Ave. & Fleet Sts.),
410-675-4022*
Curtains-up on an entertaining concept – first-run movies
paired with casual American food and drink; savvy local
talents transformed North Fells Point's historic Polish
Castle into a state of the art cinema-cum-cafe, which
debuted last summer ('97); the lofty, multilevel mix of old
oak, brass and crystal chandeliers with lightweight prices
also wins applause.

Capitol City Brewing Co. S   † | M
Harborplace, 301 Light St. Pavilion (Pratt St.), 410-539-7468
See Washington, DC, Alphabetical Directory.

Captain Larry's ◑S   † | ⌐|
601 E. Fort Ave. (Jackson St.), 410-727-4799
Some of the city's choicest crab cakes and crab soup
anchor the menu at this American relic, hard by Fort
McHenry, whose faded nautical memorabilia and colorful
barflies evoke Baltimore's seafaring past; enjoy it for what
it is – an old-fashioned workingman's bar with decent
grub and a clubby clientele.

Casa Mia's S   †† | M
40 York Rd. (Burke Ave.), Towson, 410-321-8707
Don't fix what ain't broke is the advice Towsonites would
give the new owner of this popular, upscale Italian-Greek;
it's conveniently located in an office building, yet manages to
look like it's not, and its salad, pasta and seafood menu suits
its regulars just fine.

Chameleon ⑤   ⊞ M

32 W. Main St. (bet. John St. & Railroad Ave.), Westminster, 410-751-2422
A delightful rest stop while antiquing in Westminster, this tastefully remodeled American offers a tempting array of meal or snack possibilities (phyllo pizza with vegetables, salads and fanciful entrees), along with cappuccino and house-baked sweets; the living room–like comfort of its bar seems made for wintertime soup or brandy sipping and there's a patio for warm summer nights.

City Cafe ⑤   ⊞ M

1001 Cathedral St. (Eager St.), 410-539-4252
This chic, multilevel Downtown bean bar recently boosted its salad, sandwich and dessert selections with the addition of a Contemporary American dining room; a clientele as urban as its setting keeps it busy from breakfast on.

Corks ⑤   ⊞ E

1026 S. Charles St. (bet. Cross & Hamburg Sts.), 410-752-3810
A cruvinet, some yellow paint and new owners have transformed this Federal Hill townhouse (formerly daniel's) into one of the newest outlets for Contemporary American food and wine pairings; if you're no oenophile, not to worry – the menu uncorks some of the mystery by listing a vinous suggestion for each entree.

Costas Inn ⑤   † M

4100 N. Point Blvd. (New Battle Grove Rd.), Dundalk, 410-477-1975
In this vast, no-nonsense, fluorescent-lit seafooder, local Dundalk steel workers and savvy Old Baltimoreans enjoy high-quality, reasonably priced steamed crabs, a full surf-'n'-turf menu and an unbuttoned atmosphere; its huge barroom is a bustling beer, crab and karaoke (only in Baltimore) venue.

Crew's Quarters ⑤   † M

534 Riverside Dr. (Margaret Ave.), Essex, 410-780-3928
Although the bar at this rambling Essex spot is a local preserve, the arrival of a Spanish chef gives its dining room broader appeal; its steamed crab, steak and seafood menu is being supplemented by such rich Spanish-Continental dishes as oysters stuffed with crabmeat, while sangria is supplanting beer as the beverage of choice here.

El Salvador ⑤⊄   † ⌐

207 S. Broadway (bet. Gough & Pratt Sts.), 410-522-3270
Happy Latino families devouring big bowls of seafood soup suggest that this unembellished BYO Fells Point storefront is dishing up the real thing; go for authentic versions of familiar south-of-the-border dishes or, better still, try one of the unusual preparations of shrimp or steak.

Globe Brewing Co. ⑤   † | M
1321 Key Hwy. (Webster St.), 410-347-7964
This cavernous brewery, with its pool and picnic tables and
limited Inner Harbor view, doesn't offer much decor, and
though steamers and sandwiches are served, they're not the
main event; it's the crowds that count, but it can get too loud.

Hacienda ⑤   † | I
4840 Belair Rd. (Woodlea Ave.), 410-488-9447
Colorful Mexican decorations add a fiesta feeling to this
simple Belair Road stop, while the 16 oz. margaritas ease
patrons into a party mood; the Tex-Mex standards are cheap
and filling and the staff is swell.

Hamilton's ⑤   ††† | E
Admiral Fell Inn, 888 S. Broadway (Thames St.), 410-522-2195
Lynn Patrick and his crew from the now-defunct Milton
Inn relocated to this attractive Fells Point nest (formerly
Savannah), offering a New American menu and some of
the Inn's vaunted wines; it should be interesting to see
how they fare in salty Fells Point.

Hard Rock Cafe ◑⑤   † | M
Power Plant, 601 E. Pratt St. (Gay St.), 410-347-7625
See Washington, DC, Alphabetical Directory.

Helen's Garden ⑤   †† | I
2908 O'Donnell St. (on O'Donnell Sq.), 410-276-2233
This engaging Canton coffee bar bloomed into a real
restaurant with a Continental seafood-and-veggie-oriented
menu and an ambitious brunch; upstairs is the cozy dining
room, downstairs the bean bar serves up soup for lunch.

J. Leonard's Waterside ⑤   † | E
*HarborView Marina, 500 HarborView Dr. (Key Hwy.),
410-752-6896*
The let's-get-away-from-it-all harbor view is the perennial
attraction of this marina restaurant, which has suffered from
several ownership and chef changes; now J. Leonard
Schleider brings a catering background and a seafood-
heavy Contemporary Continental menu to this destination;
the big question is: can this crew keep it afloat?

Johansson's Dining House ⑤   † | M
4 W. Main St. (Railroad Ave.), Westminster, 410-876-0101
This tarted-up Westminster British pub offers a wide-ranging
Continental menu and many beers in dark, atmospheric digs.

La Tavola ⑤   † | M
248 Albemarle St. (Fawn St.), 410-685-1859
In the heart of Little Italy, this large, touristy dining room
features the sort of Italian dishes you might find in Rome,
such as freshly made noodles and charcoal-broiled fish.

Le Bistro Midi S   ††† | M

(nka Weber's on Boston)
845 S. Montford Ave. (Boston St.), 410-276-0800
It's easy to get comfortable at this elegant yet unpretentious
Canton restoration whose post-*Survey* switch to authentic
French bistro food is tempered by the availability of burgers
and such in the cheery bar and a Southern-style brunch with
biscuits and beignets; understandably, its wide-ranging
menu attracts nongourmets and serious wine buffs alike.

Little Havana S   † | M

1325 Key Hwy. (Webster St.), 410-837-9903
Designer grunge is the backdrop for Inner Harbor mingling,
pool-playing and sunset watching on this mega-cantina's
concrete deck; its Cuban connection is exploited in the
menu (pollo à la Castro) and wall art – not to mention its
cigar-toting clientele.

Mamie's S   †† | I

911 W. 36th St. (bet. Elm & Roland Sts.), 410-366-2996
A big deal on 'The Avenue' (a booming Hampden enclave
of new restaurants and bric-a-brac shops), this sandwich
and seafood house makes imaginative use of an old movie
theater; credit the owner's grandmother for its name and
art, while its kitchen contributes updated versions of East
Baltimore classics like crab cakes and, at dinner, more
ambitious fish dishes.

Mango Grove S   †† | I

Dobbin Ctr., 6365B Dobbin Rd. (Rte. 175), 410-884-3426
In Columbia, this young South Indian is admired for its
command of that culture's complex vegetarian cuisine
and for its traditional hospitality; the spicy fare appeals to
meat eaters and abstainers alike.

Matthew's Pizza   † | I

3131 Eastern Ave. (bet. East & Linwood Sts.), 410-276-8755
For more than 50 years, this friendly, family-run storefront
has been serving Baltimore-style pizzas (with thick, bread-
like crusts) that are tasty, wholesome and unbelievably
cheap; the most expensive pie with everything on it costs
$8.95 and many go for under $5.

M. Gettier's Orchard Inn S   ††† | E

*1528 E. Joppa Rd. (½ mi. west of Loch Raven Blvd.),
East Towson, 410-823-0384*
In Spring 1997, Michael Gettier, Baltimore's top French
toque, closed his Fells Point namesake establishment and
took over Hersh's Orchard Inn in East Towson; here, he
strives to please both his and Hersh's clientele with an
imaginative, modern Continental menu, spacious, svelte
premises and suburban parking.

Morton's of Chicago   ††† | E
Sheraton Inner Harbor Hotel, 300 S. Charles St. (Conway St.),
410-547-8255
See Washington, DC, Alphabetical Directory.

Neon Moon S   ⫟ | M
2522 Fait Ave. (bet. Rose St. & Luzerne Ave.), 410-327-6366
A buzzing transformation of a seedy Canton saloon into an
American-Eclectic and spiffy watering spot where one can
sip designer martinis and microbrews beneath an eye-
catching trompe l'oeil sky; in the art deco back dining
room, Uptown twosomes look pleased with the likes of
Creole seafood wraps.

Oregon Grill S   ††† | E
1201 Shawan Rd. (Beaver Dam Rd.), Hunt Valley, 410-771-0505
The Hunt Club crowd trumpets the return of chef Mark
Henry (ex Milton Inn, Chester River Inn) to an exciting
new Hunt Valley venue – an opulently restored country
store with a sophisticated steakhouse menu; here, one
dines on aged beef, rack of lamb and wild game amid
exposed stone and mahogany splendor or on fieldstone
patios by the proverbial old mill stream.

Reister's Desire S   †† | M
1100 Westminster Pike/Rte.140 (1 mi. west of Rte. 795),
Reisterstown, 410-517-1100
New owners transformed the woody Old Forest Inn into a
decorative New American eatery while retaining its cozy,
place-to-take-Mom appeal; a trendy menu and comfy
ambiance should satisfy the desires of antique hunters
and local dress-up diners.

Rotisseria S⇗   †† | I
219 S. Broadway (bet. Gough & Pratt Sts.), 410-563-3712
The mouthwatering aromas of this Fells Point carryout's
spicy grilled chickens will have you nibbling your order
before you walk out the door; the concept's as direct as
its name suggests – a charcoal pit, a couple of tables and
a short menu of Peruvian and vegetarian sides, as well as
a terrific banana shake.

San Sushi S   †† | M
9832 York Rd. (Padonia Rd.), 410-453-0140
San Sushi Too
10 W. Pennsylvania Ave. (York Rd.), 410-825-0907
Softly lit and pristine, these young BYO Timonium and
Towson Japanese serve fresh, authentic and fairly priced
sushi, along with other specialties; everything, from their
warm greeting to their willingness to prepare creative
alternatives to raw fish, quickly turns customers into friends.

171

Santi's S (CLOSED)   † | M
3321 Eastern Blvd. (Bengies Rd.), Middle River, 410-391-2725
From the Edwardian splendor of the Belvedere to this brash
Italian watering hole, Paul Santi (ex Champagne Tony's)
reels in an appreciative crew; powerboaters mix with picky
palates who are willing to travel almost anywhere for
his linguine with clam sauce, shrimp bisque and strange
sounding specials that actually work.

Showalter's ⊄   † | ⌐
3360 Chestnut Ave. (34th St.), 410-889-0968
An ageless Hampden saloon where Baltimoreans kick back
with old chums; it's notable for the kitchen's fresh, Old
Maryland–style seafood and the call-you-Hon help – the
latter helps make amends when the former has a bad night.

Silk Road S   † | ⌐
336 N. Charles St. (bet. Saratoga & Mulberry Sts.), 410-385-9013
The ancient highway from Asia to the Near East brought
oriental influences to Afghan cuisine and inspired this Mt.
Vernon spot; simple touches like native rugs create a subtly
exotic setting for savory dishes based on familiar foodstuffs
(lamb, rice, vegetables) and there's a bargain buffet lunch.

Sushi Chalet   †† | M
105 N. Charles St. (bet. Fayette & Charles Sts.), 410-625-7811
See Washington, DC, Alphabetical Directory.

Turf Inn ◐S   † | M
*2306 York Rd. (bet. Timonium & Padonia Rds.), Timonium,
410-252-2911*
This Italian-American warhorse's steady gait, comfortable
mien and low prices keep its Timonium parking lot full; it's an
odds-on favorite for good crab cakes, steak or seafood;
the addition of a new deck for outdoor dining may be its
biggest innovation in years.

Viccino Bistro S   †† | M
1317 N. Charles St. (Mt. Royal & Preston Sts.), 410-347-0349
Modish best describes this Mt. Vernon bistro, with its yellow
sponged walls, pale wood and imaginative takes on Italian
and Contemporary American dishes, and its business, art
and pre-theater clientele; those looking for the basics stick
with its older brother, a pizza carryout and deli next door.

Winterling's S⊄   † | ⌐
3200-2 Foster Ave. (East Ave.), 410-675-7700
Cheap eats and cold beer have been the story at this
Highlandtown mainstay for some 65 years; recently reborn
as a neighborhood watering hole/diner (yep, mashed
potatoes and hot roast beef), it's been discovered by Canton
types willing to walk a few blocks for good low-priced grub.

Yianni Cafe ●S (CLOSED) ⊞ I
4701 Eastern Ave. (Oldham St.), 410-522-3076
Welcoming at 3 AM, when you're craving sweets, a late-
night snack or simply a place to shmooze with your date,
this gleaming pastry shop and cafe is equally appealing
by day; upstairs, there's an attractive dining room serving
Greek specialties and light fare, and an intimate outdoor
deck overlooking the area's Hellenic restaurants and clubs.

Annapolis and Eastern Shore

Bistro S ⊞ E
*403 S. Talbot St. (bet. Mulberry & Chester Sts.), St. Michaels,
410-745-9111*
This painstakingly remodeled St. Michaels townhouse looks
enough like a French bistro to be mistaken for the real
thing; its good looks and contemporary Continental food
draw sophisticated residents and 'second night' traffic
from the tony local inns; in season, its wisteria-covered
deck is a delightful spot for a special event.

Joss Cafe & Sushi Bar S ⊞ M
195 Main St. (Church Circle & Conduit St.), 410-263-4688
Sushi aficionados give this tiny Annapolis Japanese the
nod for its fresh fish and interesting combinations, as well
as its full menu of noodles and cooked entrees; best of all,
with just a handful of seats at the sushi counter and a
smattering of tables, solo dining isn't so self-conscious.

Tilghman Island Inn S ⊞ E
21384 Coopertown Rd., Tilghman Island, 410-886-2141
A get-away-from-it-all seafooder on Chesapeake Bay
whose dockside dining room gets national recognition for
its contemporary treatment of local produce, broad wine
list and sumptuous desserts; enjoying a relaxed meal
while watching the wildfowl in the marshes may seduce
you into spending the night.

Alphabetical Directory of Baltimore, Annapolis and the Eastern Shore Restaurants

Baltimore

Acropolis §
4714-8 Eastern Ave. (Oldham St.), 410-675-3384
☑ At this Highlandtown icon, cheapskates with "big appetites" overdose on "more than enough" Greek food in "ethnically comforting" surroundings (translation: "zero decor"); picky eaters fuss about "old mutton" dressed as lamb.

Adrian's Book Cafe §
714 S. Broadway (bet. Lancaster & Aliceanna Sts.), 410-732-1048
■ A "cozy" bookstore cafe in "manic" Fells Point with "creative" snacks, "killer" sweets and enough books to "scare off the skateboarders"; be prepared to "linger."

Akbar §
823 N. Charles St. (bet. Madison & Read Sts.), 410-539-0944
3541 Brenbrook Dr. (Liberty Rd.), Randallstown, 410-655-1600
Columbia Marketplace, 9400 Snowden River Pkwy.,
Columbia, 410-381-3600
■ This "cave-like Indian classic" in Mt. Vernon and its suburban sibs "continue to win converts to Indian food" despite stiff competition from Mughal Garden and Bombay Grill; go for the "reliable" standards, "attentive" help and "bargain" lunch buffets.

Alonso's ◐§
415 W. Coldspring Ln. (bet. Charles St. & Roland Ave.),
410-235-3433
■ Attractive "barflies, huge [1 lb.] hamburgers" and great pizza lure "aging preppies" to this "funky, unkempt" Roland Park "nabe cave"; it's a perennial winner of Baltimore's "best burger" and best "late-night-drunk" place awards – a "barbaric tribute to red meat."

Al Pacino Cafe §
811 S. Broadway (bet. Lancaster & Thomas Sts.), 410-327-0005
Belvedere Sq., 542 E. Belvedere Ave. (York Rd.), 410-323-7060
900 Cathedral St. (Read St.), 410-962-8859
Lake Forest Village, 6084 Falls Rd. (Lake Ave.), 410-377-3132
Festival at Woodholme, 1809 Reisterstown Rd. (Hooks Ln.),
Pikesville, 410-653-6868
513 Baltimore Pike (Rte. 24), Bel Air, 410-638-8057
■ Pizza "diversity" with a Middle Eastern spin at these no-frills (BYOB) brick ovens is "something to be desired" – their "cramped", "carry-out" atmosphere is not; don't miss the sharm el-sheq pizza with a side of baba ghanoush.

Amicci's S   21 | 15 | 18 | $17
231 S. High St. (bet. Stiles & Fawn Sts.), 410-528-1096
2903 O'Donnell St. (S. Linwood Ave.), 410-675-3207
■ "Fun" and "trendy", these "rock 'n' roll Italians" feature
red-sauced pasta and seafood cooked by youthful "singing
chefs"; the scene is "cramped but cute" in Little Italy,
Canton is "more roomy" and "relaxed."

Anastasia S (CLOSED)   ▽ 13 | 14 | 13 | $22
2501 Boston St. (O'Donnell St.), 410-276-7000
■ You can avoid parking problems by sailing to this Canton
anchorage, but dock only for the noisy bar scene and
"nice view"; according to most reviewers, as a seafooder,
it's an impostor.

Angelina's S   19 | 12 | 17 | $19
7135 Harford Rd. (Rosalie Ave.), 410-444-5545
■ A "softball"-sized "mound of fantastic lump crabmeat"
puts this dimly lit, North Baltimore Irish-Italian bar on the
gastronomic map; but don't expect its legendary crab
cake to come with much in the way of atmosphere – or
to come cheap.

ANTRIM 1844 S   24 | 28 | 25 | $52
Antrim 1844 Country Inn, 30 Trevanion Rd. (Rte. 140),
Taneytown, 410-756-6812
■ An excursion to this "magnificent restoration" an hour
northwest of Baltimore evokes the "age of innocence" with
an "imaginative", multicourse Contemporary American
meal and "breathtaking" setting; equally breathtaking
pricing, however, makes some reviewers decide to "go
there once, not twice."

A-1 Crab Haven ●S   17 | 11 | 17 | $19
1600 Old Eastern Ave. (Back River Neck Rd.),
410-687-6000
■ "Affluent suburbanites" frequent this "comfortable",
aptly named Essex seafooder for top-quality steamed
crabs (in season), spicy steamed shrimp and Greek salad;
you get what you pay for seafood-wise and vice versa.

Attman's Delicatessen S   20 | 8 | 14 | $10
1019 E. Lombard St. (bet. Lloyd & Watson Sts.),
410-563-2666
■ The "last of the real Lombard Street delis" is still hanging
in there, although the premises and neighborhood have
been "declining rapidly" for years; mavens report that
the "kibitzing has slipped, but the corned beef hasn't";
N.B. delivery advised.

Backfin S   10 | 6 | 11 | $16
1116 Reisterstown Rd. (Sudbrook Ln.), Pikesville, 410-484-7344
☑ Though capable of producing a "respectable" crab cake ("at times"), this "Pikesville crab dive" draws some of this *Survey*'s worst reports: "no decor or ambiance", "an anomaly in seafood city" and "two-for-one coupons have kept it afloat."

Bamboo House S   20 | 19 | 19 | $19
Harborplace, Pratt St. Pavilion, 410-625-1191 **(CLOSED)**
Yorktowne Plaza Shopping Ctr., 26 Cranbrook St. (York Rd.), Cockeysville, 410-666-9550
■ "Tasteful" settings, "unthreatening" Chinese food and Joey Chiu's "professional" oversight keep these "pretty" old-timers evergreen; add a sensational view (Harborplace) for the "best lunch in the Inner Harbor."

Bandaloops   19 | 19 | 18 | $17
1024 S. Charles St. (Cross St.), 410-727-1355
■ A "cheerful" SoBo "hangout for serious drinkers" and "interesting characters", this American with "artsy but not bizarre help" also draws "a big weekday lunch crowd" since you can hear yourself talk; its "relaxed" manners and eclectic bar food let you drop by in "dress up" or sweats.

Bangkok Place S **(CLOSED)**   21 | 13 | 19 | $16
5230 York Rd. (bet. Cold Spring Ln. & Woodbourne Ave.), 410-433-0040
■ "Daily special curries" are the "best bet" at this "well-established" North Baltimore Thai; it's "not fancy, but a good deal" and fine for a family fill-up or "dinner before the Senator" movie theater.

Banjara S   24 | 19 | 23 | $16
1017 S. Charles St. (bet. Hamburg & Cross Sts.), 410-962-1554
■ The "wonderful aroma of spices" fills this Federal Hill storefront leading Baltimore's burgeoning Indian parade; the "flavorful", fairly priced dishes taste even better because you're treated like their "most important customer."

Ban Thai   19 | 12 | 18 | $14
340 N. Charles St. (Mulberry St.), 410-727-7971
■ This "predictable" Thai won't win any creative-cooking prizes; what it offers instead is a pleasant place to talk business Downtown and "good, plentiful food for the price"; but don't be fooled by its quiet demeanor — regulars swear that some of the dishes pack such a punch "you won't know what hit you."

Bare Bones ⑤ | 18 | 15 | 17 | $16 |
617 S. Frederick Ave. (½ mi. north of Shady Grove Rd.),
Gaithersburg, 301-948-4344
St. John's Plaza, 9150 Baltimore Nat'l. Pike (1 light west of
Rte. 29), Ellicott City, 410-461-0770
■ Bones are "all that's left" when rib lovers leave these
"decently priced", family-style rib joints – and, happily,
their recent remodeling doesn't interfere with the pleasure
of messy eating; some go mostly for "Monday night football"
and the "rowdy fun" that results when the "beer selection is
better than the food."

Baugher's ⑤ | 16 | 11 | 17 | $11 |
289 W. Main St. Ext. (Rtes. 31 & 32), Westminster, 410-848-7413
■ A "relic" of "deep-fried" "country cooking" at "1940s
prices" sums up this "folksy" Carroll County farmstand/
restaurant with "crusty" servers and "farm-fresh fruit", pies
and ice cream; be prepared to contend with "busloads" of
pilgrims seeking "comfort."

Bay Cafe ●⑤ | 14 | 17 | 13 | $17 |
2809 Boston St. (Linwood Ave.), 410-522-3377
☑ "Wonderful sunsets", "awesome" shrimp salad
sandwiches and doing the "meat market mambo" are the
attractions at Canton's "beach" on the bay; but even if
you're not an "Xer or boater", this dockside watering hole
is worthwhile for a drink; and the "wonderful" view can
help you forget the "indifferent" seafood, "absurdly slow
service" and crowds.

Bel-Loc Diner ●⑤ | 11 | 12 | 14 | $9 |
Corner of Loch Raven Blvd. & Joppa Rd., East Towson,
410-668-2525
☑ "A real diner from the old days" with "burnt eggs", "gravy
from a barrel" and "cheap, bland food"; it's staffed by
"female commandos" (as "bitter as the coffee") and
frequented, sooner or later, by virtually everyone who
passes this NE Baltimore County intersection; it's also
"one of the last places left to play jukebox warfare" or go
for "3 AM munchies."

Berry & Elliot's ⑤ | 19 | 22 | 19 | $24 |
(nka Pisces)
Hyatt Regency Baltimore, 300 Light St. (bet. Pratt &
Conway Sts.), 410-605-2835
☑ With the harbor lights twinkling, the "magnificent view" is
the main draw at this Contemporary American hotel dining
perch popular with "out-of-towners and conventioneers";
although some say the steak and seafood are "surprisingly
good" accompaniments, the consensus is "go for the
view, not the food."

179

Bertha's S
18 | 17 | 16 | $17

734 S. Broadway (Lancaster St.), 410-327-5795

■ It's "hard to resist" this "salty" old Fells Point "institution" with its "great waterfront atmosphere", legendary "seafood, jazz and beer", "serious afternoon tea" (by reservation) and indefinable "charm"; despite the "hype" and quips ("gone flabby, losing its mussels"), "everyone goes and loves it."

Bertucci's S
17 | 16 | 16 | $15

8130 Corporate Pl. (bet. Honeygo & Perry Hall Blvds.), White Marsh, 410-931-0900
Owings Mills Mall, Owings Mills Blvd. at I-795, Owings Mills, 410-356-5515
1818 York Rd. (Ridgely Rd.), Timonium, 410-561-7000
12 Bel Air S. Pkwy. (Rte. 24), Bel Air, 410-569-4600
Snowden Sq., 9081 Snowden River Pkwy. (Robert Fulton Dr.), Columbia, 410-312-4800
See Washington, DC, Alphabetical Directory.

Bill Bateman's Bistro ●S
18 | 15 | 15 | $14

7800 York Rd. (Cross Campus Dr.), Towson, 410-296-2737

■ Bill Bateman's "gut-stuffing" formula – "no flash, little cash, heart-stopping ribs" and "wings to fly for" plus "beer in a frosted mug" – makes this a "family dining" place as well as a "college hangout and sports bar"; credit the "open spaces", "perky" help and irresistible appeal of "great unhealthy" eats; "if the food doesn't kill you, the noise will."

Birds of a Feather
– | – | – | E

1712 Aliceanna St. (Broadway), 410-675-8466

Serious eaters flock to this quaint, "intimate" Fells Point bar for wild fowl, game and Contemporary American fare "cooked to perfection" in a "very professional" kitchen headed by the owners' son, a Michael Rork (ex Hampton's) disciple; write-ins tap it for "future greatness", not to mention the "best scotch selection in Baltimore."

Bo Brooks Crab House S
20 | 9 | 16 | $20

5415 Belair Rd. (Frankford Ave.), 410-488-8144

■ All a "crab house needs are mallets, brown paper", cold beer and a reliable source of "big, sweet" crabs in and out of season – which explains why this "windowless factory" in NE Baltimore rates as one of the best; its "other seafood" is "acceptable", but the "uniquely Baltimore" steamed crab "experience" should not be missed.

BOCCACCIO S
25 | 24 | 24 | $34

925 Eastern Ave. (bet. Exeter & High Sts.), 410-234-1322

■ Baltimore's top Italian strikes many as the kind of "classy", "aloof", "can't loosen your belt at the table" restaurant they'd find in New York; nevertheless, the "great pastas and seafood", "outstanding veal chop", well-chosen Northern Italian wines and "romantic" setting compel admiration: a "real treasure in Little Italy."

Bombay Grill S   23 | 19 | 21 | $18
2 E. Madison St. (N. Charles St.), 410-837-2973

Cafe Bombay S
114 E. Lombard St. (Calvert St.), 410-539-2233

Bombay Peacock Grill S
*10005 Old Columbia Pike (Eden Brook Dr.), Columbia,
410-381-7111*

■ Even if Indian food is normally "not your thing", the "excellent", subtly spiced food, refined surroundings and "rajah" treatment at one of Baltimore's best Indians could sway you; aficionados "can't go wrong here" and biz lunchers swear by the "quiet-for-conversation" settings and "truly delicious" bargain buffets; check out the dosas (S. Indian crêpes) and mod take on the classics at the newish Downtown cafe.

Bowman S   18 | 16 | 18 | $19
9306 Harford Rd. (bet. Joppa Rd. & Putty Hill), 410-665-8600

✓ This Carney hub scores a bull's-eye with regulars for its crab cakes and light fare served on the "dark" bar side; "a charming older crowd" goes for the "step above church supper" fare dished out in the "small" dining room; it's one of those "likable", "good value for your dollar" places that every neighborhood needs; N.B. try the comedy club downstairs after dinner.

BRASS ELEPHANT S   24 | 27 | 23 | $33
924 N. Charles St. (bet. Read & Eager Sts.), 410-547-8480

■ A "ritzy" backdrop for anything from a "stockbroker" dinner to a TV shoot, this Downtown Edwardian showplace's "lovely" Northern Italian and Mediterranean-Continental menu and service let you go "first class" without paying "ridiculous prices" – particularly if you take advantage of the $19.95 pre-theater deal or go for a light bite in the "fabulous marble bar" upstairs.

Brasserie S   ▽ 20 | 18 | 17 | $18
*Pomona Sq., 1700 Reisterstown Rd. (Naylors Ln.),
Pikesville, 410-484-0476*

✓ It's not clear why this Pikesville Northern Italian is often "empty"; it's "roomy, comfortable, quiet and easy to park" nearby – it even has "decent", "reasonably" priced food; perhaps it's the "unlikely location" in a shopping mall, plus the somewhat dispiriting atmosphere and only "fair service."

Braznell's Caribbean Kitchen S ▽ 19 | 15 | 16 | $17
1623 E. Baltimore St. (Broadway), 410-327-2445

✓ Alfred and Esme Braznell cook up a fiery Caribbean storm at their low-rent Butcher's Hill location just like they would back home in Trinidad – slowly and "superbly"; a "real survivor in a tough area", it's a "decent place to get your goat" or "hang out" and "eat in the bar."

Burke's Cafe ◖⑤　　　　13 | 11 | 14 | $13
36 Light St. (Lombard St.), 410-752-4189
◪ A "dark, sleazy" "dinosaur" lazing on prime Downtown
corner real estate; it's a "love it, hate it" deal with onion
rings "the size of inner tubes", "greasy" burgers, steak
and beer – "no fad foods or California bull" – and "good
comedy" upstairs, if not always good service.

Cacao Lane ⑤　　　　　18 | 18 | 17 | $20
8066 Main St. (Tiber Alley), Ellicott City, 410-461-1378
◪ Reeking of "Old Ellicott City charm", this rustic little eatery
"fits in well" with the historic surroundings; the "please-
everyone" Continental menu, weekend music and multilevel
outdoor deck please most, but there are those who grouse
about "inept service" and "wait in vain for the flavor of the
food to match that of the setting."

Caesar's Den ⑤　　　　21 | 16 | 21 | $26
223 S. High St. (Stiles St.), 410-547-0820
◼ This Southern Italian's food tastes "home cooked", it
treats customers "like family" and the "cute paintings" and
"close tables" give it a "cozy", "romantic" air; go for
"consistency", not nuova cucina – it's a Little Italy "classic."

Cafe Bretton　　　　　▽ 24 | 16 | 22 | $28
*849 Baltimore-Annapolis Blvd. (McKinsey Rd.), Severna
Park, 410-647-8222*
◼ In Europe, it's not unusual for a "small, family-owned"
restaurant to use produce from its "own garden" to add
fresh flavor to its countrified food; but in a "suburban
backwater" north of Annapolis it's noteworthy – so is this
French-Continental's "good value" and "attempts to please."

Cafe Hon ⑤　　　　　18 | 16 | 17 | $12
1002 W. 36th St. (bet. Roland Ave. & Falls Rd.), 410-243-1230
◼ "Working hard in its new ['95] space to be homey" and
not run short of either chicken salad or "folksy" help, this
old-time American supplies an "eclectic mix" of Hampden
blue collars and university types with "cheap", "normal"
food; it's rapidly become "everyone's favorite for meetings
and brunch" (not to mention breakfast and lunch), raising
concerns that it's becoming too popular.

Cafe Manet　　　　　　19 | 11 | 15 | $13
1020 S. Charles St. (Cross St.), 410-837-7006
◪ "Quirky" Continental carryout (with a handful of tables
and "extremely casual" service) near the Cross Street
Market comes in handy for "picnics at the harbor", an
"after-work wind down", below-$10 wines and take-home
dinners; some marvel that "warm-up food can taste so
good", others "don't agree."

Café Pangea S
_ _ _ I
4007 Falls Rd. (bet. 40 & 41st Sts.), 410-662-0500
An engaging mix of gingerbread architecture, cyberspace access, exotic coffees, interesting wines and sophisticated snacks draws cybernauts, oenophiles, caffeine heads, TV news teams (headquartered nearby) and the curious to this Hampden cafe and wine bar; check out your E-mail at one of the sleek computer booths or settle into the sofa for an old-fashioned chat.

Cafe Tattoo
15 10 15 $12
4825 Belair Rd. (Moravia Rd.), 410-325-7427
◪ A "smoky" bar with many beers, "loud bands", "good chili", "great ribs" and a "tattoo parlor" upstairs – this roadhouse also has "fantastic burritos and peanut butter pie" and what those who don't dig the "wit" or the "rough crowd" call an "unfriendly atmosphere"; nevertheless, it "fits well in B'more."

Cafe Troia
23 20 21 $28
28 W. Allegheny Ave. (Washington Ave.), Towson, 410-337-0133
◪ Since this Towson Italian became the "rage", admirers bemoan the expansion that sometimes "overwhelms" its "excellent" kitchen and "cordial" staff and prices it "not for every day"; still, most remain enthusiastic about the "sophisticated" food and ambiance that feels "like Italy."

Cafe Zen S
21 17 18 $14
438 E. Belvedere Ave. (York Rd.), 410-532-0022
◪ Senator moviegoers flock to this dressed-up Chinese serving good "traditional" fare enlivened by sushi and a couple of "unusual" dishes; it gets points for "trying to be fresh in an area that needs freshness" and for giving vegetarians interesting things to eat, but not for being "a little slow" at night.

Candle Light Inn S
18 20 20 $24
1835 Frederick Rd. (Rolling Rd.), 410-788-6076
◪ "The established Catonsville restaurant" for anniversaries and family occasions pairs a colonial setting with "chart-topping" chicken cordon bleu and chocolate mousse; the "pleasant" atmosphere and covered porch make it a "nice little getaway" for "conservative" diners – and we hear the new chef (early '96) is serving some "new food."

Canopy, The S
16 7 12 $8
5820 Johnnycake Rd. (Ingleside Ave.), 410-744-2188
Roberts Field Shopping Ctr., 721 Hanover Pike (North Woods Trail), Hampstead, 410-239-4089
(Continues)

Canopy, The (Cont.)

5 Vernon Ave., NW (Ritchie Hwy.), Glen Burnie, 410-768-1719
9319 Baltimore Nat'l Pike (Chatham Rd.), Ellicott City,
410-465-5718
607 E. Main St. (Chartley Dr.), Reisterstown, 410-526-4229
Peddlers Sq. Shopping Ctr., 2030 Liberty Rd. (Monroe Ave.),
Eldersburg, 410-549-2880
Festival, 8125-P Ritchie Hwy. (Jumpers Hole Rd.),
Pasadena, 410-647-7722
140 Village Shopping Ctr., Westminster, 410-848-7443

■ Known for "great roast beef sandwiches", messy ribs
and fresh-cut fries, these "quick pit stops" serve simple,
tasty "fast food" in spartan, self-service settings that are
impervious to kids; they're Bawlmer's home-grown answer
to BBQ, though a minority labels them the pits – period.

Captain Harvey's 🅂 | 17 | 13 | 17 | $23 |

11510 Reisterstown Rd. (Nicodemus Rd.), Reisterstown,
410-356-7550

▨ "Decor is not available" at this Reisterstown destination –
"seafood is all that counts" here; the steady clientele is
"never let down" by the "old-fashioned" menu (shellfish,
sandwiches, steak) and motherly ("sometimes surly")
waitresses, but if you're not a part of the local scene, it'll
seem "mediocre all the way around."

Champagne Tony's/Owl Bar 🅂 | 20 | 25 | 19 | $25 |
(nka Owl Bar)

The Belvedere, 1 E. Chase St. (N. Charles St.), 410-347-0888

▨ There is no more atmospheric spot for a drink, a
designer pizza or varied American fare than the Owl Bar,
a "wonderfully restored", legendary Baltimore "beer
hall"; and while the "elegant" John Eager Howard Room
(formerly Champagne Tony's) is now a private catering
facility (outdating the above ratings), revelers can find live
music and snacks at the rooftop club.

Chapps Kosher Oriental 🅂   ▽ | 14 | 12 | 14 | $16 |

Pomona Sq., 1700 Reisterstown Rd. (Naylors Ln.),
410-653-3198

■ It may be a bit difficult to imagine "good" Chinese food
cooked "with a Jewish flair", but this Pikesville kosher
Chinese does it; it also manages to produce convincing
versions of the real thing without shrimp, shellfish or pork.

Charred Rib 🅂 | 18 | 12 | 16 | $15 |

2010 York Rd. (Timonium Rd.), Timonium, 410-561-0735

■ "Forget the tacky decor" – one goes to this dark, smoky
Timonium bar for "falling off the bone", "melt in your mouth"
ribs, fries and fellowship; an occasional salad has been
sighted, but don't let that spoil your "high cholesterol" fun

Chart House S
| 19 | 21 | 19 | $28 |

Pier 4, 601 E. Pratt St. (Marketplace St.), 410-539-6616
See Washington, DC, Alphabetical Directory.

Cheesecake Factory
| 19 | 18 | 17 | $20 |

Harborplace, Pratt St. Pavilion (South St.), 410-234-3990
See Washington, DC, Alphabetical Directory.

Chiapparelli's S
| 19 | 16 | 19 | $21 |

237 S. High St. (Fawn St.), 410-837-0309
◪ This Little Italy Italian defines the genre with its "great", garlicky salad, "heavy" pastas and veal and "family-like" atmosphere; maybe it's "outdated", but it's a beacon for tourists and the faithful because it remains, comfortingly, the "same as always."

Ciao Bella S
▽ | 21 | 20 | 23 | $20 |

236 S. High St. (bet. Stiles & Fawn Sts.), 410-685-7733
◼ When family owners take "pride in their work" (as they do here), you can taste it in the pastas and "homemade" sauces and tell it by the "royal treatment" you get; although many seemingly similar "Little Italy restaurants are not worth their price", its clientele thinks this one is.

City Lights S
| 14 | 18 | 15 | $18 |

Harborplace, Light St. Pavilion, 2nd fl. (Pratt St.), 410-244-8811
◪ Panoramic city skyline and harbor views from its terrace keep this Harborplace stalwart "in business"; otherwise, the American food is "overpriced" and "ordinary" and it seems like the "staff is always new" – however, given the alternatives, it's "ok" for lunch.

CJ's
| 15 | 10 | 15 | $18 |

10117 Reisterstown Rd. (Painters Mill Rd.), Owings Mills, 410-363-6694
◪ When Owings Mills locals don't want to drive "for midweek crabs", they dock at this "cramped", "noisy", "smoky", "dark" seafood shack; the place offers plenty of finfare choices, but as most regulars will tell you, it's best to eat steamed crabs, crab soup or possibly pizza – and "nothing else."

Claddagh Pub
▽ | 21 | 16 | 21 | $17 |

Canton Sq., 2918 O'Donnell St. (Curley St.), 410-522-4220
◼ Youthful "Irish charm" fills this Emerald Isle–themed pub in Canton that offers neighborly vibes and "perfect for the '90s food"; virtually everything from the "upscale" bar grub and the "build your own burger" Saturday lunch special ($2.95) to the "great" black Angus steaks and "excellent" mashed potatoes (before 6 PM) gets the nod.

Clyde's
| 17 | 21 | 18 | $21 |

10221 Wincopin Circle, Columbia, 301-596-4050, (DC) 410-730-2829
See Washington, DC, Alphabetical Directory.

Corner Stable 🅂   19 │ 11 │ 15 │ $15 │
9942 York Rd. (Church Ln.), Cockeysville, 410-666-8722
■ *Cheers*-like Cockeysville BBQ satisfies meat cravings
with some of Baltimore County's "best" baby back ribs
and garlic-salted fries; but ribs aren't the only reason it's
packed – this "dark" bar and its "no-nonsense waitressing"
generate so much atmosphere, "you can't be sad in here";
N.B. other locations share the name, but they ain't the same.

Crack Pot 🅂   16 │ 11 │ 15 │ $18 │
Ravenwood Shopping Ctr., 8102 Loch Raven Blvd.
(Taylor Ave.), 410-828-1095
☑ TV ads haven't changed much about this dark, "smoky"
bar near Parkville; as always, it "desperately needs to
remodel" and serves "pretty good" seafood "for the price";
neighborhood "old-timers" treat it like their "retirement
village", while others come to "experience" crabs (in
season) and "quintessential", if "pedestrian", Baltimore.

Crease, The 🅂   16 │ 15 │ 16 │ $14 │
523 York Rd. (bet. Allegheny & Pennsylvania Aves.),
Towson, 410-823-0395
☑ Unless you play lacrosse, or follow it intently, you may not
understand this "preppy" Towson sports bar's goal, which
is to give postgrad jocks a place to drink beer, swap stories
and fill up on a "smorgasbord" of "khaki" (i.e. fried) bar food;
but it has a new dining room and it scores with "good
burgers and chicken" for a "fast dinner before the movies."

Crossroads of Cross Keys   – │ – │ – │ E │
Cross Keys Inn, 5100 Falls Rd. (Northern Pkwy. & Cold
Spring Ln.), 410-435-0101
Given the lack of restaurants in the Uptown area, the
reopening of this Contemporary American hotel dining room
is good news indeed; it's where Roland Park matrons lunch
and business deals are done in an atmosphere of quiet
civility; don't miss the serious Sunday brunch.

Dalesio's of Little Italy 🅂   20 │ 19 │ 20 │ $28 │
829 Eastern Ave. (Albemarle St.), 410-539-1965
☑ An "intimate" townhouse in Little Italy offering Northern
Italian–inspired pastas and seafood and its signature "spa
cuisine"; surveyors split on service and whether one finds
"Italy in Baltimore" or a plate of "yesteryear's Italiana fare."

Da Mimmo 🅂   24 │ 20 │ 23 │ $37 │
217 S. High St. (Stiles St.), 410-727-6876
☑ Does the "limo pickup from hotels", the "glitz", the
lobster-stuffed pasta or even the "veal chop of infamy"
justify the cost of a meal at this small, crowded Little Italy
restaurant?; that depends on one's pocketbook and appetite
for luxury ingredients – many think it "doesn't get any better"
than this; P.S. the cost escalates sharply if one succumbs
to the waiter's "polished sell" of the "expensive" specials.

daniel's ⑤ (CLOSED) | – | – | – | E |
(fka Tabrizi's)
1026 S. Charles St. (bet. Cross & Hamburg Sts.),
410-752-3810
Susan Daniel has reinvented her "innovative" South
Baltimore restaurant, Tabrizi's, to celebrate Chesapeake
cuisine and international seafood; this involved a major
gentrification of the atrium-lit dining room, filling the
courtyard with greenery and glittering lights, and installing a
new chef trained at the Culinary Institute of America; the
rest of the staff remains – as does her high-profile following.

Desert Cafe ⊘ | 20 | 17 | 19 | $12 |
1605-07 Sulgrave Ave. (Newbury St.), 410-367-5808
■ If ever there was a spot for a rainy afternoon or coffee
and sweets at night, it's this "romantic, four-table hideaway
in Mt. Washington"; by most accounts, the "whole earth"
Middle Eastern nibbles are "worth a try", the atmosphere
"relaxing" and the falafel a must – now "if only they'd take
the calories out of those wonderful desserts."

Di Pasquale's Cafe (CLOSED) | ∇ 17 | 15 | 16 | $10 |
8 W. Cross St. (bet. S. Charles & Hanover Sts.),
410-276-1005
■ It's little bigger than a food stall in the nearby Cross
Street Market, yet this sunny corner of Italy builds an
"excellent porketta sandwich" and other mouth-filling
subs; every day there's a homey hot special to nourish
all the briefcases who wish it weren't "only open for
Monday–Friday lunch."

Di Vivo's ⑤ | – | – | – | M |
(nka Della Notte)
801 Eastern Ave. (President St.), 410-837-5500
Notwithstanding its garish exterior, this block long
Little Italy addition pulls a lively mix of happy eaters
with its spacious setting highlighting wonderful city
skyline views, on-site parking, a giant pastry showroom,
wood-burning pizza oven, perky salads and improved
versions of red- sauced Italian favorites; its got a new
name but the same crew.

DONNA'S AT THE BMA ⑤ | 22 | 22 | 19 | $21 |
Baltimore Museum of Art, Art Museum Dr. (N. Charles St.),
410-467-3600
■ No food could "match the art" or rival the BMA's "tree-
rimmed sculpture garden", which is the backdrop of this
"contempo" museum cafe; nevertheless, this Donna sib
produces fresh, modern American food that tastes like it
was "made from scratch" yet "does not distract" from the
"elegant" surroundings; service remains problematic and
reservations are a good idea.

Donna's Coffee Bar S | 21 | 19 | 18 | $17 |
2 W. Madison St. (N. Charles St.), 410-385-0180
22 W. Allegheny Ave. (York Rd.), Towson, 410-828-6655

Donna's at Bibelot
Festival at Woodholme, 1819 Reisterstown Rd. (1 block
north of Hooks Ln.), Pikesville, 410-653-6939
Timonium Crossing Shopping Ctr., 2080 York Rd.
(Timonium Rd.), Timonium, 410-308-2041
Harford Mall Annex, 618 Boulton St., Bel Air, 410-803-9058

Donna's at UMMS
Univ. of Maryland, 22 S. Greene St. (Baltimore St.), 410-328-1962

Donna's Espress
Calvert & Centre Sts., 410-539-1858 (carryout only; Mon.-Fri.)
■ Donna Crivello "found a niche and filled it nicely" with
"light designer fare" – roasted veggies, fresh salads, great
bread – and "minimalist", "pose or die" surroundings; but
someone should "tell those folks to wear less black" and
lighten up; her newish niche, The Ruby Lounge, is next door.

Dotson's BBQ S⧄ | _ | _ | _ | I |
7317 Furnace Branch Rd. (bet. Baltimore-Annapolis Blvd.
& Ritchie Hwy., off Rte. 10), Glen Burnie, 410-768-2784
■ BBQ fiends often won't tell you when they find the "real"
thing – they want to keep those succulent, mouthwatering
ribs and chicken for themselves; once you try this "great",
little-known pit/carryout in Glen Burnie, you'll probably
feel the same way.

Double T Diner ●S | 14 | 13 | 17 | $11 |
6300 Baltimore Nat'l Pike (Rolling Rd.), 410-744-4151
1 Mountain Rd. (Ritchie Hwy.), Glen Burnie, 410-766-9669
10741 Pulaski Hwy./Route 40 E. (Ebeneezer Rd.), 410-344-1020
☑ Only at this colorful diner near Catonsville that grew (and
grew) can you find "Peking duck on Belgian waffles . . . 24
hours a day" and hundreds of other "dizzying" choices, all
for change; N.B. the Double T on Ritchie Highway is a "too
new" relation and the other one on Rte. 40E ain't no kin.

Duda's Tavern ● | 20 | 16 | 19 | $14 |
1600 Thames St. (Bond St.), 410-276-9719
■ One of the few "genuine" waterfront bars left in Fells
Point, this "corner" local is so small that its "gargantuan"
subs, "great salads" and terrific burgers nearly fill the
place; the kitchen is even smaller (and therefore "slow"),
giving customers plenty of time to sample the 150 beers.

Due S | 24 | 22 | 22 | $29 |
25 Crossroads Dr. (McDonough Rd.), Owings Mills, 410-356-4147
■ This "uptown" trattoria in Owings Mills brings an "earthy"
Tuscan "touch" to the "imaginative bistro cuisine", "posh"
surroundings and "accommodating" dining approach
popularized at its sister Linwood's; many consider it "almost
as good" as its sib, though a few claim they're "due" more.

Elkridge Furnace Inn ▽ | 21 | 25 | 18 | $21 |
5745 Furnace Ave. (Washington Blvd.), Elkridge,
410-379-9336
■ Not many people realize that this picture-perfect wedding venue, a "delightfully restored" 18th-century property near BWI, serves weekday lunch and dinner; it's one of those "well-intentioned" places that produces a "pleasant" meal even when the Continental food and service fall short of the "lovely setting."

El Taquito Mexicano | – | – | – | ⊔ |
1744 Eastern Ave. (Broadway), 410-563-7840
This low-rent Mexican functions as a community center for Eastern Fells Point's Central American enclave, offering authentic chile rellenos, rolled tacos and other typical dishes; artists, students and adventurous diners join them for a bargain tour – "this is good" and "cheap."

Ethel & Ramone's Cafe S | 18 | 20 | 18 | $11 |
1615 Sulgrave Ave. (bet. Newbury St. & Kelly Ave.), 410-664-2971
■ "Tucked away" in Mt. Washington is a "cute, little, funky" place to "sip tea, eat pastry" (or healthy light fare), "chat and get warm"; it's very much a family affair, run by very talkative Ramone (aka Jeff), his wife, Ethel (aka Jane), and their son, who was recently installed in an "expanded" kitchen whipping out 'New Age' California cuisine.

Faidley's Seafood | 22 | 11 | 15 | $11 |
Lexington Market, 400 W. Lexington St. (Paca St.), 410-727-4898
■ A "standup" crab cake at this city market raw bar is a "Baltimore experience not to be missed" – well "worth the risky location" and "dumpster" smells; this is one eatery with no "yuppie pretensions" – just "excellent value" and the "freshest" seafood and coldest beer in town; it'll "bring out the hon'" in you.

Fazzini's Italian Kitchen S ▽ | 22 | 9 | 20 | $12 |
Cranbrook Shopping Ctr., 578 Cranbrook Rd. (York Rd.),
Cockeysville, 410-667-6104
☑ If you live or work in Cockeysville, chances are you've stopped by this "bare bones", strip stop Italian for "fresh", "delicious" carryout on your way home; it's also handy for a "cheap" pizza or a bring-the-kids, midweek dinner.

Field's Pharmacy S | 16 | 9 | 13 | $10 |
1401 Reisterstown Rd. (Walker Ave.), Pikesville,
410-486-3375
■ This "classic" drugstore lunch counter is still a Pikesville "place to eat and greet" and see what life "was like 35 years ago"; there aren't many places left offering old-fashioned shrimp salad, grilled-cheese sandwiches, milk shakes, "gravy and fries" and "great snowballs in summer", but "you could die waiting" to be served.

Fisherman's Wharf 🆂　　　| 19 | 15 | 17 | $21 |
*Dulaney Valley Shopping Ctr., 826 Dulaney Valley Rd.
(Fairmount Ave.), Towson, 410-337-2909*
▣ A "huge selection" of moderately priced seafood and a kitchen ready to prepare it "your way" explain why this Towson fish house is a favorite "everyday spot for dinner"; its "unlikely" commercial setting and dishes that sometimes "lack flavor" keep it from being more; don't overlook the "interesting specials" or the light bar menu.

Fishery, The 🆂　　　▽ 22 | 16 | 21 | $25 |
1717 Eastern Ave. (Broadway), 410-327-9340
■ "Maybe Baltimore's best seafood secret" is the "good selection" of Spanish and Chesapeake seafood dishes served in delightfully "tacky", Mediterranean-feeling surroundings and the "personal touches that make you feel welcome" at this Fells Point Iberian; note, however, that it may be "erratic."

Foster's 🆂 (CLOSED)　　　| – | – | – | M |
606 S. Broadway (Fleet St.), 410-558-3600
Reopened in June '96 following another ownership change, this Fells Point yuppie stronghold now covers the latest trendy bases with cigars, microbrews on tap, a casual raw bar, sushi, seasonal American fare and billiards upstairs.

Frazier's 🆂　　　| 14 | 11 | 15 | $15 |
857 W. 33rd St. (Elm Ave.), 410-889-1143
919 W. 36th St. (Roland Ave.), 410-662-4914
▣ Hampden has "changed over the years", but not this knotty pine "basement bar" or the picnic tables out back, the classic "beware of frozen peas" American menu or the $9.95 Sunday night dinners (for two!); the new location (36th St.) is "charmless" and finding its legs.

Friendly Farms 🆂　　　| 18 | 11 | 19 | $15 |
17434 Foreston Rd. (Mt. Carmel Rd.), Upperco, 410-239-7400
▣ The "groaning" board of farm food at this "Presbyterian picnic" in Upperco could cap a pleasant, inexpensive family outing – that is, if you're up for "serious fill 'em up", pass the bowls eating (a bit "like the Army") and no alcohol; the "lovely" grounds and duck pond will amuse the kids and you'll find some of the best crab cakes around.

Gabler's 🆂　　　▽ 23 | 19 | 19 | $21 |
*2200 Perryman Rd. (Old Philadelphia Rd.), Aberdeen,
410-272-0626*
■ Fame hasn't spoiled the "restful" atmosphere of this crab joint near Aberdeen; its "unrivaled", "wonderful setting" takes one back to the "old days on the shore" when the crabs were plump and flavorful and life seemed to stand still; since times have changed, however, be sure to reserve ahead.

Germano's Trattoria S
23 | 19 | 21 | $30

(fka Petrucci)
300 S. High St. (Fawn St.), 410-752-4515
■ "Gutsy" Tuscan-style fare, "festive", art deco, poster-filled surroundings and "Germano himself" (a "gem" of a host) keeps this trattoria a Little Italy "favorite" despite rising prices and occasional "disappointments"; unless you opt for half portions, you won't need to eat for a week.

Gibby's S
18 | 14 | 16 | $20

22 W. Padonia Rd. (I-83), Cockeysville, 410-560-0703
■ "Jammed" into this nautical fish place is a "finny feast" of "fresh seafood, plainly served" to what seems like all of Timonium; whereas food-wise it's a "great" place to celebrate crab in all its glorious guises, the atmosphere would be much improved if the "bar noise" and smoke didn't creep in.

GlasZ Cafe S
21 | 20 | 16 | $11

6080 Falls Rd. (Lake Ave.), 410-377-9060
☑ Besides "great coffee", "attractive desserts", "gourmet sandwiches and salads" and "eclectic, interesting" prepared foods, this tiny, "stylish" Falls Road "self-serve" cafe and carryout is also a "place to be seen"; but it's "not very user-friendly" and "quite expensive for takeout."

Grand Palace S
▽ 25 | 15 | 23 | $16

5721 Ritchie Hwy. (Church St.), 410-636-8333
■ "Amazingly good" daily dim sum explains the full parking lot outside this ordinary-looking Brooklyn Park Chinese; inside, it's "homey, warm" and filled with Asian-Americans eating what may be some of the best Cantonese food "outside of San Francisco."

Great American Melting Pot
15 | 14 | 16 | $15

(aka Gampy's)
904 N. Charles St. (Read St.), 410-837-9797
☑ If you're brave enough to venture Downtown "after hours", this "tatty" venue is *the* place to "see who is out and about"; the "colorful atmosphere" and "freak show" are the main draws; the "novelty" bar food is mostly (perhaps only) an attraction "in the middle of the night."

Gunning's Crab House S
18 | 10 | 16 | $21

3901 S. Hanover St. (Jeffrey St.), Brooklyn, 410-354-0085
■ The site of one of South Baltimore's old-time, "down-home", "blue-collar" crab houses; although the Gunnings moved on, it's still a destination for "messy as you want" steamed crab and seafood eating that draws faces (like Cal Ripkin) and just plain folks, too; P.S. since "crabs are the main thing", check on availability before you go.

Gunning's Seafood S 20 | 13 | 18 | $15
7304 Parkway Dr. (off Dorsey Rd., Rte. 176), Linthicun,
410-712-9404
■ "Exiled" to a "small strip mall" near BWI Airport, the
Gunnings keep on steaming crabs and clams, frying green
peppers (and "everything else") and serving them along
with all manner of seafood in a "helpful", no-fuss way;
if you want "great crabs", come here – if you want
atmosphere, go elsewhere.

HAMPTON'S S 27 | 29 | 28 | $52
Harbor Court Hotel, 550 Light St. (bet. Conway & Lee Sts.),
410-347-9744
■ Rated tops in decor and service (and No. 3 for food) in
Baltimore, this most "luxurious" hotel dining room never
fails to "impress" guests; it has the "best of everything" –
from the harbor lights view to the "refined" appointments,
pampering service, Contemporary American menu, fine wine
and a professionalism that takes chef changes in stride.

Hampton's of Towson S ▽ 21 | 20 | 22 | $25
Hampton House, 204 E. Joppa Rd. (Goucher Blvd.),
Towson, 410-821-8888
■ An "older set" dines and dances at this comfortable,
"friendly" apartment house dining room with a lovely view
overlooking Towson; while the Continental-American menu
holds few surprises, it's priced for everyday dining and the
piano bar hosts a "nice" crowd.

Hampton Tea Room ⇗ ▽ 16 | 22 | 19 | $16
Hampton Mansion, 535 Hampton Ln. (Dulaney Valley Rd.),
Towson, 410-583-7401
◩ This aptly named, "sweet" old Towson historic site feels
like you're sipping tea or sherry and nibbling sandwiches in
your great aunt's parlor – if she lived in a "historic mansion"
and entertained her "blue-haired" friends en masse; limited
hours (Tuesday–Saturday, lunch) and menu.

Harryman House S 21 | 20 | 20 | $25
340 Main St. (1¼ mi. north of Franklin Blvd.), Reisterstown,
410-833-8850
■ It's a little "drafty", but what else would you expect
when the middle room of this "woody" charmer is a log
cabin dating from the 1790s?; the "great bar" (with lots of
beers) and rustic dining rooms (with American "light fare
or full dinners") are where Reisterstown locals "socialize",
antique hunters lunch and lovers come when they "don't
want to be seen."

Harvey's S 19 | 18 | 19 | $21
Greenspring Station, 2360 W. Joppa Rd. (Falls Rd.),
Brooklandville, 410-296-9526

◼ The problem with this contemporary "neighborhood fixture" and its please-everyone California and spa menus – and ability to accommodate everything from a "short business meeting" to a casual family snack – is that it gets "monotonous" (also "uneven") because people go so much; it's best "outdoors in the summer" with live music; N.B. there's a carryout/gourmet shop next door.

HAUSSNER'S 19 | 25 | 22 | $23
3242 Eastern Ave. (Clinton St.), 410-327-8365

◼ "Worth a trip" for its "unique", floor-to-ceiling art and kitsch, "stag bar", "gruff" waitresses and the experience, if not the actual eating, of its German and Old Maryland food, this vast Highlandtown "landmark" is a Baltimore tourist's "must"-see; be sure to take home a strawberry shortcake.

HELMAND, THE S 25 | 22 | 22 | $20
806 N. Charles St. (bet. Read & Madison Sts.),
410-752-0311

◼ Imagine a restaurant with food that's inoffensively spicy, "health-conscious", vegetarian-friendly and "affordable", then add an "intimate", ethnic, modern setting and really "helpful" help; even if it didn't do "amazing things with pumpkin", this Mt. Vernon Afghan would be a winner; N.B. be careful at night.

HENNINGER'S TAVERN 25 | 22 | 21 | $24
1812 Bank St. (bet. Ann & Wolfe Sts.), 410-342-2172

◼ Not only is this "classic" Fells Point tavern a great neighborhood watering hole with top-notch bar food, its tiny back room is "sort of elegant", very "civilized" and serves "excellent" Contemporary American–Continental food; the no-reserving policy often makes it tough to get a table on weekends.

Hersh's Orchard Inn – | – | – | M
(nka M. Gettier's Orchard Inn)
1528 E. Joppa Rd. (½ mi. west of Loch Raven Blvd.), East Towson, 410-823-0384
See review in Baltimore, Annapolis and Eastern Shore 1998 Additions section.

Hoang's Seafood Grill & Sushi Bar S

21 | 16 | 19 | $20

1619 Sulgrave Ave. (Kelly Ave.), 410-466-1000
6805 York Rd. (Regester Ave.), 410-377-2500 ⊘
■ This "professionally" run Mt. Washington Asian's menu sweeps from Tokyo to Thailand, making stops in Korea, China and Vietnam for "beautifully presented", fresh-tasting food; despite occasional sputters, it's a "great" engine for an edible tour of the Orient, as is the York Road eat-in/carryout (try one of the Vietnamese meal-in-a-bowl phos).

Holy Frijole

– | – | – | I

908 W. 36th St. (Roland Ave.), 410-235-2326
The tasty Mexican eats at this hot Hampden hole for the multipierced and tattooed are not its main attraction; if you can squeeze into this narrow corner slot, the colorful, modern decor – walking as well as on the walls – will command your attention.

Hull St. Blues Cafe S

19 | 18 | 19 | $18

1222 Hull St. (bet. Fort Ave. & Cuba St.), Locust Point, 410-727-7476
■ In a "scrubbed-step neighborhood" near Fort McHenry, this "charming but erratic" pub-plus gets citywide attention for its "heart attack brunch", "cheap bar food" and "simple American favorites" served in the "dressier dining room"; be sure to leave room for the homemade desserts.

Hunan Manor S

22 | 20 | 22 | $18

7091 Deepage Dr. (off Snowden River Pkwy. at corner of Carved Stone Rd.), Columbia, 410-381-1134
■ "Really good" multiregional Chinese with the ability to attractively accommodate a large group as well as a briefcase lunch or family dinner while satisfying a range of tastes – it does "wonderful vegetarian dishes" and things "not on the menu"; in Columbia, where such amenities are scarce, it's "popular" and "business-minded."

Hunt Ridge S (CLOSED)

15 | 13 | 18 | $18

Yorkridge Shopping Ctr., Ridgely Rd. at York Rd., Lutherville, 410-252-2122
◪ "Comfortable" Towson shopping strip standby catering to a seasoned clientele with the sounds and "generous" bites of the '50s, '60s and '70s; if you "stick with" a "favorite" from the seafood-strong American menu, you'll do alright.

Hunt Valley Szechuan S

20 | 17 | 18 | $18

9 Schilling Rd. (York Rd.), Hunt Valley, 410-527-1818
◪ A "nice enough Chinese restaurant" in terms of food and decor, its multiregional menu and sushi are just what most Hunt Valley diners have come to expect; only a few wonder how food can be "hot 'n' spicy" and "still lack flavor" and whether the usually "polite" servers were having a bad day.

Ikaros S
21 16 19 $18
4805 Eastern Ave. (bet. Oldham & Ponca Sts.), 410-633-3750
◪ For many Baltimoreans, this "Highlandtown haunt" is synonymous with "you'll never leave hungry" portions of inexpensive Greek food and being treated "like family" while you feast; the rest insist there's "better, cheaper" Aegean food, "without the wait", nearby.

Jeannier's
23 19 21 $29
Broadview Apts., 105 W. 39th St. (University Pkwy.), 410-889-3303
■ Some occasions demand a "classic" béarnaise and genteel, "take your mom" surroundings, while others call for "great" onion soup, gumbo or a soft-crab sandwich in a casual, "hand-holding" cafe; at this Uptown apartment-house French, all of the above (plus light fare) are "made with care", fairly priced and served by "college types."

Jenning's Cafe ◑
▽ 17 11 15 $14
808 Frederick Rd. (Ingleside Ave.), Catonsville, 410-744-3824
■ Food-wise, this 1950s relic is a "fat-o-rama" with possibly the best fried chicken, fried oyster sandwiches and cheeseburgers extant; you can blow your cholesterol count in "very Baltimore" company at this "smoky" old bar in Catonsville.

Jerry D's Saloon ◑S
18 10 14 $15
7808 Harford Rd. (Taylor Ave.), 410-665-0525
◪ "Best bar dining – bar none" or big drinks, big steaks and "bar food that plays at being homemade" – however you slice it, this "expanded" Parkville saloon serves a lot of food "for the price", threatening your waist but not your wallet.

Jilly's S
14 11 14 $14
1012 Reisterstown Rd. (Waldron Ave.), Pikesville, 410-653-0610
Enchanted Forest Shopping Ctr., 10030 Baltimore Nat'l Pike (Bethany Ln.), Ellicott City, 410-461-3093
◪ "If you're looking for a place to watch an O's game", meet friends, get some ribs or a shrimp salad sandwich (or "see your boss with the other woman"), this Pikesville "dump" will do; everyone complains about the Styrofoam, the servers, the sonics and the smoke – and everyone goes; P.S. its Ellicott City upstart also hosts "neighborly" fun.

Jimmy's S
16 12 18 $9
801 S. Broadway (Lancaster St.), 410-327-3273
■ In a town that takes justifiable pride in its diner "dives", this Fells Point "grease pit" stands out; whether you go for one of Baltimore's cheapest morning-after breakfasts ("with draft beer"), Sunday AM sightings, a pork chop lunch or simply to observe the "gritty" Damon Runyonesque scene, you "gotta love it."

Jimmy's Famous Seafood ◐🅂   20 | 10 | 17 | $22
6526 Holabird Ave. (bet. Dundalk Ave. & Broening Hwy.),
410-633-4040
■ Steamed "crabs are a tradition" at this massive "Dundalk seafood hall for blue collars" (it's also frequented by an "old-time" Bawlmer crowd); many picky pickers consider its steamed crabs the best "seasoned", its Greek salad impossible to finish and its shrimp and finfare a "dream"; the help is down-to-earth.

Joey Chiu's Greenspring Inn   22 | 22 | 21 | $22
10801 Falls Rd. (Greenspring Valley Rd.), Brooklandville,
410-823-1125
■ Although this Brooklandville Chinese takes the same "pretty place with pretty food" approach to ethnic dining as its Baltimore sibs (Bamboo House), it deserves separate mention for its "predictable but very well prepared food, good sushi" and for giving customers a chance to "need their best bib and tucker."

John Steven, Ltd. ◐🅂   21 | 19 | 17 | $18
1800 Thames St. (Ann St.), 410-327-5561
■ American sushi and steamers in the bar are only one side of this "hard-working" Fells Point tavern's gastronomy — its "patio possibilities" extend to "ambitious" Contemporary American fare; but what really packs the joint is a "genuine" waterfront atmosphere that persists even though the "local riffraff" are outnumbered by "yuppies."

Josef's Country Inn 🅂   24 | 20 | 21 | $27
2410 Pleasantville Rd. (Rte. 152), Fallston, 410-877-7800
◪ A "country drive" and a flashback to the "good old days" of "fräulein-served" German-Continental dining are the major attractions of this Harford "getaway"; the older dining rooms are "noisy, crowded" and kitschy, but we hear that a "back room" done up as a Victorian library is a "delight."

JOY AMERICA CAFE 🅂   25 | 25 | 23 | $35
American Visionary Art Museum, 800 Key Hwy. (Covington St.),
410-244-6500
◪ Despite concerns that its pricey "tall food" would be too visionary for Baltimore, this "cutting edge" American garnered high ratings; a Spring '98 chef change augurs lower prices and plates, while its minimalist decor, harbor views and the folk art museum in which it's housed are well worth a look.

J. Patrick's ◐🅂⇗   ▽ 18 | 17 | 16 | $14
1371 Andre St. (Fort Ave.), 410-244-8613
◪ A "congenial" place to celebrate St. Patrick's Day or listen to traditional Irish bands, this Locust Point pub's Irish-American menu is a "little more varied than bar food" and can be eaten in a "nice dining room"; but boisterous boozing is its main thing.

Jpn. 🅂　　　　　21　17　19　$22
(fka Shogun)
316 N. Charles St. (bet. Saratoga & Pleasant Sts.), 410-962-1130
■ "Asian food buffs" give this Charles Street sushi "master"
points for its shoes-off tea room, "high standards" and non-
sushi items like seafood teriyaki and yakitori.

Jumbo Seafood 🅂　　　　23　18　21　$18
48 E. Sudbrook Sq. (Old Court Rd.), Pikesville, 410-602-1441
■ When "jumbo" portions of some of the area's "best"
Chinese food are served in "too small" Pikesville premises,
the result is "long lines" and a brisk carry-out trade; at
this very popular Asian, the menu doesn't stray far from the
standards, but the kitchen prepares "unusual" specials
and is "very accommodating with special requests."

Kaufmann's Tavern 🅂　　　▽ 19　15　18　$20
329 Gambrills Rd. (Rte. 175), Gambrills, 410-923-2005
■ "Seafood the way it should be done" – in timeworn,
"after-the-game" simplicity; this "nice place in nowhere
land" proves that if you steam a great crab and "treat
patrons like gold", the world will come to you.

Kawasaki　　　　　　21　19　20　$22
413 N. Charles St. (bet. Franklin & Mulberry Sts.), 410-659-7600
■ "Despite the Chesapeake Bay", Baltimore lacks the
rarefied sushi found in LA or NYC; but that doesn't mean
"cold fish addicts" can't get "good", "fresh" sushi at
this "steady" Charles Street Japanese (especially when
it's not "pressured") or that less "daring" appetites
can't find a "nice selection" of tempura, teriyaki and
noodle-based entrees.

Kelly's ◗🅂　　　　　▽ 23　15　20　$15
2108 Eastern Ave. (bet. Duncan & Chester Sts.), 410-327-2312
■ This may be the "finest neighborhood bar" in a great bar
town, not to mention its serving some of the "most perfectly
seasoned", best-quality steamed crabs in Crab City (and
very good everyday grub, too); but its real specialty is
"fun times" – only Kelly and Mary Sheridan could pull off
karaoke in an East Baltimore Irish pub.

Kelsey's 🅂　　　　　▽ 17　16　16　$18
*Normandy Shopping Ctr., 8480 Baltimore Nat'l Pike
(Center Ave.), Ellicott City, 410-418-9076*
◪ A "good neighborhood saloon" in an area near Ellicott
City lacking one, this "comfortable" storefront offers "steak
value", burgers and "great" french fries along with a
"bountiful" shrimp salad sandwich and American entrees to
a suburban clientele that has "just discovered" it; in their
view, "service could improve."

KING'S CONTRIVANCE ⑤   23 | 24 | 22 | $32

10150 Shaker Dr. (bet. Rtes. 29 & 32), Columbia, 410-995-0500
◪ Though the Continental food and service sometimes seem
to be "coasting", this "magnificent" Victorian mansion
emains "the place for private parties in Columbia" (the
dining rooms aren't "private enough for romance"); the
"pre-theater special" is the "only way to go" to
Merriweather events.

Kisling's Tavern ●⑤   18 | 12 | 16 | $14

2100 Fleet St. (Chester St.), 410-327-5477
◪ Bay fries and blaring sports TV mark this "reliable way
station on a Fells Point pub crawl" frequented by "youngish"
types; while beer is the name of its game, the "finger food" is
"cheap", comes in "substantial quantities" and affords
"occasional pleasant surprises"; "grouchy" help and grunge
go with the territory.

La Scala ⑤   – | – | – | E

411 S. High St. (Eastern Ave.), 410-783-9209
A relaxed, contemporary Italian meal in this well-appointed
Little Italy row house is a bit like dining at a friend's home;
staffers, who clearly want patrons to like them and their
food, create a cozy, inclusive atmosphere in a space that's
way too small for secrets.

La Tesso Tana ⑤   22 | 19 | 18 | $29

Abarcrombie Badger Bed & Breakfast, 58 W. Biddle St.
(Cathedral St.), 410-837-3630
■ With "reservations necessary" before a "BSO or Lyric
event", this "cozy" step-down "treasure" across from the
Meyerhoff displays its "romantic" potential when unrushed;
at such times, the "rich" Italian cuisine is a "masterful"
prelude to whatever you have planned and "tight" seating
could be turned into an advantage.

Ledo Pizza ⑤⇄   17 | 10 | 15 | $12

1020-40 W. 41st St. (Falls Rd.), 410-243-4222
*Snowden Ctr., 6955 Oakland Mills Rd. (Snowden River Pkwy.),
Columbia, 410-381-5550*
*Park Plaza, 552 E. Ritchie Hwy. (Baltimore-Annapolis Blvd.),
Severna Park, 410-544-3344*
11321 York Rd. (Shawan Rd.), Hunt Valley, 410-785-5336
405 N. Center St. (Cranberry St.), Westminster, 410-857-3500
2657-A Old Annapolis Rd. (Rte. 175), Hanover, 410-551-0220
16-18 E. Ordinance Rd. (Ritchie Hwy.), Glen Burnie, 410-590-2222
110 Kent Landing, (Rtes. 50 & 8), Stevensville, 410-643-7979
See Washington, DC, Alphabetical Directory.

Liberatore's Bistro ⑤   21 | 19 | 20 | $29

*Timonium Corporate Ctr., 9515 Deereco Rd. (Padonia Rd.),
Timonium, 410-561-3300*
*Freedom Village Shopping Ctr., 6300 Georgetown Blvd.
(Liberty Rd.), Eldersburg, 410-781-4114*

Liberatore's Bistro (Cont.)
New Town Village Ctr., 9712 Groffs Mills Dr.
(Lakeside Blvd.), Owings Mills, 410-356-3100
■ "Chubby cherubs" may be an incongruous backdrop for doing lunchtime deals, but Timonium briefcase toters seem to take it in stride; in the evening, this "office park" Northern Italian's "luxuriant" civility, "excellent" traditional menu and easy parking seem more in keeping with its status as the "suburban place to go" – ditto at its other locations.

LINWOOD'S S   27 | 26 | 25 | $35
25 Crossroads Dr. (McDonough Rd.), Owings Mills, 410-356-3030
■ Linwood Dame "got it together" at this "stylish" Owings Mills Contemporary American; his food is "imaginative", the help is "accommodating" and the room is "hopping" with "heavy-hitters" reminiscent of the "old Pimlico Hotel"; a few wish it weren't quite so "mink"-lined, but no one can deny it's a real "value at lunch."

Lista's S   15 | 20 | 16 | $19
Brown's Wharf, 1637 Thames St. (bet. Broadway & Bond St.),
410-327-0040
☑ At Margaritaville on the Fells Point waterfront, the atmosphere is so "zippy" most don't notice the "faux" SW decor, "fake" Tex-Mex fare and flawed service – especially if they're seated at a patio table, listening to live music and watching the ships go by; call it "partying" with a "price tag."

Loco Hombre S   18 | 15 | 16 | $17
413 W. Coldspring Ln. (bet. Charles St. & Roland Ave.),
410-889-2233
☑ This "colorful" Roland Park Tex-Mex isn't big enough to seat its many amigos – that's not surprising given the college neighborhood and "very good yuppie Mexican cuisine" (i.e "greaseless", gringoized and "overspiced"); the artwork is 'with it', which is more than you can always say for the help.

Louie's Bookstore Cafe ◐ S   17 | 20 | 14 | $14
518 N. Charles St. (bet. Franklin & Centre Sts.), 410-962-1224
☑ Baltimore's "Left Bank" runs up Charles Street to this bookstore/cafe where "artists and musicians serve playful Eclectic food and excellent desserts" to "diverse" types who go for "stimulation" (books, music, art, people-watching and conversation) as much as for sustenance and who shrug philosophically that "when the service is good, the food is so-so" and vice versa; N.B. be careful at night.

Luigi Petti ◐ S   19 | 17 | 19 | $20
1002 Eastern Ave. (Exeter St.), 410-685-0055
☑ It's easy to "love this place in the summer" when you're eating some of the "best gnocchi in Little Italy" or a "good red sauce" staple on the terrace; it's less enjoyable inside when there are "interminable waits" or the food tastes like "they stopped trying"; petti-good or petti-bad – it's a toss-up.

Mai Thai 🆂 (CLOSED) ▽ 20 | 14 | 18 | $17 |
1032 Light St. (bet. Cross & Hamburg Sts.), 410-539-5611
■ South Baltimore foodies can't understand why more
people don't know about their "secret" Thai, an offshoot of
the Thai Restaurant in Waverly, since the traditional dishes
are well-prepared and "not very hot" and the hospitality
is usually "great too"; perhaps it's because the white
tablecloths and chandeliers belie the "inexpensive" tab.

Mama Lucia 🆂 17 | 11 | 15 | $14 |
*Valley Ctr., 9616 Reisterstown Rd. (Greenspring Valley Rd.),
Owings Mills, 410-363-0496*
☑ When you cash in your "coupon" at this "shopping center
Italian", you'll "doggie-bag tomorrow's dinner"; the double-
sized portions of "hearty" pastas, pizza and subs help offset
the "mediocre surroundings" and some misses in the menu;
carryout is another way to deal with the "cheesy" decor.

Manor Tavern 🆂 19 | 20 | 18 | $24 |
15819 Old York Rd. (Manor Rd.), Monkton, 410-771-8155
☑ "A great spot in horse country for a burger", a full
American-Continental meal in formal candlelight or mingling
with the "horsey set" in the rustic bar; but some feel this
atmospheric coach stop could be improved by teaching
the "college kids" to "pace a meal."

MARCONI'S 23 | 18 | 23 | $26 |
106 W. Saratoga St. (bet. Park Ave. & Cathedral St.), 410-727-9522
■ They say that "if you're not a Baltimorean, you don't
understand" this "Old Maryland" "townhouse treasure"
however much you relish the "fabulous" lobster Cardinale,
fried eggplant, creamed spinach and "chocolate sundae
without equal", the courtliness of the "shuffling waiters"
and the fact that it "retains its old-time dowdiness" and
"time-warp" prices – nevertheless, you should go.

Margaret's Cafe 🆂 21 | 21 | 19 | $14 |
909 Fell St. (bet. Thames & Wolfe Sts.), 410-276-5605
■ Margaret Footner's "spare", "healthy and hip" Fells Point
cafe is hailed as a "gem" and her customers look upon her
"innovative, light", vegetarian-minded cooking as an "eating
adventure" and shrug off an occasional "disappointment"
and the "eccentric" help; they even "support local artists"
whose works hang in the nonprofit gallery upstairs.

Martick's 21 | 17 | 17 | $24 |
214 W. Mulberry St. (bet. Park Ave. & Howard St.), 410-752-5155
☑ Straining the envelope of "quirkiness", Morris Martick
holds court (at his "whim") in his family's "run-down"
Baltimore speakeasy (no sign, light or doorknob – ring the
"buzzer" above the door) with his "unique" French food
and "early aircraft carrier" decor; "on a good night it can
be lots of fun, on a bad night it's a disaster"; but neither
the restaurant nor the neighborhood is for timid souls.

Matsuri | 24 | 17 | 19 | $18 |
1105 S. Charles St. (Cross St.), 410-752-8561
■ "Baltimore's hippest sushi bar", and probably its best Japanese restaurant, packs a lot of excellent eating into a smart-looking, "closet"-like space in South Baltimore; however, with the chef and the owners changing, the above ratings and the "agonizing waits" may also change.

McCabe's S | – | – | – | M |
3845 Falls Rd. (Cox St.), Hampden, 410-467-1000
"Known for perfect burgers, great crusted fries" and "exceptional bar food", this "tiny local pub in Hampden" recently reopened to citywide applause; diverse local diners "sit at the bar" – the best place to soak up the "atmosphere."

McCafferty's S | 22 | 21 | 20 | $31 |
1501 Sulgrave Ave. (Newbury St.), 410-664-2200
■ If you "don't eat red meat", it could be because you've never succumbed to the "great beef" and lamb served in "chummy" comfort at this Mt. Washington "testosterone" palace; Montana meat, "delicious garlic mashed potatoes", "personalized service", football memorabilia and plenty of polished wood are just a few of the disparate elements that come together here.

Metropol Cafe & Gallery S | 20 | 20 | 16 | $18 |
1718 N. Charles St. (Lafayette St., 1 block north of Penn Station), 410-385-3018
☑ Although it can be a "neat place to visit for art and a cup of joe", "innovative" smoked seafood, veggies and "great desserts", people forget about this cafe/culturama unless "there's a good flick at the Charles"; perhaps better service would help, not to mention a safer location.

M. Gettier's Orchard Inn | – | – | – | E |
1528 E. Joppa Rd (½ mi. west of Loch Raven Blvd.), East Towson, 410-823-0384
See review in Baltimore, Annapolis and Eastern Shore 1998 Additions section.

Michael's ●S | 18 | 15 | 16 | $20 |
2119 York Rd. (Gerard Ave.), Timonium, 410-252-2022
☑ There's no mystery about this Timonium pub's popularity – it has "location" and "excellent" crab cakes as well as a raw bar, "good happy hour" grub and lots of attractive customers playing the singles game or the "19th hole" (or both); consequently, the "expanded" premises can't seem to accommodate the crowds.

Mick's S (CLOSED)　　16 | 16 | 16 | $16 |
Towson Commons, 425 York Rd. (bet. Pennsylvania &
Chesapeake Aves.), Towson, 410-825-0071
See Washington, DC, Alphabetical Directory.

Miller's Delicatessen S　　13 | 9 | 10 | $12 |
Greenspring Shopping Ctr., 2849 Smith Ave. (Sanzo Rd.),
Pikesville, 410-602-2233
☑ When deli mavens want a corned beef fix, chicken soup
or a "good Reuben", they're willing to endure "standing
on line and being yelled at" in this relocated cafeteria-style
entry in Pikesville; P.S. dining at its prior premises was
really a "desperation measure."

Milton Inn S　　– | – | – | E |
14833 York Rd. (bet. Hunt Valley Mall & Belfast Rd.),
Sparks, 410-771-4366
New owners that are seasoned pros (Brass Elephant, King's
Contrivance) have rekindled the hearth room fire at this
romantic country inn to heartwarming cheers; long
considered the place to celebrate, its sudden fall '97 closing
saddened many, but now a contemporary Continental menu
and brightened decor open a new chapter for this 240-
year-old legend.

Minato S　　– | – | – | M |
(fka CoChin)
800 N. Charles St. (Madison St.), 410-332-0332
Replacing CoChin in its brick-walled Mt. Vernon basement,
this thoroughgoing Japanese touches all of that cuisine's
bases – sushi, sashimi, hot and cold noodle dishes, yakitori
and tiny grilled tidbits are just some of the possibilities; N.B.
care advised at night.

Morgan Millard S　　18 | 18 | 18 | $20 |
4800 Roland Ave. (bet. Upland & Elmhurst Rds.),
410-889-0030
☑ Where Roland Park "matrons lunch" while "preppies"
crunch numbers and assorted neighborhood "50-year-olds
go to feel young"; this "arts 'n' crafts" restaurant in a historic
building specializes in "home cooking outside of the home"
and remains as "sleepy" as ever.

Morning Edition Cafe S　　21 | 20 | 14 | $15 |
153 N. Patterson Park Ave. (Fayette St.), 410-732-5133
☑ Heroic patience is rewarded with "delicious fresh-baked
breads, muffins" and "brunch offerings" at this "Vermont"-
feeling "haven in the Highlandtown war zone"; "clearly,
the servers are better artists than waiters", but the "Jerry
Garcia" vibes and the "entire Sunday paper" should help
pass the time.

Mo's Crab & Pasta Factory 19 | 14 | 16 | $22
502 Albemarle St. (Eastern Ave.), 410-837-1600 ◐Ⓢ

Mo's Fisherman's Exchange
Satyr Hill Shopping Ctr., 2025 E. Joppa Rd. (Satyr Hill Rd.), Parkville, 410-665-8800 ◐Ⓢ

Mo's Fisherman's Wharf Inner Harbor
219 President St. (Stiles St.), 410-837-8600 ◐Ⓢ

Mo's Seafood Factory
7146 Ritchie Hwy. (Furnace Branch Rd.), Glen Burnie, 410-768-1000 ◐Ⓢ

2403 Belair Rd. (Mountain Rd.), Fallston, 410-893-6666 Ⓢ

■ Doggie bags the size of shopping bags indicate these seafood factories don't skimp on portions; here, you'll find a big catch of "very fresh" seafood cooked "101 ways" (mostly garlicky and "rich") but not much finesse, causing some to carp about "too much" of a not so good thing.

Mt. Washington Tavern Ⓢ 15 | 17 | 14 | $18
5700 Newbury St. (Sulgrave Ave.), 410-367-6903

☑ Bashing this Mt. Washington brew hole and its clientele is a cottage industry – "Beavis and Butt-head with bank accounts", "lacrosse nirvana: bring a jock", "very J. Crew"; nevertheless, hundreds of surveyors find a "nice niche in the sun room" or go to "meet friends", rating the "surroundings more enjoyable than the service" or "fair" "tavern fare."

Mughal Garden Ⓢ 22 | 17 | 20 | $18
920 N. Charles St. (bet. Read & Eager Sts.), 410-547-0001

■ The "third jewel in the Little India crown"; reviewers laud this "roomy", "cheerful" Charles Street Indian for its "great vindaloos and curries", "American portions", "tasteful decor" and, especially, for its "superb" midday spread – "calling it another lunch buffet is like calling the Taj Mahal another tomb", "there's so much food at Sunday brunch you'll go home and go back to sleep."

Nacho Mama's ◐Ⓢ 19 | 19 | 19 | $14
2907 O'Donnell St. (Linwood Ave.), 410-675-0898

■ "Tex-Mex with a sense of humor" in a happening area is the short of it; the rest of the story is this Canton hangout mixes Elvis kitsch, "chips in a hubcap", Texas chili and other "good, hearty, unpretentious feed" to come up with a "good place for a guy to meet his brother for dinner" – that is, "if they can get in the door."

Nam Kang ◐Ⓢ – | – | – | I
2126 Maryland Ave. (Charles St.), 410-685-6237

Write-ins draw attention to this Little Korea community center with a comprehensive Korean menu plus "good sushi" and other Asian dishes; it's a good place to expand your vocabulary with words like bulgoki (marinated sliced beef) and kimchi (spicy fermented cabbage).

Nates & Leons ⑤
300 W. Pratt St. (Howard St.), 410-234-8100

– | – | – | M |

Nostalgia for overstuffed corned beef sandwiches, chicken salad and banana cream pie, along with a savvy regard for Convention Center, Oriole Park and Inner Harbor traffic, prompted the revival of this legendary deli on prime turf; early returns range from "needs more practice" and "better food" to "fun place."

New No Da Ji ⑤
2501 N. Charles St. (25th St.), 410-235-4846

19 | 11 | 17 | $17 |

☑ The bargain "all-u-can-du" sushi buffet, which "ranges from fair to excellent depending on when you go", lures an "eclectic collection" of "adventurous" students and suits to this Charles Street Asian, but it's the "superior Korean part of the menu" that turns them into regulars; P.S. this place has "no charisma, no charm" and "not a great location" (i.e. "always lock your car").

New Orleans Cafe (CLOSED)
322 N. Charles St. (bet. Saratoga & Mulberry Sts.), 410-727-6317

– | – | – | M |

Gumbo fiends head to this Charles Street storefront for a local sampler of Louisiana music and eats; here, le bon temps roule in a laid-back way that makes tourists feel as comfortable as the hip types who used to frequent this weekend evening hot spot when it was Profusions.

New Towne Diner ◑⑤
11316 Reisterstown Rd., Reisterstown, 410-654-0066

14 | 14 | 16 | $11 |

☑ In Reisterstown (on the site of Twin Kiss), this phoenix-like diner proves that if you give folks "lots of food at a fair price", "tolerate" their kids and position a mouthwatering bakery as they come in the door, you'll have to double your size in a year; critics cite "too long lines" and "bland food."

Nichi Bei Kai ⑤
1524 York Rd. (Seminary Ave.), Lutherville, 410-321-7090
Columbia Market Pl., 9400 Snowden River Pkwy. (Oakland Mills Rd.), Columbia, 410-381-5800

21 | 18 | 21 | $23 |

☑ The enduring popularity of Japanese slice 'n' dice shows, like these suburban samurai, irritates purists – the lunch specials at the "decent sushi bars" are more their style; but hey, as long as you provide a "good dinner at a reasonable price", what's wrong with making "food fun"?

Nick's Inner Harbor Seafood
Cross Street Market, 1065 S. Charles St. (Cross St.), 410-685-2020

– | – | – | I |

Construction workers rub elbows with young professionals over an inexpensive bite and a brew at this much-expanded fish stall in the Cross Street Market; most nights, it's a "happy-hour happening" with hundreds swarming the sushi bar, lobster bar, raw bar, beer bar, and soup and crab cake station – so if you want to sit, go before 5 PM.

No Way Jose 🖪
16 | 14 | 15 | $15

1041 Marshall St. (Cross St.), 410-752-2837

☑ Where twentysomethings fill up on "good, greasy" (translation: "authentic") Tex-Mex "before a night out in Federal Hill", this border cafe near the Cross Street Market is also known for its margarita-fueled bar scene; note that the kitchen really loves to play with fire – watch out for the killer-spiced wings and BBQ.

Obrycki's 🖪
20 | 14 | 18 | $25

1727 E. Pratt St. (bet. Broadway & Regester St.), 410-732-6399

☑ Whether this venerable Baltimore crab house is everything "it's cracked up to be" is the question; naysayers list "poor quality", "seafood dishes swimming in butter", "bad attitude", "horrendous waits" and "chancy 'hood; still, the fans smile "have had my best crabs here."

Ocean Pride
18 | 10 | 15 | $19

1534 York Rd. (bet. Seminary Rd. & Bellona Ave.), Lutherville, 410-321-7744

☑ "Great crabs and cold beer – what else do you need to know" about this Lutherville crab joint?; possibly that it's "willing to be flexible", has one of the "best raw bars" and cream of crab soup around and doesn't promise more than it can deliver.

One World Cafe 🖪
18 | 21 | 17 | $10

904 S. Charles St. (E. Henrietta St.), 410-234-0235

■ This atmospheric Federal Hill bean bar with veggie fare, recently expanded to include a full kitchen, is variously described as a "great black bean burrito coffee place" and a "hang out, read a book, watch the crowd, listen to the music, relax and enjoy the atmosphere" place – you get the drift.

OPA ❷🖪
– | – | – | M

1911 Aliceanna St. (Wolfe St.), 410-522-4466

An "Inner Harbor transplant" (Taverna Athena's stepchild) brings a "nice Greek menu" and festive spirit to Fells Point; here, you'll find 'Athenian pasta' and lots of seafood besides the "fresh Greek salad" and lamb that locals used to have to contend with tourists to enjoy.

Orchard Market & Cafe 🖪
24 | 18 | 22 | $18

8815 Orchard Tree Ln. (Joppa Rd.), East Towson, 410-339-7700

■ "Hidden in the suburbs", where it "doesn't get enough credit" for bringing "delicious" Persian food, "extraordinary hospitality" and "striking decor" within reach of families "on a budget" (in addition to "parking at the door" and a "BYOB bonus"); if you've never tried the rich, flavorful cuisine of Persia, this ethnic market and cafe will be a "treat."

Orient 🖻   ▽ | 22 | 17 | 18 | $17 |
319 York Rd., Towson, 410-296-9000
■ It's ostensibly Chinese, but the "very fresh" sushi is a big seller at this "dependable", tastefully turned out Towsonite; the "huge portions of unadorned sushi" and possibly the "best California roll in town" more than satisfy such yens; P.S. there are "wonderful eggplant dishes" for those otherwise inclined.

OUTBACK STEAKHOUSE 🖻 | 20 | 16 | 19 | $21 |
Perry Hall Sq., 4215 Ebenezer Rd. (Belair Rd.), 410-529-7200
Tollgate Plaza, 615 Belair Rd. (Rte. 24), Bel Air, 410-893-0110
Target Shopping Ctr., 4420 Long Gate Pkwy. (St. Johns Ln.),
Ellicott City, 410-480-0472
See Washington, DC, Alphabetical Directory.

Pacific Rim 🖻   ▽ | 17 | 15 | 18 | $20 |
9726 York Rd. (Padonia Rd.), Cockeysville, 410-666-2336
☑ The Pacific Rim in Cockeysville stretches from Southeast Asia to New Orleans – an "eclectic mix" reflected in the "creative" menu and designer decor; reactions vary from "great sushi" to "new name, old food."

Palermo's Grill   (CLOSED) | 20 | 18 | 18 | $21 |
Padonia Park Plaza, 106 W. Padonia Rd., Timonium, 410-252-0600
☑ In keeping with the generous spirit of namesake Steve Palermo, portions are sized large and "extra large" at this sports-themed Italian-American bar and grill in Timonium; but notwithstanding the "nice-looking" surroundings, "pleasant" help and "decent prices", the call is just "ok" ("good bar, but the restaurant needs help").

Paolo's 🖻 | 20 | 19 | 18 | $22 |
Harborplace, 301 Light St. Pavilion (Pratt St.), 410-539-7060 🌒
Towson Commons, 1 W. Pennsylvania Ave. (York Rd.),
Towson, 410-321-7000
See Washington, DC, Alphabetical Directory.

PaperMoon Diner 🌒🖻 | 13 | 19 | 12 | $11 |
227 W. 29th St. (bet. Howard & Remington Sts.), 410-889-4444
☑ "Weird and wacky" (in a "dicey area", too) Remington comfort-food station that's strictly for "young, zany, late-night snackers" and "slackers" – smokers preferred; unless you're into "headless Barbie Dolls", "Pez dispensers", "stale desserts", "Soviet-style service" and questionable housekeeping, this place is not for you.

PAVILION AT THE WALTERS 🖻 | 22 | 25 | 20 | $21 |
(nka Troia the Bistro at the Walters)
600 N. Charles St. (Centre St.), 410-752-2887
■ In early 1997, Cafe Troia moved into the skylit atrium at the Walters Art Gallery, softening this dining space to frame its mainly Italian menu (and putting a question mark next to the above ratings); still, there is no more "elegant" backdrop for a business or special occasion lunch or dinner.

Peerce's Gourmet ⑤ (CLOSED)　21 14 17 $16
9624 Deereco Rd. (Padonia Rd.), Timonium, 410-561-2233
■ This American "overachiever in a culinary wasteland" on Deereco Road, an offshoot of the "real Peerce's" (Peerce's Plantation) and Josef's Country Inn, offers "excellent carry-out" and eat-in lunch options ranging from a "roasted veg sandwich", soups and "great specials" to a comprehensive Sunday brunch buffet.

PEERCE'S PLANTATION ⑤　23 24 23 $31
12460 Dulaney Valley Rd. (Loch Raven Dr.), Phoenix, 410-252-3100
◪ The tradition of "Sunday drives to the country" for family celebrations may be "better than the Continental food", but that doesn't diminish this lovely Loch Raven Reservoir overlook's appeal; for many, being served "seafood in puff pastry" by a "personable" waiter defines fine dining the "way it used to be."

Perring Place ⑤　▽ 23 16 22 $20
Perring Crossing, Perring Pkwy. (McLean Blvd.), 410-661-0630
■ "Good eats at a good price" draws crowds anywhere, so it's hardly surprising that a Northeast suburban strip mall location hasn't hurt this fixture's bottom line; long ago, word of its old-fashioned "comfort food", "huge slab servings" and "friendly" folks spread in the neighborhood – since then it's been a local "favorite."

Peppermill ●⑤　17 15 19 $19
Heaver Plaza, 1301 York Rd. (Seminary Ave.), Lutherville, 410-583-1107
◪ In a Lutherville office building, this unimpressive old trouper plays to a mature ("blue-haired") audience that "goes here frequently to see all their friends"; management sees no reason to change the "wholesome" American menu or "hire a decorator" – after all, the place is always full.

Peter's Inn ⌀　24 19 20 $14
504 S. Ann St. (Eastern Ave.), 410-675-7313
■ "Artists" took over this "funky" Fells Point "biker bar" and the Eclectic "gourmet" fare is "truly creative"; a meal here is something "like going to Mom's house" – if she wore "Harley accessories."

Phillips Harborplace ⑤　15 15 15 $23
Harborplace, 301 Light St. Pavilion (bet. Calvert & Pratt Sts.), 410-685-6600

Phillips Seafood Grill ⑤
White Marsh Mall, 8200 Perry Hall Blvd. (Honeygo Blvd.), 410-931-0077
See Washington, DC, Alphabetical Directory.

Piccolo's S
17 | 20 | 17 | $23

Brown's Wharf, 1629 Thames St. (foot of Broadway on Pier), 410-522-6600

◪ When approached by water taxi (or private yacht) with moderate expectations and not on weekends ("to avoid crowds"), this "upscale" Italian on a Fells Point pier does fine – especially if you nab an "awesome" waterside seat, watch the tugboats in the harbor and order pasta and one of its winning wines; in contrast, the "large dining room feels impersonal and touristy."

Pier 500 S (CLOSED)
18 | 20 | 18 | $27

HarborView Marina, 500 HarborView Dr. (Key Hwy.), 410-625-0500

◪ A "straight-up" martini and an "away from everything" Harbor view are the highlights of a visit to this marina restaurant; the "cramped, crowded" interior and comings and goings of too many chefs have left its identity in disarray, but perhaps the latest menu of regional Maryland seafood (a "mixed success") will stick.

PIERPOINT S
26 | 18 | 21 | $31

1822 Aliceanna St. (bet. Ann & Wolfe Sts.), 410-675-2080

■ Nancy Longo's "national stature" derives from her "imaginative" interpretations of Maryland seafood classics, her ability to transform the freshest ingredients into "memorable" comfort food and her generosity as a teacher; the major complaint about her "cozy, stylish", "intelligent" Fells Point bistro is that it's "too small."

POLO GRILL S
26 | 25 | 24 | $38

Inn at the Colonnade, 4 W. University Pkwy. (bet. Canterbury & Charles Sts.), 410-235-8200

■ Say what you will about its "who's who" "power scene" and "snooty" attitude – this Contemporary American's grill-room updates are "almost always impeccably prepared" and served "whether it's New Year's Eve or brunch"; and if you "know everyone" in the "clubby" room "it's fun" – if not, you can always eat the same "good food" at the bar; N.B. a new chef (summer 1996) should not rock this solid ship.

PRIME RIB ◖S
28 | 25 | 27 | $41

1101 N. Calvert St. (Chase St.), 410-539-1804

■ The epitome of "swanky", "let's get dressed up dining", this "fancy" Downtowner brings a "touch of NY to town" and demonstrates the timeless appeal of "consistently excellent" beef, seafood and dry martinis and "solicitous service" by earning top ratings for food (No. 2 for popularity and service) in this year's *Survey*; N.B. be sure to park in the garage.

Puffin's S   23 | 18 | 21 | $22 |
1000 Reisterstown Rd. (Sherwood Ave.), Pikesville,
410-486-8811
■ "Upscale" (a bit "expensive for Formica tabletops")
Pikesville crowd-pleaser offering a "very California (for
Baltimore)" take on healthy eating; the focus here is on
fresh vegetables, grains and grilled fish in an "artistic"
environment; new owners (post-*Survey*) haven't fixed
what ain't broke.

Purim Oak   - | - | - | I |
321 York Rd. (Chesapeake Ave.), Towson, 410-583-7770
This cavernous Korean with Pan-Asian aspirations draws
Towson business types for lunch, students, families and
moviegoers for dinner; penny-pinchers head straight for
the all-you-can-eat buffet.

Purple Orchid S   24 | 20 | 21 | $27 |
(fka Orchid)
419 N. Charles St. (Franklin St.), 410-837-0080
■ A new name flags renewed emphasis on fusing Asian and
French dining experiences (with "outstanding presentation"
and service complementing "interesting" food) as well
as a refurbishing of this "quietly elegant" Mt. Vernon
townhouse; best of all, it's seldom crowded, making it a
good "last-minute" bet.

Ralphie's Diner S   16 | 17 | 16 | $16 |
9690 Deereco Rd. (Padonia Rd.), Timonium,
410-252-3990
◪ A "run-of-the-mill place to eat during the week" with
enough dineresque dishes and blue plate specials to
occupy the kids; although many reviewers find this
Timonium faux-diner useful for a good, "informal" meal,
some say what was once fresh and "trendy" now seems
like they're "faking it."

Ransome's Harbor Hill Cafe S   19 | 14 | 18 | $17 |
1032 Riverside Ave. (Cross St.), 410-576-9720
■ This "cute" neighborhood tavern "tucked away" near
Federal Hill serves duck salad, "fresh-baked bread" and
inventive pasta along with burgers and brews to a gentrified
'hood; there's a division between those who would "like
to love it" (a minority) and those who do.

Red Hot & Blue S (CLOSED)   20 | 15 | 17 | $17 |
11308 Reisterstown Rd. (High Falcon Rd.), Owings Mills,
410-356-6959
See Washington, DC, Alphabetical Directory.

Red Star 🖪
| 17 | 14 | 16 | $18 |

906 S. Wolfe St. (Thames St.), 410-327-2212
✦ A red star points the way to this former Fells Point "brothel" that's now a gentrified place for lunch – that is, "when it's not too crowded" and you can take advantage of the "varied" menu of bar eats and "unusual" American choices; at night, you'll find raucous, "smoky", "crowded" goings-on that are often labeled "fun."

Redwood Grill 🖪
▽ | 15 | 18 | 17 | $17 |

12 S. Calvert St. (bet. Baltimore & Redwood Sts.), 410-244-8550
✦ Updated bar and grill bidding for the Downtown lunch trade that makes dramatic use of a former car dealership's soaring space; but its shaky start in a "tough location" gives rise to comments like "tries hard, but doesn't quite make it"; N.B. it gets noisy and flashy at night.

Regi's
| 18 | 18 | 16 | $17 |

1002 Light St. (Hamburg St.), 410-539-7344
✦ Diehards lament that this "nice Federal Hill bar with average food and good atmosphere" is "not the same since Regi sold it"; apparently, the new owners have "changed the American menu" and introduced "rotating art shows complete with curators" – which strikes some as a distinct "improvement"; service remains familiarly "slow."

River Watch 🖪
| 19 | 19 | 18 | $20 |

207 Nanticoke Rd. (Middleborough Rd.), Essex, 410-687-1422
✦ This "redneck riviera" on Hopkins Creek offers something for everyone – "crabs with a view", "savory seafood and sensational sunsets", a chance to "meet men with boats", a summertime singles scene, "great music", dancing, family dining and "good value"; sometimes you can even "catch a great meal" at this seafooder.

Ruby Lounge 🖪
▽ | 24 | 24 | 21 | $25 |

(fka Donna's Restaurant)
800 N. Charles St. (Madison St.), 410-539-8051
■ Once again, Donna Crivello and company "score big" with this "dark, stylish", high-energy Mt. Vernon supper club where "martinis replace roasted vegetable salad" on a "superb" Eclectic menu designed for "regular eating"; the air of "NYC chic" is heightened by small tables and "waitresses with attitude"; N.B. park on Charles Street.

RUDYS' 2900 🖪
| 27 | 23 | 25 | $37 |

2900 Baltimore Blvd. (Rte. 91), Finksburg, 410-833-5777
■ It's a "bit of a drive" to Finksburg, but that doesn't dampen admiration for this Continental-American's "dynamic, interesting food" (ranked No. 2 in Baltimore); here, a "pair of Rudys" display their "mastery" – one elevates service to an art form, while the other does "fabulous fish", game and dishes with "Austrian accents"; decor isn't bad, but not masterful.

Rusty Scupper ⑤   16 21 17 $22
402 Key Hwy. (Light St.), 410-727-3678
☑ Commanding Baltimore's "best" Inner Harbor view from
virtually every seat and a spectacular deck for outdoor
dining, this nautical tourist stop is "much better looking"
since its post-*Survey* "overhaul"; but it remains to be
seen if the seafood and service "are as good."

RUTH'S CHRIS STEAK HOUSE ⑤   24 21 22 $39
34 Market Pl., 600 Water St. (bet. Market Pl. & Gay St.),
410-783-0033
See Washington, DC, Alphabetical Directory.

SABATINO'S ◗⑤   18 15 18 $22
901 Fawn St. (S. High St.), 410-727-9414
■ "A quintessential Baltimore restaurant – "average" food
and decor "but appealing all the same" – this famous Little
Italy "spaghetti house" is known for its "great" Bookmaker
salad, massive red-sauced pastas and entrees and for
staying open after the "bars close"; note that nonregulars
are "sent to Siberia."

Saguaro's ⑤   17 16 15 $18
2 W. Pennsylvania Ave. (York Rd.), Towson, 410-339-7774
☑ This "attractive" SW range rider gets borderline reviews
for its "colorful" Tex-Mex eats, grills and modern desert
fare: "barely ok" vs. "very good even when the waiter
brings the wrong dish"; but located where it is, in collegiate
and suburban Towson, you can bet the bar is "full."

Saigon ⑤   ▽ 23 8 19 $13
3345 Belair Rd. (Erdman Ave.), 410-276-0055
■ The food's so reasonable at this "linoleum Vietnamese"
on Belair Road "that if you get a bad dish", you can easily
afford another; but chances are you'll love everything you
try – "a Vietnam tour you'll want to repeat"; BYOB.

Samos ⊘   ▽ 24 7 19 $11
600 S. Oldham St. (Fleet St.), 410-675-5292
■ The highly edible outcomes of this archetypal Greek
"hole-in-the-wall" include "excellent calamari", "wonderful
stuffed grape leaves" and the "best chicken souvlaki", gyros
and hamburgers in Highlandtown; prices couldn't be lower
or customer satisfaction greater; if only it "were more than a
carryout" with a few tables.

Sanders' Corner ⑤   15 17 15 $14
2260 Cromwell Bridge Rd. (Loch Raven Dr.), Glen Arm,
410-825-5187
☑ Whether you go to this "damn quaint" American "in the
woods north of Towson" for a breakfast "like Mom's", an
"extra-thick malted", a "romantic sandwich" or a drink
with a "view on the porch", it can be "family-friendly" or
"disorganized" depending on the hour; many prescribe "a
chef transplant" before they'll go for dinner.

211

SAVANNAH S (CLOSED)   25 | 23 | 23 | $32
Admiral Fell Inn, 888 S. Broadway (Thames St.), 410-522-2195
■ Native and born-again Southerners salute Baltimore's
"best new restaurant" – a "cheerful" Fells Point "nest" of
Dixie living; besides "excellent", "refined" (but not fat-free),
"new Southern food", it features a "creative selection" of
martinis, cigars and award-winning wines; N.B. however,
a late fall 97 chef and staff relocation is in the offing.

Schultz's Crab House S   ▽ 21 | 13 | 19 | $18
1732 Old Eastern Ave. (Walkern Rd.), Essex, 410-687-1020
■ "Call ahead to check if steamed crabs are in season" (and
available) because that's the right time to visit this timeless,
"real blue-collar" Essex seafooder; there's nothing fancy
about the knotty pine dining rooms or the down-to-earth
help, but, eat-in or carryout, its crabs are among the "best."

Sevilla's ◗S   ▽ 17 | 15 | 14 | $22
(fka Rio Madrid)
4700 Eastern Ave. (Newkirk St.), 410-522-5092
☑ "Flamenco dancers", "great sangria" and a Spanish
tapas bar and dancing (downstairs) reflect a shift from
Lisbon to Madrid for this Brazilian hybrid in Highlandtown;
the hokey "La Cucaracha" festivities are the drawing card,
not the "hit-or-miss" food and service.

Sfuzzi S   18 | 19 | 17 | $22
100 E. Pratt St. (Calvert St.), 410-576-8500
☑ Baltimore's link in this forged-in-Texas "Tuscan" chain is
only a few minutes from Little Italy, but its California salads,
"nouvelle" pasta and pizza and trendy "trappings" are
decades apart in style; N.B. it's expected to become
one of Pino Luongo's Coco Pazzo's in fall of '97.

Sidestreets S   ▽ 17 | 18 | 17 | $21
8069 Tiber Alley (Main St.), Ellicott City, 410-461-5577
☑ "Adequate" for lunch or as an "end to a day in Ellicott
City", this "middle-range" American's "musty" charms
strike some as "quaint", others as "unpredictable and
average"; still, it's hard to go wrong with Sunday brunch.

Silver Diner ◗S   14 | 16 | 16 | $13
*Towson Town Ctr., 825 Dulaney Valley Rd. (Fairmount Ave.),
Towson, 410-823-5566*
See Washington, DC, Alphabetical Directory.

Silver Spring Mining Co. S   ▽ 23 | 16 | 18 | $15
(fka Silver Spring Inn)
8634 Belair Rd. (Link Ave.), Perry Hall, 410-256-6809
☑ This recently remodeled Belair Road standby still satisfies
the basics – "sit, eat, pay, leave full and not feeling ripped
off" – and has kept predecessor Marvin & George's sour
beef and dumplings on its updated all-American bar food
menu; note that the "upstairs dining room is better than
the downstairs bar" for eaters.

Sisson's S   19 | 18 | 18 | $21
36 E. Cross St. (bet. Light & Charles Sts.),
410-539-2093

■ "Order blackened anything" at Baltimore's original microbrewery, where the spicy Cajun eats (and newfangled American grills) "go great with the beer"; but most go to "enjoy the Baltimore-ness" of "Federal Hill's best" pub – "noisy", "crowded", and "hearty good fun."

Sotto Sopra S   – | – | – | M
405 N. Charles St. (Mulberry St.), 410-625-0534

Turning Baltimore's image of mod Italian dining topsy-turvy with its talented young chef from Milano cooking la vera cucina, and its "hip" gilded age decor, this "hot" young Italian on Charles Street has been having its moment; although sotto sopra means 'upside down', it seems like some knowledgeable folks are getting things right.

Speakeasy S   19 | 20 | 18 | $23
2840 O'Donnell St. (Linwood Ave.), 410-276-2977

☑ For "plain and fancy", mostly Mediterranean food in a "very pretty", vaguely Edwardian room, this gussied-up Canton speakeasy has its takers – mainly those not "watching their cholesterol" and into desserts; those who "just have drinks" in the neat-looking bar tag upstairs as being "for people who eat with their wallets."

SPIKE & CHARLIE'S S   24 | 20 | 20 | $29
1225 Cathedral St. (Preston St.), 410-752-8144

☑ Serving "adventurous, architectural" light fare and wine samplings in spare designer surroundings is no big deal in some cities, but across from the Meyerhoff & Lyric concert halls it is; despite some missteps ("slow" service), this "chichi but not imposing" New American "comes through" for everything from a "simple pizza at the bar" to "an elegant night out."

Stixx Cafe   18 | 18 | 17 | $21
Club Ctr., 1500 Reisterstown Rd. (bet. McHenry Ave. & Old Court Rd.), Pikesville, 410-484-7787

☑ Pikesville's "in crowd" recommends this slick Cal-Asian for its "excellent sushi", "varied menu", "close to home" and shopping convenience and getting you "in and out without feeling rushed"; ratings are up a notch after an ownership change last year, although a few note it "needs to shape up."

STONE MILL BAKERY S⊅   23 | 15 | 19 | $22
1609 Sulgrave Ave. (Newbury St. & Kelly Ave.),
410-542-2233
(Continues)

STONE MILL BAKERY (Cont.)
5127 Roland Ave. (Deepdene St.), 410-532-8669
1838 Green Tree Rd. (Reisterstown Rd.), Pikesville, 410-415-5961

STONE MILL BAKERY & ECOLE S
Greenspring Station, 10751 Falls Rd. (Greenspring Valley Rd.),
Brooklandville, 410-821-1358

▨ "Billy Himmelrich deserves the credit" for bringing
seriously excellent bread and croissants to Baltimore; his
"heavenly" loaves and a few choice sandwiches and
desserts make his bakery/cafes good "alternative" breakfast
and lunch venues; prix fixe, BYO dinners at the Ecole on
Friday and Saturday reflect a "passionate commitment"
to "cutting edge" cuisine, but prompt some patrons to say
"stick to the bread."

Strapazza S   16 13 16 $15
300 Pratt St. (bet. Howard & Eutaw Sts.), 410-547-1160
1330 Reisterstown Rd. (Walker Ave.), Pikesville, 410-484-6906
Palace 9, 8775 Centre Park Dr. (Rte. 108), Columbia,
410-997-6144
12 W. Allegheny Ave. (Washington Ave. & York Rd.),
Towson, 410-296-5577

▨ Given the inevitable "crying baby" and the flavors of
"Chef Boyardee", it may "feel like the relatives invited you
over" when you take the kids to these "cheap Southern
Italians" for "lots of pasta", pizza and "garlicky" entrees; of
course, quality, appearance and service "vary" by location –
the one near Camden Yards is the high-profile place.

Sunset S   20 19 17 $20
625 Greenway Ave. (Aquahart Rd.), Glen Burnie,
410-768-1417

▨ If you thought that "country club–style decor" and "large,
varied menus" of seafood, steak and American-Continental
entrees went out with the '50s, think again; efforts to revive
this Glen Burnie "suburban strip" eatery are welcomed in
an "area that needs it"; it's "romantic" and "cozy around
Christmas", but some find service "amateurish and familiar."

Surfin' Bull S   – – – M
2821 O'Donnell St. (Streeper St.), 410-675-9155
Dos hermanos "are striking out on their own" in an
attractive room above a Canton bar with Latino seafood,
flavorful beef, "homemade sangria" and their guitars;
and, just like the American "immigrant dream" movies,
it's a real family operation.

Sushi Cafe S   ▽ 17 11 16 $16
1640 Thames St. (Broadway), 410-732-3570

■ As trim and tidy as its well-made maki, this tiny Fells Point
sushi bar does "great takeout" and slices a "quick",
"cheap", "friendly" lunch; it's perfectly situated for a late-
night "sushi fix" – but do remember that the "spicy" special
rolls deliver a karate kick.

Sushi-Ya 🅂
21 | 15 | 22 | $18

*Valley Ctr., 9616 Reisterstown Rd. (Greenspring Valley Rd.),
Owings Mills, 410-356-9996*

■ A warm greeting puts diners at ease at this "clean",
personable Owings Mills Japanese; the "nicely rolled,
fresh-tasting maki, greaseless tempura", seaweed salad
and lots of cooked things to slurp and crunch please their
palates – and the BYO policy is kind to their pocketbooks.

Swallow at the Hollow 🅂
11 | 7 | 14 | $12

5921 York Rd. (Northern Pkwy.), 410-532-7542

▣ Looking "older than" most of its customers, this "smoky"
York Road "neighborhood pub would fit nicely in a pub
crawl" for "local color"; the equally "classic", "deep-fried
everything" bar fare is "cheap, filling, not very nutritious"
and tasty – and, of course, the place is filled with regulars
who "just drink."

Szechuan
22 | 11 | 20 | $16

1125 S. Charles St. (Cross St.), 410-752-8409

▣ This "plain" South Baltimore BYO Chinese has many
years of cheap, "high-quality cooking" under its belt; dubbed
"Baltimore's Szechuan pioneer", it's the locale for fiery tofu
and eggplant dishes, "excellent fish" and whatever the
staff says is good.

Szechuan Best 🅂
24 | 14 | 20 | $16

8625 Liberty Rd. (Old Court Rd.), Randallstown, 410-521-0020

▣ Try to go to this Randallstown Taiwanese with someone
who can order from the Chinese menu, or "just ask and
they help"; that way you'll be able to sample the pick of
its "authentic" Cantonese seafood, dim sum and other
multiregional specialties; "when it's on" (usually), "it's
the best in the area."

Szechuan House 🅂
▽ 22 | 18 | 23 | $15

1427 York Rd. (Seminary Ave.), Lutherville, 410-825-8181

■ Although this Lutherville Chinese has a "nice room" and
"excellent personal service", a surprising number of its
customers have never seen the place; on the other hand,
ordering the "good, cheap" carryout and delivery as often
as they do, most have gotten "to know off-the-menu items"
intimately – "and they're great."

Tenosix 🅂
▽ 18 | 16 | 18 | $20

1006 Light St. (Hamburg St.), 410-528-2146

Noodles, pasta, spaghetti, soba, bean threads – call it what
you will; if it whirls, twirls, sops up sauce or serves as
ballast in a soup, you can get it fast, cheap and "beautifully
arranged" at this multicultural noodle shop south of the
Inner Harbor; the fast food, veggie-friendly concept (and
"exceptional" desserts) seem right in line with dining trends.

TERSIGUEL'S **S**   25 | 24 | 24 | $35
8293 Main St. (Forrest St.), Ellicott City, 410-465-4004
■ No one knows how to make Americans feel comfortable
with Classic French cuisine better than Fernand Tersiguel;
his "warm, welcoming" red townhouse in Ellicott City is
"cheaper than going to Paris (but just as good)" and his
customers feel they "can't go wrong" with his menu of
"comforting favorites"; maybe the space is "cramped"
and "best seen in a dim light", but so are plenty of
lesser places in France.

T.G.I. Friday's **◑S**   14 | 14 | 15 | $15
Towson Town Ctr., 668 Fairmount Ave. (Dulaney Valley Rd.),
Towson, 410-828-4556
4921 Campbell Blvd. (Honeygo Blvd.), White Marsh, 410-931-3091
Restaurant Park, 5330 Benson Dr., Columbia, 410-312-2719
See Washington, DC, Alphabetical Directory.

Thai **S**   23 | 14 | 19 | $17
3316-18 Greenmount Ave. (33rd St.), 410-889-7303
◪ Despite the influx of newer Thai restaurants in less
"dubious" (safer) locales, this Waverly storefront is a
"real survivor"; chalk it up to the "fabulous seafood in
outstanding sauces, stunning use of herbs and spices"
and doing "great things with squid"; even when you
factor in occasional slips, it delivers a "mega-value" meal.

Thai Landing   23 | 14 | 21 | $18
1207 N. Charles St. (bet. Biddle & Preston Sts.), 410-727-1234
◪ In a city "blessed with good Thai food", this Charles
Street offering provides a bit of "atmosphere", "even
better" service and a chance to test your tolerance for
heat; "even the nonstarred dishes are too spicy" for some
and if you "ask for extra hot" – watch out; that advice also
applies to the neighborhood.

Thai Orient **S**   ▽ 23 | 20 | 21 | $17
Valley Ctr., 9616-I Reisterstown Rd. (Greenspring Valley Rd.),
Owings Mills, 410-363-3488
■ Shopping center Asian with the "right formula" for
Owings Mills – "excellent Thai", "fantastic Chinese",
crystal chandeliers, elaborate murals and "good advice"
from polite help; too bad that "it's become so popular" it
gets crowded at times.

Thames Street Tavern **S**   ▽ 15 | 15 | 15 | $13
1702 Thames St. (Broadway), 410-563-5423
◪ Before Hollywood film crews gave this Fells Point
waterfront bar visibility beyond its upstairs harbor view, it
was best known for major bedlam during "happy hour on
Fridays", "classic" bar food and what passes for service
in a twentysomething "hangout"; since then, it hired a chef
(internationally inspired).

That's Amore S 19 | 16 | 18 | $21
720 Kenilworth Dr. (West Rd.), Towson, 410-825-5255
See Washington, DC, Alphabetical Directory.

Timbuktu S – | – | – | M
1726 Dorsey Rd. (off I-295), Dorsey, 410-796-0733
Don't let the exotic "name fool you", this dark-paneled
dining room near BWI Airport is as Baltimore as can be;
indisputable proof are its "great crab cakes" and seafare-
oriented American menu.

TIO PEPE S 26 | 23 | 23 | $35
10 E. Franklin St. (bet. St. Paul & Charles Sts.), 410-539-4675
☑ A Baltimore perennial "favorite", this "Spanish wine
cellar" in the heart of Downtown has a compelling,
sangria-fueled "party" atmosphere with dungeonesque
decor, dated but good Continental dishes and courtly
bows; ups and downs last year resulted in some
unprecedented slow nights.

Tomato Palace S 19 | 17 | 18 | $16
10221 Wincopin Circle (Rte. 175), Columbia, 410-715-0211
■ On the lakefront in Columbia is "Clyde's Italian cousin",
a lighthearted, child-friendly pasta and pizza place with
"calzone so good you'll weep" and a combo of fresh,
"interesting" food, wine, "value" and "fast" service that
mostly works; a "must" on a nice day.

Tomcat Alley (CLOSED) ▽ 22 | 19 | 22 | $21
1705 Aliceanna St. (Broadway), 410-327-7037
■ There's always room for another atmospheric bar and
grill – especially one with a brick-walled courtyard; now
under new management (putting the above ratings in
question), this revamped locale goes upscale with a trendy,
ever-changing Eclectic fusion menu to complement its
new decor; lunch served weekends only.

Tony Cheng's Szechuan S 21 | 20 | 19 | $22
801 N. Charles St. (Madison St.), 410-539-6666
☑ This "spacious, quiet" Mt. Vernon townhouse is an
unexpected (and relatively expensive) setting for "better
than most" Chinese food and service; regulars have
"liked it for years", others say "used to be good, but I still
go anyway", and many feel it would be "best if they could
build a parking lot."

Trattoria Alberto ▽ 26 | 19 | 22 | $37
*1660 Crain Hwy. (Underpass Rte. 100), Glen Burnie,
410-761-0922*
■ Italian expats don't judge a restaurant's pasta and veal
by its "strip mall" location and neither should you; they
consider this somewhat "pricey" Glen Burnie Northern
Italian a "real find", with a "commendable" chef and a
willingness to "remember your name"; "make arrangements
to sit back and eat a lot."

Tully's S   17 | 16 | 15 | $15
Putty Hill Plaza, 7934 Belair Rd. (I-695), Perry Hall,
410-665-9100
◪ "A model train runs around the ceiling perimeter, a
magician comes to the table" (weekend nights), there's
wing night and shrimp night and a Monday-night band –
were it not for these "positives", this Perry Hall bar would
have little to recommend it, except as a "place for greasy
bar food, many beers" and mating possibilities.

Turtle Bay Grille S   ▽ 12 | 14 | 15 | $16
Hunt Valley Mall, 118 Shawan Rd. (bet. I-83 & York Rd.),
Hunt Valley, 410-584-2625
◪ A desert-toned, "barn"-like eatery in Hunt Valley with
an open-ended menu that covers all the casual American
food bases from the Islands to the Southwest with "typical
mall" results; given the sprawling space, it's "good the
waiters are so full of energy."

Valley Inn S   15 | 17 | 17 | $24
10501 Falls Rd. (Hillside Rd.), Brooklandville, 410-828-8080
◪ "Some things never change" – notably, this "old
plantation" in Brooklandville whose "down at the heels,
romantic" appearance, "reliable" seafood and steak menu,
"experienced servers" and "gin and tonic" clientele have
been around forever; "if you know what Old Maryland
means", you can attend this "private club."

Velleggia's S   18 | 17 | 18 | $20
829 E. Pratt St. (Albemarle St.), 410-685-2620
◪ "An old name with an older cookbook" of "heavy"-
handed pastas and veal, the self-proclaimed 'oldest
restaurant in Little Italy' could use some updating; some go
to this "large, impersonal", ornate operation for its "old-
world charm" – most on a "two-for-one."

Victor's Cafe S   18 | 20 | 17 | $25
Pier 7, 801 Lancaster St. (President St.), 410-244-1722
◪ The wrap-around deck offers "fabulous" Downtown
skyline and harbor views "worth the price of admission",
which was just as well given the need for "fine tuning" its
"strongly flavored", around-the-world-menu and for staff
training, as well as the "few things in the kitchen that
need[ed] to be worked out"; but perhaps all was smoothed
out during last spring's renovations.

Vito's Cafe   – | – | – | I
10249 York Rd., (Warren Rd.), Cockeysville, 410-666-3100
"You don't have to go to Little Italy for good, reasonable
Italian food" say supporters of this strip-mall Italian in
Cockeysville; it's cheerful and bustling – not a place for
intimate dining – but the food tastes "homemade and
delicious" and the price is right; P.S. bring your own vino.

Waterfront Hotel ⑤   ▽ 17 | 19 | 18 | $20
1710 Thames St. (bet. Broadway & Ann St.),
410-327-4886

◪ A familiar scene to TV viewers ("*Homicide* films here") as
well as to Fells Point pub crawlers, this "quaint" ("gloomy")
old bar has become a "great people-watching place"; since
it has "decent" American food and ok help, it's surprising
that it's not that hard "to get a table on a Saturday night"
in the upstairs dining room.

Weber's on Boston ⑤   – | – | – | M
(nka Le Bistro Midi)
845 S. Montford Ave. (Boston St.), 410-276-0800
See review in Baltimore/Annapolis and Eastern Shore
1998 Additions section.

Wharf Rat ⑤   15 | 18 | 15 | $15
206 W. Pratt St. (Sharp St.), 410-244-8900

◪ Close enough to Camden Yards that many virtually
"go through on the way to the ball game", this brewpub
inevitably hosts a major 'before and after' scene; although
most go to sample the "unbelievable variety" of microbrews,
we hear that the British pub fare and pizza "isn't bad."

Wild Mushroom   23 | 20 | 20 | $20
641 S. Montford Ave. (Foster Ave.), 410-675-4225

Wild Mushroom Merchant
1641 Fleet St. (bet. Broadway & Bond St.), 410-522-7277
(carryout only)

■ Mushrooms and Belgian beer would seem to be an
odd coupling, yet those specialties have made this newish
Canton bar in a vintage building "wildly popular"; it offers
plenty of portobellos (some meat and fish as well), "youthful
energy", a few tables and creatively mismatched chairs,
long waits and "innovation with a smile" – all of which make
its upstairs expansion and Canton sprouting good news.

WINDOWS ⑤   21 | 24 | 21 | $24
Renaissance Harborplace Hotel, 202 E. Pratt St.,
410-685-8439

■ "The view is stunning", the space "attractive" (if a bit
hotelish) and the Contemporary American food and service
can be a notch or two above what's needed for a "nice
business lunch"; this Downtown dining room is a "good
choice" for meetings, with a "great lunch buffet" and a
view-and-then-some Sunday brunch.

Windows on the Bay ⑤   22 | 21 | 19 | $23
White Rock Marina, 1402 Colony Rd. (Ft. Smallwood Rd.),
Pasadena, 410-255-1413

■ At "sunset in warm weather", this "lovely" marina setting
near Severna Park glows best; it's a "fine" place to soak
up "local color" and eat "terrific fish" (or unsurprising
American food); call ahead – it's "not easy to find."

Wing Wah ⑤   ▽ 18 | 13 | 21 | $13
509 Reisterstown Rd. (Slade Ave.), 410-653-0606

☑ A "throwback" to the "egg roll" and "fried rice" dynasty of suburban Chinese food, this offering's carry-out business was so popular that it set up a dining room; but takeout is still the recommended option for a "tasty", "predictable" fast-food fix in Pikesville.

Woman's Industrial Exchange   18 | 16 | 23 | $10
333 N. Charles St. (Pleasant St.), 410-685-4388

■ "Wonderful" "turn-of-the-century tearoom" that evokes a "kind and gentle" era with every bite; it's presided over by the "original staff" ("where else can you be waited on by a 90-year-old?") serving "homemade", white-bread food for what seems like the original prices; check out the handicrafts before you leave; N.B. breakfast and lunch, weekdays only.

Ze Mean Bean Cafe ⑤   ▽ 20 | 22 | 19 | $11
1739 Fleet St. (bet. Broadway & S. Ann St.), 410-675-5999

■ This "mellow" coffeehouse in Fells Point has the "added bonus" of some interesting Eastern European food, especially at dinner; if you're not "in a hurry", sink into the red damask couch, taste some brewed beans and find out what "pierogi" means.

Zorba's ⑤   ▽ 18 | 15 | 17 | $18
4710 Eastern Ave. (bet. Oldham & Newkirk Sts.), 410-276-4484

■ "Lots of regulars" at the bar of this Highlandtown nook lend it "old-time atmosphere"; while the kitchen does an "excellent" job with steak and grilled fish, "the chops and octopus" are also recommended (on a "hit-or-miss" basis); expect the help to be "low key."

F	D	S	C

Adam's Ribs S
| 19 | 13 | 18 | $16 |

East Port Shopping Ctr., 321-C Chesapeake Ave. (Bay Ridge Ave.), 410-267-0064
589 Baltimore-Annapolis Blvd. (MacKenzie Rd.), Severna Park, 410-647-5757
219 N. Fruitland Blvd./Rte. 13, Salisbury, 410-749-6961
2200 Solomon's Island Rd./Rte. 4, Prince Frederick, 410-586-0001
169 Mayo Rd. (Old Solomon Rd.), Edgewater, 410-956-2995
■ "Absolutely the best ribs in the USA (including Texas)" and the "best value" too – once such a secret leaks, this "plain" suburban Annapolis BBQ could be mobbed by Baltimore and DC BBQ freaks; right now, it's a family-oriented, neighborhood place near the movies, where waiters "enjoy their work."

Angler S
| ▽ 18 | 15 | 18 | $17 |

3015 Kent Narrows Way S. (Rte. 18), Grasonville, 410-827-6717
■ A "convenient" stop "after sailing" or for a home-cooked "dinner on the way to the beach"; local "hunters and fishermen" eat steak and fried chicken, while tourists find a "Chesapeake seafood experience" and kind folks – no one goes to this "unpretentious" restaurant "for the decor."

Armadillo's ◑ S
| ▽ 15 | 15 | 16 | $18 |

City Dock, 132 Dock St. (Main St.), 410-268-6680
☑ "Great margaritas and the band upstairs" parlay an Annapolis City Dock location into big-time party time; think of it as "a friendly bar" with a "great waterfront location" and treat the Tex-Mex food as "pricey" fuel.

Bertucci's S
| 17 | 16 | 16 | $15 |

2207 Forest Dr. (bet. Rte. 2 & Riva Rd.), 410-266-5800
See Washington, DC, Alphabetical Directory.

Buddy's Crabs & Ribs S
| 14 | 13 | 15 | $17 |

100 Main St. (Market St.), 410-269-1800
■ "Other places have better" steamed crabs, BBQ, bar food, housekeeping and help (not to mention smaller crowds and shorter waits), but they don't have a "down by City Dock" location, which is why it's easy to "spot Navy cadets" and virtually everyone else at this hurly-burly "tourist trap."

Cafe du Vin S (CLOSED)   – | – | – | M |
Clocktower Plaza, 1410 Forest Dr. (Gemini Dr.), 410-268-6677
Blessed for bringing house-baked breads and well-selected
wines to the Annapolis area, plus "creative sandwiches",
pastries and "imaginative" Continental-American entrees,
this take-out market/bakery/cafe offers multiple solutions
to the 'what do we do about dinner' dilemma; for added
inspiration, you can sample "over 40 wines by the glass."

Cafe Normandie S   23 | 21 | 20 | $26 |
185 Main St. (bet. Church Circle & Conduit St.), 410-263-3382
✓ A "charming" French bistro in historic Annapolis is bound
to attract tourists, especially when its fireplace looks so
"inviting on cold winter nights"; this one is also a "local
favorite", highly praised by most, but not all ("nice but
uninspired"), for its provincial fare and early-bird deals.

Cafe Sophie S⌿ (CLOSED)   – | – | – | M |
401 Lovepoint Rd. (Historic Stevensville), Stevensville,
410-643-8811
If more people knew about this "jewel", a "lovely, small,
owner-run" French boîte in Stevensville, it might lose its
"refreshing" appeal; here, Lyon-born Suzanne Peach cooks
carefully chosen, market-based bistro fare to order – as
she would in her home; N.B. lunch Wednesday–Sunday,
dinner Friday and Saturday.

California Pizza Kitchen S   18 | 14 | 17 | $16 |
Annapolis Mall, 22 Annapolis Mall (Jennifer Rd.), 410-573-2060
See Washington, DC, Alphabetical Directory.

Calvert House S   ▽ 19 | 14 | 18 | $21 |
401 Solomon's Island Rd. (Parole Plaza), 410-266-9210
■ Although there's "nothing exceptional" about its
American food or clean-cut appearance, this Parole
seafooder will come as a "real surprise"; seldom does one
find the combination of simplicity, "good quality" and "good
value" – traits much appreciated by its early-bird clientele.

Cantler's Riverside Inn S   21 | 15 | 18 | $21 |
458 Forest Beach Rd. (on Mills Creek), 410-757-1311
■ There's "no better crab pickin'" than at this "true riverside
crab joint" near Annapolis; the crabs arrive "fresh off
the boat daily", along with other local seafood, and the
atmosphere is "great"; the "challenge is finding it" (call
for directions) and being prepared to wait (even to park).

Carrol's Creek Cafe S   20 | 23 | 20 | $26 |
410 Severn Ave. (East Port Bridge), 410-263-8102, in
Baltimore call 410-269-1406
✓ This contemporary seafood "vantage point" overlooking
the harbor draws two kinds of trade – those who "go for a
drink on the deck" and those who say the "imaginative"
kitchen "doesn't rely" on the "scenic location"; P.S. if you
lean toward the latter, ask for a "view table."

Chart House
19 21 19 $28
300 Second St. (Severn Ave.), 410-265-7166
See Washington, DC, Alphabetical Directory.

CHESTER RIVER INN S (CLOSED)
27 18 23 $32
Castle Harbour Marina, 205 Tackle Circle (1 mi. off Rte. 50), Chester, 410-643-3886
■ Mark Henry (ex Milton Inn) gets rave reviews and near top marks in this *Survey* for "wonderful high-end and low-end", classically based Contemporary American fare at his Kent Island venue: "excellent food, great presentation", "pleasant people and place", "worth a detour, but don't dress up"; N.B. it's especially nice on the porch in summer.

Chick & Ruth's Delly ●S⌀
18 14 18 $11
165 Main St. (Conduit St.), 410-269-6737
■ From the "breakfast pledge of allegiance" (recited at 8:30 AM during the week, 9:30 AM on weekends) until after the bars close, Annapolis locals "meet their legislators" and everyone else at this Downtown "1930s-style" diner/deli; go for "local color", magic tricks, milk shakes, chopped liver, a cheap feed, whatever – just go.

Corinthian S
▽ 25 26 25 $30
Loews Annapolis Hotel, 126 West St. (Lafayette St.), 410-263-1299
■ "Crisp tablecloths" and "elegant" appointments tag this Annapolis hotel dining room as *the* "fine dining" place; although "sometimes ordinary", it's capable of "five-star service", "steak cooked to perfection" and a "nice variety" of Contemporary American dishes.

Crab Claw S⌀
21 17 17 $21
Navy Point, 156 Mill St. (Talbot St.), St. Michaels, 410-745-2900
☑ "One of St. Michaels' oldest, most bustling crab houses", beloved by boaters, lets you watch the river traffic from its pierside prospect, and the "seafood and crabs are great"; unfortunately, it's "now haunted by the tour bus crowd", which overwhelms the help.

Fergie's S
▽ 17 19 21 $24
Oak Grove Marina, 2840 Solomon's Island Rd. (off Rte. 2 next to South River Blvd.), Edgewater, 410-573-1371
■ The South River window view "at sunset" (and "value" deals) season the "good, not great" food at this "aim-to-please" American "suitable for a businessman's lunch."

Giolitti Deli S
▽ 22 8 15 $11
2068 Summerville Rd. (bet. Rte. 2 & West St.), 410-266-8600
■ This "authentic Italian cafe and grocery store outside Annapolis is not to be missed" for its breads, pastas and entrees – they often inspire "spur-of-the-moment" meals; it's also a treasure trove of "specialty ingredients" and good wine so you can "do it yourself" at home.

Griffin's at City Dock ◐Ⓢ
18 | 19 | 17 | $19

2224 Market Space (Main St.), 410-268-2576

Griffin's West St. Grill
2049 West St. (Rte. 2), 410-266-7662

■ "Good management", "good bar", "good atmosphere", "good American food in the heart of Annapolis", "good everything" – why can't those City Dock tourist traps learn from this well-designed, gargoyle-themed pub?; P.S. go for "oysters at the bar" paired with "wine by the glass."

Harris' Crab House Ⓢ
21 | 15 | 19 | $20

433 N. Kent Narrows Way (off Rte. 50 under Kent Narrows Bridge), Grasonville, 410-827-9500

■ Cracking crabs at this "real Maryland crab house" just over the Bay Bridge will "extend your vacation" – the picnic tables on the upper deck, "water, water everywhere" and "great sunsets" are the "essence of the shore"; it's "family-owned", locally favored and hard to find.

Harry Browne's Ⓢ
23 | 22 | 23 | $28

66 State Circle (bet. Maryland Ave. & East St.), 410-263-4332, in Baltimore call 410-269-5124

■ If it were possible to keep a "secret" near the State House, this classy Continental would be it; it brings a touch of *Casablanca* to the "Circle" with strong drinks, "well-served", "reliably good" food and a location "far enough from the tourists to provide a lovely, leisurely meal"; in summer, the patio is a "popular" retreat.

Holly's Ⓢ
∇ 15 | 10 | 18 | $18

108 Jackson Creek Rd. (Rte. 50), Grasonville, 410-827-8711

■ For travelers, this "old-fashioned diner" offers a chance to eat the "best chicken salad in the US", "great fried chicken" and "vanilla milk shakes" instead of "Route 50 fast food"; for locals, it's "of extreme importance" as a meeting place.

Imperial Hotel Ⓢ
∇ 27 | 27 | 27 | $37

Imperial Hotel, 208 High St. (Cross St.), Chestertown, 410-778-5000

■ Cap "a wonderful escape" to a colonial-era Chesapeake Bay port with a "most enjoyable" Contemporary American meal in this "charming" inn's dining room; Carla and Al Missoni, who were responsible for its "lovely" restoration, "know and care, especially about wine."

INN AT PERRY CABIN Ⓢ
27 | 29 | 26 | $49

Inn at Perry Cabin, 308 Watkins Ln. (Talbot St.), St. Michaels, 410-745-2200

■ Maybe it's a "schlep and a bit too fussy", but very few would turn down a meal (or overnight stay) at this luxurious manor on the Eastern Shore; it's "definitely a special-occasion experience" with "beautifully served", modern Continental food matched by award-winning wines and a patio with a breathtaking water view.

Ironstone Cafe
▽ 27 | 23 | 24 | $28

236 Cannon St. (Cross St.), Chestertown, 410-778-0188

■ This "informal" eatery in historic Chestertown has "character" – a rough-edged, "creative simplicity" reflected in the short, eclectic, Regional American menu and "pleasant" atmosphere; it looks like a "real find", but with a chef change who knows?

LA PICCOLA ROMA S
24 | 21 | 22 | $29

200 Main St. (bet. Church Circle & Conduit St.), 410-268-7898

■ In historic Annapolis, this "intimate", Victorian-feeling storefront's Northern Italian food and "gracious" hospitality reflect Mary and Gino Giolitti's Roman restaurant family roots; many consider it Annapolis' "best."

Lewnes' Steakhouse S
▽ 29 | 21 | 22 | $42

401 Fourth St. (Severn Ave.), 410-263-1617

■ Sometimes there's nothing like a big, juicy steak – "cholesterol be damned"; when so inclined in the Annapolis area, this "men's club" steakhouse with its "big portions, big prices" approach to "excellent steak and seafood" is "the only place to go."

Maria's Italian Ristorante ◑S
▽ 20 | 16 | 18 | $23

12 Market Space (Randall St.), 410-268-2112

☑ It's on Market Square, but it has the air of a side-street trattoria in Rome; this Southern Italian is a "local place" with a "home-like atmosphere" and "predictable" fare; surrounded by tourist meccas, it's a "good solid choice."

Marmaduke's Pub S (CLOSED)
▽ 16 | 17 | 16 | $18

301 Severn Ave. (3rd St.), 410-268-1656, in Baltimore call 410-269-5420

■ At Eastport's semi-official "sailboat racing headquarters", a polished mahogany pub with "pretty good" burgers and "seasonal seafood", docksiders swap scuttlebutt "after Wednesday night races"; for those less nautically inclined, there's a weekend sing-along upstairs.

McGarvey's ◑S
19 | 18 | 18 | $19

8 Market Space (Pinkney St.), 410-263-5700

■ After the sails go down, "tourists and shoppers" make way for a "rowdy yachty crowd" at this popular seaporter where the "classic American saloon food" (chili, burgers, black bean soup) is "good" and the bar is "better" – "this is the place for oysters and a real taste of Annapolis."

Michael Rork's Town Dock S
▽ 22 | 17 | 20 | $28

125 Mulberry St. (waterfront), St. Michaels, 410-745-5577

☑ Boaters can dock at Michael Rork's (ex Hampton's) St. Michaels "crowd-pleaser" – a sprawling indoor-outdoor, casual-serious dining and entertainment complex with "seafood galore", a "great staff" and "sunset on the bay" views; those who "order from the daily specials" are most likely to get one of his "great" meals.

Mick's
16 | 16 | 16 | $16

*Annapolis Mall, 187 Annapolis Mall (off Parole Rd.),
410-224-4225*
See Washington, DC, Alphabetical Directory.

Middleton Tavern
20 | 21 | 18 | $23

2 Market Space (Randall St.), 410-263-3323
◪ "Cozy", colonial-era tavern with "lots of history", a
"working fireplace", "great oyster shooters", "good pub
grub" and seafood – no wonder it's swamped by tourists
and "preppy sailors"; the bar is a hangout for an "older
crowd" – with "food secondary" and service in third place.

Mike's Crab House ⑤
▽ 16 | 15 | 14 | $18

3030 Riva Rd. (White Point Rd.), Riva, 410-956-2784
◪ "Ok for crabs" and beer, with a "pretty setting by the
river", an outdoor deck and its "own dock for boats", this
Annapolis-area crab house is decidedly less appealing
inside; at night, "casual slumming" in the bar is more of a
draw than the "average" burgers and seafood, although
local workers come here for lunch.

NARROWS ⑤
23 | 23 | 21 | $27

3023 Kent Narrows Way S. (Rte. 18), Grasonville, 410-827-8113
■ A contender for "best crab cakes" and crab soup in the
area; this Kent Narrows viewspot mixes a "great Bloody
Mary" and its "traditional and nontraditional shore menu is
always good", too; though it seems "almost too fancy" to
be fixing shore food, it's "very relaxing", "not overpriced"
and will cook your catch, at the lowest entree price, as long
as it's gutted and scaled.

NORTHWOODS ⑤
27 | 22 | 25 | $35

*609 Melvin Ave. (Ridgely Ave.), 410-268-2609, in Baltimore
call 410-269-6775*
■ The "lovely prix fixe meal" ($25.95 Sunday–Friday) is
Continental ("not cutting edge"), the candlelit residential
setting "pleasant" (if "slightly cramped") and the service
"unsurpassed"; this "special-occasion place" rates a spot
on almost everyone's 'Tops in Annapolis' list because it's
"consistent", "quietly festive" and "a good deal."

O'Brien's ◗⑤
▽ 16 | 17 | 16 | $21

*113 Main St. (Green St.), 410-268-6288, in Baltimore call
410-269-0099, in DC call 301-261-2100*
■ Don't take a politico to this clubby Annapolis tavern
"when the assembly is in session" – there will be "too many
handshake interruptions" to your spiel (later in the evening,
the distractions are youthful meetings of a different kind);
the raw bar, steak and seafood won't overwhelm, and,
though we're told "the place has improved dramatically",
it still "could use some decor."

O'Leary's Seafood ⑤
23 | 20 | 21 | $32

310 Third St. (Severn Ave.), 410-263-0884

■ Recommended by Annapolis 'finatics' for "swimmingly" fresh fish "prepared to your request"; the cottagelike premises are as simple as the "casual" concept (which translates service-wise as "expect to wait"), and though prices may seem high for the setting, they're reasonable for high-quality seafare.

Outback Steakhouse
20 | 16 | 19 | $21

Hechinger Plaza, 2207 Forest Dr. (Riva Rd.), 410-266-7229
See Washington, DC, Alphabetical Directory.

Paul's on the South River ⑤
▽ 22 | 23 | 22 | $34

3027 Riva Rd. (Old Riva Rd.), Riva, 410-798-5272

☑ "Walking out on the pier" is a pleasant coda to a business lunch at this "nice"-looking "water place" near Annapolis, or you can sail in for a "romantic" meal; the "varied" American menu "emphasizes seafood" – understandably, as it has three seafood market sibs; some find it "ho-hum."

Rams Head Tavern ◗⑤
18 | 19 | 17 | $20

33 West St. (bet. Church Circle & Calvert St.), 410-268-4545

■ "Annapolis' best bet" for "good microbrews to wash down innovative pub fare"; this handsome brewpub with a "historic atmosphere" has one of the "best beer selections in Maryland" – over 130 bottled brews and 24 on draft along with a trellised brick patio for summertime quaffs; service is not on "par."

Red Hot & Blue
20 | 15 | 17 | $17

201 Revell Hwy. (Rte. 50 at Old Mill Bottom Rd.), 410-626-7427
See Washington, DC, Alphabetical Directory.

Reynolds Tavern ⑤
▽ 20 | 24 | 20 | $26

7 Church Circle (Franklin St.), 410-626-0380

☑ "Filled with history and good food", this "Williamsburg-like", colonial-era re-creation is a "wonderful location for a reception"; the "Chesapeake Bay dishes", rack of lamb and plain American food can be very "good if you hit it right" – the same goes for the service.

Riordan's ◗⑤
19 | 17 | 18 | $20

26 Market Space (Main St.), 410-263-5449

☑ One of several "middle of the road" Market Space taverns where "what you see is what you get" – "friendly" fun, a "good steak" or "some of the best bar food" and a "perfect place for Sunday brunch"; what you don't get is innovation or much service or, unless you go upstairs, "quiet" conversation.

Saigon Palace S ▽ 23 | 13 | 19 | $20

West Annapolis Shopping Ctr., 609-B Taylor Ave. (Rowe Blvd.), 410-268-4463

■ A welcome "change of pace" for Annapolis dwellers, their local Vietnamese offers lots of "vegetarian choices" and "good specials" in a "try-hard" storefront setting; occasional "French twists" are a reminder of colonial Indochina – it's all very "not terrifying."

Scirocco Mediterranean Grill S ▽ 24 | 23 | 22 | $30

(nka Michelangelo)

2552 Riva Rd. (Rte. 665), Riva, 410-573-0970

◪ There aren't many Annapolis-area restaurants suitable for business and dress-up dining, and fewer still with the ambition to offer a menu spanning Africa, Spain, Italy and Greece; while this Mediterranean villa is sometimes "uneven" and "amateurish", its emphasis on seafood and open-hearth and grill catch the prevailing breeze.

T.G.I. Friday's 14 | 14 | 15 | $15

Annapolis Harbour Ctr., 2582 Solomon's Island Rd. (Patuxent Blvd.), 410-224-4870

See Washington, DC, Alphabetical Directory.

TREATY OF PARIS S 24 | 25 | 23 | $34

Maryland Inn, 16 Church Circle (bet. Main & Duke of Gloucester Sts.), 410-216-6340, in Baltimore call 410-269-0990

◪ "Colonial atmosphere" and "all that jazz" sums up historic Annapolis' "finest", a Revolutionary War–era relic with a blend of Chesapeake seafood and contemporary classics, "erratic" charm and a "food orgy" brunch; weekend sounds in the tavern feature the likes of Charlie Byrd.

208 Talbot S ▽ 28 | 23 | 26 | $37

208 N. Talbot St. (bet. North St. & Dodson Ave.), St. Michaels, 410-745-3838

■ This enchanting St. Michaels Contemporary American townhouse earns accolades from nearly all quarters: "professional, serious, very pleasant", "most imaginative", "reasonable prices for quality", "as near perfect as you can get"; it's "best when the chef-owner is behind the range", which he mostly is; N.B. Saturday night is prix fixe only.

Indexes to Baltimore Restaurants

Special Features and Appeals

TYPES OF CUISINE

Afghan
Helmand

American
Adrian's
Alonso's
Anastasia
Angelina's
Bare Bones
Baugher's
Bay Cafe
Bel-Loc Diner
Berry & Elliot's
Bertha's
Bill Bateman's
Bowman
Buddy's
Burke's
Cafe Hon
Calvert House
Canopy
Charred Rib
Cheesecake Factory
City Lights
Claddagh Pub
Corner Stable
Crack Pot
Crease
Double T Diner
Duda's Tavern
Fergie's
Field's Pharmacy
Fisherman's Wharf
Foster's
Frazier's
Friendly Farms
Gr. Amer. Melt. Pot
Griffin's
Hampton's of Towson
Hampton Tea Room
Harryman House
Harvey's
Hersh's Orchard Inn
Holly's
Hull St. Blues
Hunt Ridge
Jenning's Cafe
Jerry D's Saloon
Jilly's
Jimmy's
John Steven, Ltd.
J. Patrick's
Kaufmann's Tavern
Kelly's
Kelsey's
Kisling's Tavern
Louie's Bookstore
Manor Tavern

Marmaduke's Pub
McCabe's
McCafferty's
McGarvey's
Michael's
Mick's
Middleton Tavern
Morgan Millard
Morning Edition
Mt. Washington
Narrows
Nates & Leons
New Towne Diner
Ocean Pride
Palermo's Grill
PaperMoon Diner
Paul's
Peerce's Gourmet
Peppermill
Perring Place
Peter's Inn
Phillips Harborplace
Phillips Seafood
Pier 500
Polo Grill
Prime Rib
Ralphie's Diner
Rams Head Tavern
Ransome's
Red Star
Redwood Grill
Regi's
Reynolds Tavern
Riordan's
River Watch
Rusty Scupper
Saguaro's
Sanders' Corner
Sidestreets
Silver Diner
Silver Spring
Sunset
Surfin' Bull
Swallow at Hollow
T.G.I. Friday's
Thames St. Tavern
Treaty of Paris
Tully's
Turtle Bay
Valley Inn
Waterfront Hotel
Weber's
Wharf Rat
Windows
Woman's Ind. Exchange

NEIGHBORHOOD LOCATIONS

BALTIMORE

Downtown/Charles Street/Mt. Vernon
Akbar
Al Pacino Cafe
Ban Thai
Bombay Grill
Brass Elephant
Braznell's
Champagne Tony's
Donna's Coffee Bar
Gr. Amer. Melt. Pot
Helmand
Jpn.
Kawasaki
La Tesso Tana
Louie's Bookstore
Metropol Cafe
Minato
Mughal Garden
Nam Kang
New Orleans Cafe
Pavilion at Walters
Prime Rib
Purple Orchid
Ruby Lounge
Sotto Sopra
Spike & Charlie's
Thai Landing
Tio Pepe
Tony Cheng's
Woman's Ind. Exchange

Downtown/Convention Center/Camden Yards/Inner Harbor
Berry & Elliot's
Burke's
Cafe Bombay
Chart House
Cheesecake Factory
City Lights
Faidley's
Hampton's
Marconi's
Martick's
Nates & Leons
Phillips Harborplace
Pier 500
Redwood Grill
Rusty Scupper
Ruth's Chris
Sfuzzi
Strapazza
Victor's Cafe

Wharf Rat
Windows

East Baltimore/Canton/Highlandtown
Acropolis
Amicci's
Anastasia
Attman's Deli
Bay Cafe
Claddagh Pub
Haussner's
Ikaros
Jimmy's Famous Sea.
Kelly's
Kisling's Tavern
Morning Edition
Nacho Mama's
Obrycki's
OPA
Samos
Sevilla's
Speakeasy
Surfin' Bull
Weber's
Wild Mushroom
Zorba's

Essex
A-1 Crab Haven
River Watch
Schultz's Crab Hse.

Fells Point
Adrian's
Al Pacino Cafe
Bertha's
Birds of a Feather
Duda's Tavern
El Taquito
Fishery
Foster's
Henninger's Tavern
Jimmy's
John Steven, Ltd.
Lista's
Margaret's Cafe
Peter's Inn
Piccolo's
Pierpoint
Red Star
Savannah
Sushi Cafe
Thames St. Tavern
Tomcat Alley

NEARBY MARYLAND

ANNAPOLIS/EASTERN SHORE

SPECIAL FEATURES AND APPEALS

Breakfast
(All major hotels and the
following best bets)
Baugher's
Bel-Loc Diner
Cafe du Vin
Cafe Hon
Cafe Normandie
Chick & Ruth's
Donna's Coffee Bar
Double T Diner
Holly's
Jimmy's
Morning Edition
Nates & Leons
New Towne Diner
One World Cafe
Stone Mill Bakery
Woman's Ind. Exchange
Ze Mean Bean

Brunch
(Best of many)
Anastasia
Bertha's
Cafe Hon
Carrol's Creek Cafe
Champagne Tony's
Chart House
Clyde's
Corinthian
Donna's at BMA
Hampton's
Harry Browne's
Harryman House
Hersh's Orchard Inn
Hull St. Blues
Imperial Hotel
Josef's Country Inn
Kelsey's
Lista's
Louie's Bookstore
Manor Tavern
Margaret's Cafe
Marmaduke's Pub
Metropol Cafe
Michael Rork's
Morgan Millard
Morning Edition
Paolo's
Pavilion at Walters
Peerce's Plantation
Phillips Harborplace
Pier 500
Pierpoint
Polo Grill
Rams Head Tavern
Ransome's

Red Star
Savannah
Sidestreets
Spike & Charlie's
Thames St. Tavern
Treaty of Paris
208 Talbot
Victor's Cafe
Waterfront Hotel
Weber's
Windows
Windows on the Bay
Ze Mean Bean

Buffet Served
(B = brunch; L = lunch;
D = dinner)
Akbar (B,L)
Anastasia (B)
Banjara (L)
Bombay Grill (L)
Bombay Peacock (L)
Cafe Bombay (L)
Carrol's Creek Cafe (B)
Corinthian (B)
Fergie's (L)
Harry Browne's (B)
Harvey's (B)
Hull St. Blues (B)
Manor Tavern (B)
Metropol Cafe (B)
Michael Rork's (B,D)
Mughal Garden (L)
New No Da Ji (L,D)
Orchard Market (B)
Peerce's Gourmet (B)
Phillips Seafood (B)
Polo Grill (B)
Purim Oak
Saigon Palace (L)
Scirocco (B)
Treaty of Paris (B)
Weber's (B)
Windows (B)

Business Dining
Bamboo House
Berry & Elliot's
Boccaccio
Bombay Grill
Brass Elephant
Cafe Bombay
Corinthian
Due
Hampton's
Helmand
Hersh's Orchard Inn
King's Contrivance
Liberatore's

Delivers*/Takeout

(Nearly all Asians, coffee shops, delis, diners and pizzerias deliver or do takeout; here are some interesting possibilities;
D = delivery, T = takeout)

(* Call to check range and charges, if any)

Dessert & Ice Cream

Dining Alone
(Other than hotels)
Cafe Hon
Café Pangea
Donna's
John Steven, Ltd.
Linwood's
Louie's Bookstore
Margaret's Cafe
Matsuri
Pavilion at Walters
Samos
Sushi Cafe
Windows

Family Style
Friendly Farms
That's Amore

Fireplaces
Anastasia
Antrim 1844
A-1 Crab Haven
Bandaloops
Bombay Grill
Bowman
Cacao Lane
Cafe Normandie
Chart House
Da Mimmo
daniel's
Elkridge Furnace
Foster's
Harryman House
Hull St. Blues
Imperial Hotel
Inn at Perry Cabin
La Piccola Roma
Luigi Petti
Manor Tavern
Middleton Tavern
Milton Inn
O'Brien's
Ocean Pride
Peerce's Plantation
Regi's
Reynolds Tavern
River Watch
Sanders' Corner
Thames St. Tavern
Tony Cheng's
Treaty of Paris
Turtle Bay
Valley Inn
Velleggia's
Weber's
Ze Mean Bean

Game in Season
Birds of a Feather
Brass Elephant
Cafe Sophie

daniel's
Hampton's
Imperial Hotel
Inn at Perry Cabin
Joy America
La Tesso Tana
Metropol Cafe
Polo Grill
Rudys' 2900
Sotto Sopra
Tersiguel's
Trattoria Alberto

Health/Spa Menus
(Most places cook to order to meet any dietary request; call in advance to check; almost all health-food spots, Chinese, Indian and other ethnics have health-conscious meals, as do the following)
Akbar
Dalesio's
Harvey's
Hoang's
Kelly's
Margaret's Cafe
One World Cafe
Puffin's
Thai
Wild Mushroom

Historic Interest
(Year Opened)
1740 Milton Inn*
1740 Rams Head Tavern*
1744 Elkridge Furnace*
1747 Reynolds Tavern
1750 Middleton Tavern*
1762 Savannah*
1772 Treaty of Paris*
1774 O'Brien's
1790 Harryman House*
1797 Hampton Tea Room*
1808 daniel's*
1820 Bertha's*
1820 La Piccola Roma*
1830 Valley Inn*
1844 Antrim 1844*
1850 Brass Elephant*
1850 Martick's*
1850 Wild Mushroom*
1860 Cacao Lane*
1860 Weber's*
1860 Woman's Ind. Exchange*
1871 McGarvey's*
1871 208 Talbot*
1880 Henninger's Tavern*
1880 Manor Tavern*
1886 Sanders' Corner*
1887 Hull St. Blues

Hotel Dining

"In" Places

Jacket Required

Late Late – After 12:30

Meet for a Drink

Noteworthy Newcomers

T.G.I. Friday's
Thai Landing
That's Amore
Wild Mushroom

Romantic Spots
Akbar
Antrim 1844
Cacao Lane
Desert Cafe
Henninger's Tavern
La Tesso Tana
Milton Inn
Northwoods
Prime Rib
Sotto Sopra
Treaty of Paris
208 Talbot

Saturday Dining
(B=brunch; L=lunch;
best of many)
Angler (L)
Baugher's (L)
Cacao Lane (L)
Cafe Hon (B,L)
Cafe Normandie (L)
Cafe Sophie (L)
Cantler's Riverside (L)
Charred Rib (L)
Chester River Inn (L)
Donna's at BMA (L)
Gabler's (L)
Grand Palace (L)
Haussner's (L)
Inn at Perry Cabin (L)
John Steven, Ltd. (L)
Josef's Country Inn (L)
La Tesso Tana (L)
Liberatore's (L)
Linwood's (L)
Louie's Bookstore (L)
Marconi's (L)
Michael Rork's (L)
Middleton Tavern (L)
Narrows (L)
One World Cafe (L)
Pavilion at Walters (B,L)
Piccolo's (L)
Polo Grill (L)
Sabatino's (L)
Sanders' Corner (L)
Treaty of Paris (L)
Wild Mushroom (L)
Windows on the Bay (L)

Sunday Dining
(B=brunch; L=lunch;
D=dinner; best of many)
Amicci's (L,D)
Baugher's (L,D)
Cacao Lane (L,D)

Cafe Normandie (L,D)
Cafe Sophie (L)
Cafe Zen (L,D)
Carrol's Creek Cafe (B,D)
Cheesecake Factory (L,D)
Dalesio's (D)
daniel's (D)
Donna's at BMA (B,D)
Double T Diner (L,D)
Due (D)
Friendly Farms (L,D)
Grand Palace (L,D)
Harry Browne's (B,D)
Harryman House (B,D)
Hull St. Blues (B,D)
Imperial Hotel (B)
Inn at Perry Cabin (L,D)
Jimmy's Famous Sea. (L,D)
Joy America (L,D)
La Piccola Roma (D)
La Tesso Tana (L,D)
Linwood's (D)
Louie's Bookstore (B,L,D)
Margaret's Cafe (B,L,D)
Michael Rork's (B,L,D)
Morning Edition (B,L)
Narrows (L,D)
Northwoods (D)
O'Leary's (D)
Paolo's (B,L,D)
Pavilion at Walters (B,L)
Piccolo's (L,D)
Pierpoint (B,D)
Polo Grill (B,D)
Prime Rib (D)
Ruby Lounge (D)
Rudys' 2900 (D)
Saigon (L,D)
Sanders' Corner (B,L,D)
Savannah (B,D)
Sotto Sopra (D)
Trattoria Alberto (D)
Treaty of Paris (B,L,D)
208 Talbot (B,D)
Weber's (B,D)
Ze Mean Bean (B,D)

Singles Scenes
Bay Cafe
Bill Bateman's
Hersh's Orchard Inn
Jilly's
Marmaduke's Pub
McGarvey's
Michael's
Middleton Tavern
Mt. Washington
Nacho Mama's
Nick's
Obrien's
Rams Head Tavern

Red Star
River Watch
Rusty Scupper

Sleepers

(Good to excellent food, but little known)

Antrim 1844
Cafe Bretton
Cafe Sophie
Cafe Zen
Chester River Inn
Ciao Bella
Claddagh Pub
Elkridge Furnace
Fazzini's
Giolitti Deli
Grand Palace
Gunning's (Dorsey)
Hampton's of Towson
Harris' Crab House
Imperial Hotel
Ironstone Cafe
Lewnes' Steakhouse
Matsuri
Perring Place
Peter's Inn
Reynolds Tavern
Saigon
Saigon Palace
Samos
Thai Orient
Tomcat Alley
208 Talbot
Windows on the Bay

Teflons

(Gets lots of business, despite so-so food, i.e. they have other attractions that prevent criticism from sticking)

Bay Cafe
Bel-Loc Diner
Double T Diner
Mt. Washington
Phillips Harborplace
Silver Diner
T.G.I. Friday's

Teas

(See also *Coffeehouses* & *Dessert* Indexes)

Bertha's
Hampton Tea Room
Harbor Court Hotel
Inn at Perry Cabin
Ze Mean Bean

Visitors on Expense Accounts

Corinthian
Da Mimmo

Due
Hampton's
Harry Browne's
Inn at Perry Cabin
Joy America
King's Contrivance
Lewnes' Steakhouse
Liberatore's
Linwood's
Marconi's
Michael Rork's
Milton Inn
Northwoods
Pierpoint
Polo Grill
Prime Rib
Rudys' 2900
Ruth's Chris
Savannah
Scirocco
Sotto Sopra
Tersiguel's
Tio Pepe
Treaty of Paris
208 Talbot

Wheelchair Access

(Check for bathroom access; almost all hotels plus the following)

Adam's Rib
Akbar
Al Pacino Cafe
Amicci's
Anastasia
Angelina's
Angler
Bamboo House
Ban Thai
Bare Bones
Baugher's
Bay Cafe
Berry & Elliot's
Bertucci's
Bill Bateman's
Bo Brooks
Boccaccio
Bombay Peacock
Bowman
Brasserie
Burke's
Cafe Bretton
Cafe Hon
Cafe Normandie
Cafe Tattoo
Cafe Troia
Cafe Zen
Cal. Pizza Kit.
Candle Light Inn
Captain Harvey's
Carrol's Creek Cafe

Wine Vintage Chart 1983-1995

This chart is designed to help you select wine to go with your meal. It is based on the same 0 to 30 scale used throughout this *Survey*. The ratings (prepared by our friend Howard Stravitz, a law professor at the University of South Carolina) reflect both the quality of the vintage and the wine's readiness for present consumption. Thus, if a wine is not fully mature or is over the hill, its rating has been reduced. We do not include 1984 and 1987 because, with the exception of '87 cabernets, those vintages are not recommended.

WHITES	'83	'85	'86	'88	'89	'90	'91	'92	'93	'94	'95
French:											
Burgundy	20	28	29	21	29	24	19	28	20	25	24
Loire Valley	–	–	–	–	24	23	15	19	22	23	24
Champagne	22	28	25	24	26	28	–	–	–	–	23
Sauternes	25	22	28	29	25	26	–	–	–	19	22
California:											
Chardonnay	–	–	–	–	–	24	22	27	26	23	22
REDS											
French:											
Bordeaux	25	27	26	25	28	27	16	19	23	24	25
Burgundy	23	26	13	26	27	29	21	23	25	22	23
Rhône	25	26	20	26	28	27	26*	16	23*	22	24
Beaujolais	–	–	–	–	–	–	22	15	22	23	24
California:											
Cab./Merlot	18	27	25	16	22	27	26	25	24	23	24
Zinfandel	–	–	–	–	–	20	20	20	20	21	20
Italian:											
Tuscany	–	27	16	25	–	25	17	–	19	–	20
Piedmont	–	26	–	24	27	27	–	–	19	20	25

*Rating and recommendation is only for Northern Rhône wine in 1991 and Southern Rhône wine in 1993.

Bargain sippers take note: Some wines are reliable year in, year out, and are reasonably priced as well. These wines are best bought in the most recent vintages. They include: Alsatian Pinot Blancs, Côtes du Rhône, Muscadet, Bardolino, Valpolicella and inexpensive Spanish Rioja and California Zinfandel.